Andreas Sonnenbichler

An Access Definition and Query Language

Towards a Unified Access Control Model

An Access Definition and Query Language

Towards a Unified Access Control Model

by
Andreas Sonnenbichler

Dissertation, Karlsruher Institut für Technologie (KIT)
Fakultät für Wirtschaftswissenschaften
Tag der mündlichen Prüfung: 25. Juli 2013
Referenten: Prof. Dr. Andreas Geyer-Schulz, Prof. Dr. Andreas Oberweis

Impressum

 Scientific Publishing

Karlsruher Institut für Technologie (KIT)
KIT Scientific Publishing
Straße am Forum 2
D-76131 Karlsruhe

KIT Scientific Publishing is a registered trademark of Karlsruhe
Institute of Technology. Reprint using the book cover is not allowed.

www.ksp.kit.edu

Print on Demand 2013

ISBN 978-3-7315-0088-9

An Access Definition and Query Language

Towards a Unified Access Control Model

Zur Erlangung des akademischen Grades eines
Doktors der Ingenieurwissenschaften
(Dr.-Ing.)

bei der Fakultät für Wirtschaftswissenschaften
des Karlsruher Instituts für Technologie (KIT)

genehmigte
DISSERTATION

von

Dipl.-Wi.-Ing. Andreas Sonnenbichler

Datum der mündlichen Prüfung: 25. Juli 2013
Referent: Prof. Dr. Andreas Geyer-Schulz
Korreferent: Prof. Dr. Andreas Oberweis

Credits

I like to carry on the tradition to give credits to my partners, co-workers, supervisor and family.

First of all, I would like to thank Andreas Geyer-Schulz, head of our department, for his continuing support. It is a rare case and huge asset that an academic supervisor can be bothered almost at any time. Andreas owns an incredible creativity and always shares his helpful new ideas and insights.

I further want to thank our students who have been working on several aspects of the implementation of the access control service. These are especially Stefan Geretschläger and Frederik Haxel. I want to thank Diana Lauer for her good mood, cookies, coffee, and other sweeties. Jens Kleineheismann provided me advise and support concerning IT tools and infrastructure.

There are three more persons I would like to say thank you. Without their help, this work would never have been finished: First of all, my wife, for all her support, for supporting my crazy idea to give up a well paid job in industry and go back to university. For her love. For her encouragement. Thank you! Then, my mother, for always knowing the right words when the work seemed never-ending. And my daughter, Isabelle, for just being who she is and filling the world with sunlight by her laughter. You are teaching me every day that one is a valuable person even without achieving goals. Maybe, one day I will believe you.

Abstract (English Version)

In this dissertation we suggest a meta access control model emulating established access control models by configuration and offering enhanced features like the delegation of rights, ego-centered roles, and decentralized administration. The suggested meta access control model is named "Access Definition and Query Language" (ADQL). ADQL is represented by a formal, context-free grammar allowing to express the targeted access control model, policies, facts, and access queries as a formal language. ADQL is available as executable, ready-to-use software service with its performance high enough to be used by company software as third party access control component.

The aim of all access control models is to protect information in computer systems. For this purpose, conditions are formulated granting or denying access. The method how these conditions are formulated and constructed is described by the underlying access control model. Since the middle of the 20th century a large number of such models has been suggested, e.g., DAC, MAC, RBAC, and RBAC-derived models, logic-based models and models stemming from the "semantic web". All models follow a fixed approach and cannot be flexibly substituted by each other: policy structure, model definition, and the way facts are represented cannot be transferred. In business software, components for access control are specifically implemented for each use case and are almost never re-used for other software.

The "Access Definition and Query Language" is a meta model allowing to emulate access control models in a flexible and demand-specific way, i.e., it may behave like an established access control model or support new requirements like ego-centered roles, the delegation of rights or decentralized approaches. The language utilizes concepts from mathematics, especially set theory. The structure is oriented to the well-known Lambda calculus utilizing definitions and applications. Hereby, definitions correspond to state changes of the system (configuration), evaluations ("access checks") assess policies and their access conditions. The dissertation comprehends the definition of the language, its semantics, its underlying concepts, and examples how established access control models are represented in ADQL.

The dissertation includes the implementation of a software service. The service comprises of an access control system processing ADQL language expressions.

A context-free LL(2) parser is included. The implementation is scalable and distributed. The performance is high enough for the deployment in production business environments. Business software can utilize the ADQL software service to delegate the administration and enforcement of access control rules based on the chosen model. Hereby, the business software is disburdened of essential parts of access control and administration.

This work has been supervised by Prof. Dr. Andreas Geyer-Schulz at the Institute of Information Systems and Marketing. It is written in English language. Dr.-Ing. is the targeted academic degree.

Abstract (German Version)

Die Dissertation schlägt ein Meta-Zugriffskontroll-Modell vor, das mittels Konfiguration flexibel Zugriffskontroll-Modelle nachbilden kann. Hierzu gehört u.a. die Unterstützung von Rechte-Delegation, ego-zentrierten Rollen und Dezentralität. Der flexible Ansatz erlaubt zudem die Nachbildung diverser bekannter Zugriffskontroll-Modelle. Die Konfiguration erfolgt durch eine formale, kontextfreie Sprache, die "Access Definition and Query Language" (ADQL). ADQL wurde als lauffähiger, verwendbarer Softwareservice implementiert und ist performant genug, um von Unternehmenssoftware zur Zugriffsverwaltung und -prüfung verwendet zu werden.

Das Ziel aller Zugriffskontroll-Modelle ist der Schutz von Informationen in Computersystemen. Hierzu werden Bedingungen formuliert, wann Zugriff auf Daten gewährt werden darf oder verboten werden muss. Wie diese Bedingungen formuliert werden und aufgebaut sind, beschreibt das zu Grunde liegende Zugriffskontroll-Modell. Seit Mitte des 20. Jahrhunderts wurde eine große Zahl solcher Modelle vorgeschlagen, z.B. DAC-, MAC-Modelle, RBAC- und RBAC-abgeleitete Modelle, logikbasierte Modelle und Modelle aus dem "Semantischen Web". Alle Modelle folgende einem festen Ansatz und sind nicht flexibel untereinander austauschbar: Policy-Struktur, Modelldefinition und Fakten-Repräsentation sind nicht übertragbar. In Unternehmenssoftware werden Komponenten für die Zugriffskontrolle spezifisch und kaum wiederverwendbar immer wieder neu implementiert.

Die "Access Definition and Query Language" ist ein Meta-Modell, das es erlaubt, flexibel und bedarfsspezifisch Zugriffskontrollmodelle abzubilden, d.h. wie bekannte Zugriffskontroll-Modelle zu funktionieren oder neue Anforderungen, wie ego-zentrierte Rollen, Rechte-Delegation oder dezentrale Ansätze zu unterstützen. Die Sprache bedient sich Konzepten der Mathematik, insbesondere der Mengenlehre. Der Aufbau orientiert sich am bekannten Lambda-Kalkül, das Definitionen und Applikationen erlaubt. Definitionen entsprechen hierbei Zustandsänderungen des Systems (Konfiguration), Evaluationen ("access checks") werten Policies und deren Zugriffsbedingungen aus. Die Dissertation umfasst die Beschreibung der Sprache, ihrer Semantik, ihrer zugrundeliegenden Konzepte und Beispiele, wie bekannte Zugriffskontroll-Modelle in ADQL repräsentiert werden.

Die Dissertation beinhaltet die Implementierung eines Softwareservices. Dieser umfasst ein Zugriffskontroll-System, das Ausdrücke der Sprache ADQL verarbeitet. Es wird ein kontextfreier LL(2)-Parser verwendet. Die Implementierung ist skalierbar und verteilt. Die Performanz ist schnell genug für den Einsatz in Unternehmen. Unternehmenssoftware kann den ADQL-Softwareservice verwenden, um diesem die Verwaltung und Prüfung der Zugriffsregeln auf Basis des gewählten Modells zu übertragen. Für die Unternehmenssoftware entfallen damit wesentliche Teile der Zugriffsprüfung und -verwaltung.

Die Arbeit wurde von Herrn Prof. Dr. Andreas Geyer-Schulz am Institut für Informationsdienste und Marketing betreut. Sie ist in englischer Sprache verfasst. Dr.-Ing. ist der angestrebte Doktorgrad.

Contents

1. Introduction   **1**

2. An Introduction to Access Control   **11**

2.1. Design Principles 12

2.2. Triple-A – Authentication, Authorization, Accounting 16

2.3. Important Definitions and Concepts 17

2.4. A Short History of Access Control 19

2.5. Discretionary Access Control Models (DAC) 21

     2.5.1. The Access Matrix Model 21

     2.5.2. Authorization Tables 23

     2.5.3. Access Control Lists 23

     2.5.4. Capability Lists 25

     2.5.5. Vulnerability of Discretionary Access Control Models . . . 26

     2.5.6. The General Safety Problem 27

2.6. Mandatory Access Control Models (MAC) 27

     2.6.1. The Bell-LaPadula model 27

     2.6.2. Biba's Integrity Model 28

2.7. The Clark-Wilson model 29

2.8. The Chinese Wall Policy 30

2.9. Role Based Access Control 30

     2.9.1. Derived Role Based Access Control Models 33

2.10. Standards in Authorization 35

     2.10.1. RFC 2753 Framework for Policy-Based Admission Control   35

     2.10.2. RFC 2904-2906 AAA Authorization Framework 37

     2.10.3. RFC 3198 Terminology for Policy-Based Management . . . 37

2.11. XACML - The eXtensible Access Control Markup Language . . . 38

     2.11.1. XACML Language Definition 38

     2.11.2. XACMLs Architectural Elements 39

     2.11.3. XACMLs Data Flow 40

     2.11.4. Problems of XACML 42

2.12. Access Control and the Semantic Web 44

2.13. Logic-Based Authorization Models 45

     2.13.1. Woo and Lam's approach 45

     2.13.2. Jajodia et al. 47

2.14. Summary 48

Contents

3. Motivating Example   **49**
  3.1. Components of ADQL 49
  3.2. Motivating Example 51

4. The Access Definition and Query Language (ADQL)   **61**
  4.1. The Syntax of ADQL 61
  4.2. Expression 62
  4.3. Term 62
  4.4. Symbols and Identifier 63
    4.4.1. Symbols 63
    4.4.2. Identifiers 64
  4.5. Definitions 64
    4.5.1. Definition of Entities 66
    4.5.2. Definitions of Containers 66
    4.5.3. Usage of Variables 68
    4.5.4. Definition of Relations 70
    4.5.5. Definition of Filtered 1-Projections 72
    4.5.6. Definition of Tests 74
    4.5.7. Definition of Policies 75
    4.5.8. Definition of Scopes 76
  4.6. Applications 77
    4.6.1. Application of Entities 78
    4.6.2. Application of Containers 79
    4.6.3. Applications of Relations 83
    4.6.4. Applications of F1-Projections 84
    4.6.5. Application of Tests 84
    4.6.6. Application of Policies 86
    4.6.7. Application of Scopes 88
  4.7. Summary 88

5. The Concepts of the Access Definition and Query Language   **91**
  5.1. Overview of ADQL's Concepts 91
  5.2. The Logical Layers of ADQL 92
  5.3. Entities 94
  5.4. Containers 98
  5.5. Relations 104
  5.6. Variables, Bindings, Scopes 110
    5.6.1. Scopes 113
    5.6.2. Access Control on Variables and Scopes 114
  5.7. Tests 114
  5.8. Policies 118

5.9. Operators 119
    5.9.1. Set Operators 120
    5.9.2. Equal Operators 121
    5.9.3. Order Operators 122
5.10. Summary of ADQL's Concepts 125

6. Use Cases for ADQL   127

6.1. Bell-LaPadula Access Control Model 128
6.2. A Real-World Example: SAP R/3 133
6.3. Extended RBAC: An E-Science Example 139
    6.3.1. Check Access Requests 148
6.4. Summary 150

7. Implementing ADQL as Software Service   153

7.1. ADQL's Implementation: General Architecture 153
7.2. Back End Design and Architecture 154
    7.2.1. Back End Architecture and Modules 155
    7.2.2. Persistence Layer 156
    7.2.3. Persistence Module and Database Cache 164
    7.2.4. ADQL's Core Layer, Controller, and Parser 165
    7.2.5. Network Server Layer 169
7.3. Front End Design and Architecture 171
7.4. Intermediate Layer: Design and Architecture 174
7.5. Using ADQL as Software Service 175
    7.5.1. Decide on the Model 175
    7.5.2. Implement Access Checks in the Software 176
    7.5.3. Provide the Facts 177
    7.5.4. Learn the Current System State 178
    7.5.5. Defining Policies 179
7.6. ADQL Back End Performance 179
7.7. Performance of Other Access Control Implementation 184
7.8. Summary 186

8. Conclusion   187

Appendix   191

A. Backus-Naur-Form of ADQL v3.0   193

B. Traveler Scenario   197

1. Introduction

Imagine computer applications without access control: a total transparent Facebook[1] for example. There are no limits to what a user can do. No limits which data anybody can access. No restrictions or controls apply. Total transparency. No more secrets.

At the first glance, this idea might look like a desirable utopia. At the second glance the idea evolves to a nightmare: In our total-transparent Facebook, any user can access any private data. Can even modify it. Can change anybody's pictures, postings, or comments. Surely, a scenario, many of us would not agree on.

Wikipedia and the Seigenthaler incidence

There has been a project which almost totally avoided access control in its beginnings: Wikipedia. In its early days, from about 2001 to 2005, Wikipedia had (almost) no access control. Anybody was able to read, create, modify, and delete any article or parts of articles [wik12a]. In 2005, the so-called Seigenthaler incident occurred [wik12b]. John Seigenthaler is a well-known American journalist and writer. In May 2005, an anonymous article was posted about him falsely stating that Seigenthaler has been a suspect in John F. Kennedy's assassination. The false text version was accessible at Wikipedia from May to September 2005. It read: "John Seigenthaler Sr. was the assistant to Attorney General Robert Kennedy in the early 1960s. For a short time, he was thought to have been directly involved in the Kennedy assassinations of both John, and his brother, Bobby. Nothing was ever proven. John Seigenthaler moved to the Soviet Union in 1972, and returned to the United States in 1984. He started one of the country's largest public relations firms shortly thereafter." [wik12b][2]

This hoax article was not corrected for more than four months. In the process of the Seigenthaler incident the anonymous author could not be identified (although the IP address was leading to the company the author was employed

---

[1] http://www.facebook.com, last accessed 2012-10-25

[2] We cite indirectly as the hoax versions have been hidden from public during the process of the Seigenthaler incident.

in) [Ter05b]. Brian Chase, the hoax's author, uncovered himself by delivering a confessional letter to Seigenthaler's office. The CNET News.com author Daniel Terdiman did an interview with Daniel Brandt. Brandt was running the investigation on the Seigenthaler incident to find out, who the author of the wrong Wikipedia article was. Brandt summarized on Wikipedia's access control policy "The whole model is basically flawed. [...] When you get into stuff like biographies and particularly biographies of living people, the quality is much more iffy, the potential for libel is much greater and the controls just are not appropriate." [Ter05b, p.2].

The Seigenthaler incident led to the introduction of access control in Wikipedia [Ter05a]: "These included a new "checkuser" privilege policy update to assist in sock puppetry investigations, a new feature called semi-protection, a more strict policy on biographies of living people and the tagging of such articles for stricter review. A restriction of new article creation to registered users only was put in place in December 2005." [wik12a].

The utopia of an online encyclopedia without any restrictions (thus, access control) had failed. However, the incident offered some learning points. The target of Wikipedia is to offer a freely accessible encyclopedia which is created and maintained by its users. Furthermore, Wikipedia has no commercial interests. Although Wikipedia saves any version of a document, and deletion, and changing of old versions are not possible due to Wikipedia's inherent logic, Wikipedia had to learn that access control cannot be omitted completely. Generally, encyclopedias offer their knowledge to all human beings. So there is no need to hide or protect information. However, misuse makes it necessary to establish access control even for an online encyclopedia.

Examples of Access Control in Practice

Let us now turn to other examples, where we think it is obvious that access control is required: Any standard PC running Linux, Windows, or iOS is using access control on its file systems. Without such control anyone could do anything on the PC which would make it highly vulnerable to any kind of malware. Windows latest security improvements in Windows Vista, Windows 7 and Windows 8 are also based on the introduction of a kind of supervisor mode. If the supervisor mode, e.g. for a software installation, is required, the user has to confirm this mode switch explicitly. The user is stripping his rights as a regular user and entering an administrator role. Without this role change the whole access control concept of Microsoft since Windows Vista would be impossible.

Another example are web applications running on a server or in a cloud somewhere in the internet. Such services normally offer their services to several users. It is of high importance that access control limits the usage of data, services, certain service functionality or other aspects of services and applications. A good example is online banking where access control is a major issue.

We even assume that any application used by more than a single user will require access control.

Privacy and Access Control

Two concepts are very closely related: Privacy and access control. Although almost anybody has an intuitive definition of privacy, in the literature a consequent definition of the term is not present [Int97]. L. Introna offers and discusses several definitions, one of them reads "privacy as control over personal information" [Int97, p.261], a definition we see appropriate for our work. In contrast, "access control constrains what a user can do directly, as well as what programs executing on behalf of the users are allowed to do" [SS94, p.40]. Comparing both definitions we see that access control is one major tool to aim for the target privacy. Thus, access control is a tool, privacy is the target.

Will privacy be of importance in the future? B. Debatin et al. [DLHH09] did a quantitative and qualitative study in user behavior on Facebook. The authors came to the result that "[the study] shows that the gratifications of using Facebook tend to outweigh the perceived threats to privacy" [DLHH09, p.103]. Does "generation Facebook" require much less or no privacy than the older generations do?

Brandtzaeg et al. [BLS10] suggest a so-called "privacy dilemma" of social network sites like Facebook. The dilemma unfolds to three different dimensions: "Social capital versus privacy" means that the more content and friends a user shares the higher his social capital, his social rank is within his community. This, of course, is at the price of privacy, it is "a contradiction between high levels of sociability and the need for privacy" ([BLS10, p.1010],[ST83]). The second dimension is "conformity and privacy". Social conformity can be observed when someone's actions "are exposed to increased visibility (...) by other members of a group (e.g., "followers" on Twitter and "friends" on Facebook"([BLS10, p.1011]). This social conformity effect is observed to decrease in private discussions, thus, when certain aspects of privacy apply. Social conformity (as external pressure) decreases when privacy increases. The third dimension is called "Ease of Use". It is simply the fact that hiding and protecting content on Facebook not seldom requires a lot of manual setting which many users simply avoid as they do not know how or because they are too lazy.

Framework/library	Authentication	Authorization
OpenID	+	−
Facebook Connect/Login	+	−
Twitter Connect	+	−
Radius	(relay)	(relay)
OAuth	(relay)	(relay)
Spring Security	(see OAuth)	(see OAuth)

Table 1.1.: Overview of existing software frameworks / libraries and their authentication and authorization features.

Nevertheless, coming back to our question "will privacy be of importance in the future", we can conclude that, although, studies exist pointing in the direction that privacy is sacrificed for other benefits, privacy will not disappear. Actually, we have the impression following the discussions in press and literature over the last years that the value of privacy is intensively discussed.

Authorization and Authentication

Access control basically is the combination of authentication and authorization. We will come back to proper definitions of these terms in chapter 2. While authentication is about to identify a user ("who are you?"), authorization aims to decide if a user may do what he wants to do ("what is a user allowed to do?"). Authorization is not possible without authentication. Without knowing which user is trying to access a file no authorization system will be able to make a decision. To be exact: No authorization system where the user is a part of the access control model.

Recurring tasks

Let us view the world of access control from the eyes of a system designer or software developer who is designing or coding an application with any kind of access control, thus authorization and authentication. Both tasks are recurring for any application. For any software developer doing recurring tasks the usual idea is to make use of existing libraries or software frameworks: Why write code which already exists?

Table 1.1 provides an overview of widely-used software frameworks in the field of access control. We qualitatively assess the features offered by the framework in authentication and authorization.

OpenID[3] [RR06] is a decentralized authentication protocol. A user authenticates at a central point ("single-sign-on"). The identification is transferred to the application which wants to know if the user actually is who he says he is. Software developer can simply import available libraries of the OpenID project (e.g. available for PHP, Ruby, Java, ...)[4]. On the authorization side OpenID does not offer any features. OpenID is all about authentication but not about authorization.

A proprietary solution is offered by Facebook. Facebook Login[5] is a web service offered by Facebook. Like OpenID, Facebook Login is an authentication service allowing users to login with their Facebook credentials on third party web sites. Software developers can integrate this authentication service on their own web site or applications. Users may login on the third party web page by making use of their Facebook login and password. Basically, this has two advantages: The user can re-use existing logins and passwords. The web site developer can omit user login code and re-use existing (assumable safe) Facebook technology. There are also some disadvantages: If Facebook's login service suffers problems (is not reachable), all other web sites making use of Facebook's login service are also affected and cannot authenticate users. If Facebook is hacked and user data is lost, the lost user data can be used to access not only Facebook but all connected services making use of its login service. However, Facebook's login service does not offer functionality concerning authorization.

A similar approach is offered by Twitter[6]: Twitter's authentication service offers the same features as Facebook's login service and thus shares the same advantages and disadvantages. Like Facebook, only authentication but no authorization features are supported.

RADIUS is an acronym for the Remote Authentication Dial In User Service. It is a networking protocol standardized by the IETF. RADIUS utilizes UDP as transport protocol and defines the communication between a RADIUS client and a RADIUS server about authentication, authorization, and accounting. The authentication and authorization parts are described in RFC 2865 [WRRS00], the accounting part is described in RFC 2866 [Rig00]. However, RADIUS is only a forwarding protocol in the sense that a requester (the RADIUS client) can relay an authentication or authorization request to the RADIUS server. RADIUS does not specify how authentication or authorization requests are handled by the RADIUS server. This is why we call RADIUS a relaying or forwarding service but not a full authentication of authorization service. RADIUS cannot

---

[3] http://www.openid.net, last accessed 2012-09-27
[4] cf. http://openid.net/developers, last accessed 2012-09-27
[5] https://developers.facebook.com/docs/technical-guides/login, last accessed 2013-03-11
[6] https://dev.twitter.com/docs/auth/sign-twitter, last accessed 2013-03-11

decide if a user is allowed to login (or execute an operation). It can only forward such requests to a RADIUS server which then has to make this decision. How this decision is made, is not within the scope of RADIUS.

OAuth [Har12] is an "authorization framework [enabling] a third-party application to obtain limited access to an HTTP service, either on behalf of a resource owner by orchestrating an approval interaction between the resource owner and the HTTP service, or by allowing the third-party application to obtain access on its own behalf." [Har12, p.1]. OAuth is, like RADIUS, a protocol to propagate access grants from one server to another, but not a framework to decide upon access requests. The decision whether access is granted or not is omitted from OAuth.

Spring, a well-known and often used framework library for Java applications, offers the Spring Security sub-project[7]. It calls itself "a powerful and highly customizable authentication and access-control framework. It is the de-facto standard for securing Spring-based applications"[8] it actually offers an OAuth implementation and some very basic and limited code snippets.

Other very specialized attempts for libraries implementing access control do exist: The wildly-used PHP library Zend Framework (Zend ACL)[9], Java's Spring Security mentioned above, Python libraries like AuthKit[10]. However, none of the libraries or services we found are able to encapsulate a component dealing with authorization.

We see that for authentication some frameworks like OpenID, Facebook Login and Twitter Login exist. However, a software developer will not find anything equivalent for authorization. Instead he may stumble upon certain sub-modules of software frameworks offering very limited and very specialized aspects of access control.

Scientific Goals

These findings lead to the first of our scientific goals: We want to design and implement a software service that is able to decide upon access requests. A software developer can issue a call to the service component from a piece of code he is writing. He does not need to know about the details how the access control component really works but simply checks the return value of his call. In the positive case, the code of the software developer may continue its normal way

---

[7]`http://static.springsource.org/spring-security/site`, last accessed 2012-10-23
[8]`http://static.springsource.org/spring-security/site`, last accessed 2012-10-23
[9]`http://framework.zend.com/manual/1.12/en/zend.acl.html`,
   last accessed 2012-10-25
[10]`http://pypi.python.org/pypi/AuthKit/0.4.5`, last accessed 2012-10-25

of execution, in the negative case, the access is denied. We call this first goal
"access control as a service" (ACaaS), obviously mimicking the phrases "software as a service" (Saas), "platform as a service" (PaaS), and "infrastructure as
a service" (IaaS) from cloud computing.

Our second scientific goal stems from the observation that there seems to be
a huge gap between science and industry/practice: In science an enormous
number of different access control models can be found in the literature. An
access control model is the way access control is modeled, e.g. Role-Based Access Control, Bell-LaPadula, Chinese Wall ... We explain important models in
chapter 2. In contrast, in industry/practice we found mainly three models:
Windows' way to model access rights, Unix/Linux' way, and different flavors
of role-based access control. (Of course, many more OS-specific access control models exist, like IBM system 360/370). Our impression was, that while
academia invents model after model, industry/practice re-uses the same basic
models over and over again. So our second aim is to try to unify both worlds
again. We want our access control service being able to emulate as many access
control models as possible.

Our second goal was confirmed when we became aware of Steve Barker's paper about the "Next 700 Access Control Models or a Unifying Meta-Model"
[Bar09]. In his work, Barker laid out that scientists working in this field should
not focus on inventing one specialized access control model after the other, but
try to develop a unified access control model. This unified model should then
mimic the already existing specialized models. Barker shows that such a model
can theoretically exist as most existing models seem to be based on the same
principles and concepts. This mirrors our third goal: We see our service as a
step towards such a unified model.

This third goal includes features like flexibility, delegation, and (user) empowerment. Flexibility is meant in a sense, that our service can be configured to
work like many standard access control models. Delegation means, that access
control is based on delegation and must support features like proxies and delegation of access rights from one user to another. This results in empowerment
of the user enabling the user to decide upon the access control model being
used for his data. Our article "Social Access Control" [Son13] describes this
approach for Facebook. Flexible and configurable access control mechanisms
allow the user to decide which access control model and policies are used to
protect his data. Subjects like company representatives may require very limited access control, only more or less sharing all content in Facebook freely.
Privacy-unaware users require only basic content protection allowing them to
decide if certain content elements like pictures may be shared or not. Privacy-
aware users prefer to decide upon content availability on a fine-grained level,

e.g. based on a group level. "Paranoid" users want to define the exact conditions for access, e.g. they want to share pictures only with certain users for a specific period of time. These different approaches require different access control models. The corresponding access control model must be chosen by the user. It therefore cannot be made by a software developer or administrator. This requires a flexible (meta) access control model supporting delegation and user empowerment and enablement.

Our fourth and last target is based on the insight that access control is very asymmetric concerning time restrictions. A change of an access right can in the most cases allow more time to pass to take effect while check "access queries" must be answered much faster. Furthermore, access checks may occur distributed and with a high request rate. To provide an order of magnitude, the change of an access right may be sufficient to be processed within seconds (or even minutes). On the other hand, the check of access rights must be finished at least several orders of magnitudes faster (within at most milliseconds of time). We can illustrate this assumption by a software service running at our institution, a quite large database of scientific literature. While co-workers of our chair can see almost any paper stored in this database, the access of our students is rather limited. When querying for a certain topic, e.g. "access control", the resulting list includes about 200 papers. Each of these search hits has to be filtered by our access control service to decide whether the result is presented or not. If each access control check would last only 1/10 of a second, the resulting query time would be additional 20 seconds, plus the query time for the search operation. This is unacceptable. So we come to our fourth goal: Access queries must be answered within a very short time period.

Structure of our work

Chapter 2 will provide an overview of related work in the scientific field of access control. We aim to give a short overview of the development of access control models of the last 50 years. However, we already mentioned that an enormous number of access control models have been developed. Consequently, we cannot describe all of these models in our work, but we focus on some milestones. Which model exactly is a milestone or not can only be judged by our best knowledge and we apologize for any errors in our judgment.

In chapter 3 we provide a motivation example of the Access Definition and Query Language (ADQL). In an informal way and with an example we demonstrate how the syntax of ADQL looks like, what steps are required to create an access control model, and we introduce the concepts of ADQL.

Next, chapter 4 describes the formal language ADQL we introduce in-depth. The language allows to express the concepts described in chapter 5 for the definition of the access control model to be used, the defined policies and facts, and to express access check queries. The formal language is the (user) interface of our software service as it allows defining, maintaining, and querying all concepts.

Chapter 5 describes the underlying concepts and principles of ADQL. We focus only on concepts here and try to explain them in-depth. The concepts are completely independent of any service design, implementation or use case. They describe the concepts and the interaction of our concepts in order to do a step towards a unified (meta) access control model.

Chapter 6 provides then use case examples how some well-known access control models can be modeled by our meta model, the ADQL. We re-use some models of chapter 2 and provide the ADQL statements to construct these models in ADQL. We complement the chapter by providing use case examples, policies, facts, and sample queries.

So far, all chapters abstracted from implementation and just focused on concepts, formal language and constructive proofs. Chapter 7 provides details about the implemented software service realizing ADQL. Here we describe the software design, architecture, and component layout and implementation details.

We summarize our work in chapter 8 by providing the conclusion and planned further work.

Acknowledgments

This work is based on some ideas developed during the EU-project WeKnowIt (7th Framework Program FP7/2007-2013 under grant agreement no 215453). The access control mechanism developed during the WeKnowIt project was called "Community Administration Platform" (CAP). This CAP is a predecessor of the Access Definition and Query Language described in this work.

The code was mostly and in major parts written by the author of this work, Andreas Sonnenbichler. We received support from our student assistants Stefan Geretschläger and Frederik Haxel, whom we want to thank for their high-quality work and good support. As time passed, the code was re-written and adapted many times by all of the above three persons. Today, it is impossible to say exactly, which line was written by whom and modified when by someone else without comparing all code versions step by step. Additional extensions were provided by some of our bachelor and master students working on their bachelor, respectively master thesis.

2. An Introduction to Access Control

This chapter aims to provide an overview of the work in access control models for the last 50 years. For computer science, 50 years span almost all technological eras (mainframes, workstations, PC, mobile devices, cloud computing). Consequently, a very large number of access control models has been suggested and implemented. We try to provide an overview of milestones in access control in this long tradition.

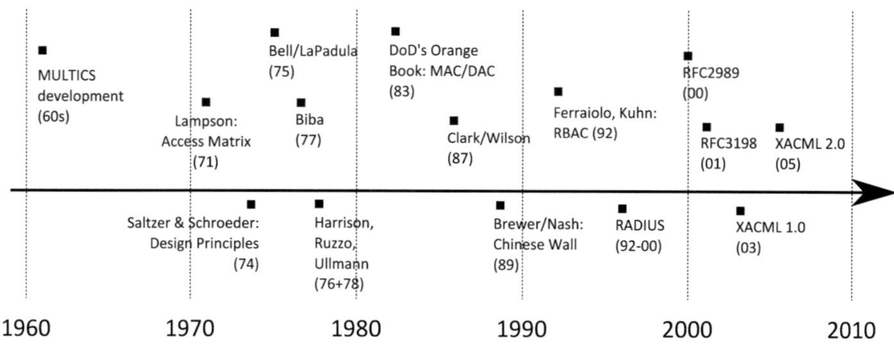

Figure 2.1.: Timeline of a selection of historically important contributions in access control

Figure 2.1 is a timeline from the 1960s until today. It shows some important contributions for access control during the last 50 years. We marked several influential pieces of work together with their authors and their first publications as far as it has come to our knowledge. In this chapter we will describe these contributions.

We start with the development of MULTICs which highly influenced the remarkable work of Saltzer and Schroeder [Sal74]. Saltzer and Schroeder lay out design principles for access control models. In 1971 Lampson [Lam71] published his "access matrix", the earliest formal definition of access control of subjects and objects. Lampsons work lead directly to the famous "HRU-model" of Harrison, Ruzzo, and Ullman [HRU76, HR78]. The HRU-model is still one of the most important access control models. A little earlier, in 1973, Bell and LaPadula [BL73] developed their well-known access control model based on military requirements. Bell and LaPadulas work was enhanced by K. Biba with the Biba model [Bib77]. With the publication of the "Orange Book" [oD83] by the U.S. Department of Defense, the access control model families of HRU and Bell-LaPadula and Biba where classified as discretionary and mandatory access control models. These phrases are still of high importance for today's access control models. In 1989, the work of Clark and Wilson [CW87] and later Brewer and Nash [BN89] led to the commercially initiated Chinese Wall model. It was followed by the path-breaking role-based access control model of Ferraiolo and Kuhn [FK92] in 1992. In the 1990s the important authorization, authentication and accounting protocol RADIUS was developed and standardized [Vol06]. The 2000s brought two important RFC standards, RFC 2989 [ZCH+00] and RFC 3198 [SHC+01], providing definitions of important terms related to access control and in 2003 the publication of the first XACML standard v1.0 ([GM03]).

All the models mentioned above will be explained in this chapter.

Another part of this chapter are definitions of important terms in order to clarify what we speak about during the rest of this work. The chapter is finished by an outlook on access control in the semantic web.

2.1. Design Principles

Before we start explaining concrete access control models, we want to provide a high-level perspective on access control models: The way, how (good) access control models should be designed, thus, design principles. Saltzer and Schroeder published an article about this topic already in the 1970s. This chapter is dedicated to this remarkable piece of work. It has its roots in the development of MULTICS and, later, UNIX.

The path-breaking system MULTICS (Multiplexed Information and Computing Service) was developed in cooperation with the MIT, General Electric, and AT&T in the 1960s. The development of UNIX (and all of its derivatives) was heavily influenced by MULTICS. Therefore, many see MULTICS as the ancestor of UNIX. For further information about MULTICS, we refer for example to [Org72, CSC72].

Jerome Saltzer was the leader of the design team for the MULTICS security kernel [HS10]. While designing the security sub-system, he defined some general principles for the design of security systems [Sal74]. He refined them later together with his colleague Schroeder. It was their aim to provide "useful principles that can guide the design [of a security system] and contribute to an implementation without security flaws" [SS75, p.1282].

According to Saltzer and Schroeder the following 10 general principles should be taken into account when designing protection and authentication mechanisms:

1. *Economy of mechanism*: The design of the security system should be "as simple and small as possible" [SS75, p.1282]. With complicated mechanisms the chance for unintended consequences, e.g. "unwanted access paths", becomes more likely. These unintended consequences will probably not occur during daily use and may be hard to detect, especially if the mechanism is too complex.

2. *Fail-safe defaults*: Access decisions should be based on permissions rather than on exclusions[1]. The principle requires, that the default situation should be the lack of access while the "protection scheme identifies conditions under which access is permitted" [SS75, p.1282]. Psychologically, the formulation of negative rights - the conditions under which no access must be granted - is seen as the wrong way. "A design or implementation mistake in a mechanism that gives explicit permission tends to fail by refusing permission, a safe situation, since it will quickly be detected" [SS75, p.1282]. In contrast, the opposite can result in an unnoticed security leak. As a consequence, any access control mechanism should rely on positive policies only and avoid negative policies. A positive policy defines conditions when access is granted. Negative policies define conditions when access is denied.

   However, from today's perspective we do not fully agree on this strict formulation of positive access rights. It might be necessary to explicitly forbid certain access cases as it might not always be possible to express all access rights in a positive manner. It might be out of convenience (when one can enumerate all relevant conditions) or might even be unavoidable (when not all positive conditions can be enumerated, e.g. in an open-world assumption).

3. *Complete mediation*: Access control must be seen system-wide (and today even beyond that). Every access to each resource must be checked for authority. Although Saltzer and Schroeder only focused on a single multi-user system, this principle becomes even more important nowadays, where systems are connected by networks like the internet: Access

---

[1]Saltzer and Schroeder cite this principle from Glaser. We (like Saltzer and Schroeder) could not identify a written reference, so we rely on the reference of Saltzer and Schroeder.

control should be designed in a way, which allows crossing these borders and still relies on the principle of complete mediation.

4. *Open design*: The design should not be secret and its mechanisms should not depend on the ignorance of potential attackers, but on advanced algorithms and techniques. Working on the U.S. Air Force project RAND[2] P. Baran argues in [Bar64, p.6] that a (system) design involves probably several people, so that "our enemies" will always learn the mechanisms. Instead it makes more sense to involve as many specialists as possible in reviewing the mechanism.

5. *Separation of privilege*: "Where feasible, a protection mechanism that requires two keys to unlock is more robust and flexible than one that allows access to the presenter of one key. [...] In a computer system, separated keys apply to any situation in which two or more conditions must be met" [SS75, p.1282]. We interpret this principle in such a way, that all conditions necessary to access a piece of information must be definable and that relying on one condition only is not a good idea.

6. *Least privilege:* Any principal (program, application, user) should be assigned the least set of privileges to be able to fulfill the job. This limits the possible damage which can arise from accident, error or purpose.

7. *Least common mechanism*: Functionality of mechanisms (code) being common to more than one user and depending on all users should be minimized. If one has the choice to implement a function on a very general level needing comprehensive access rights or on a more specialized level but requiring only limited access rights, the latter course is recommended. This approach minimizes security leaks and prioritizes security over generality and comfort.

8. *Psychological acceptability*: This factor is two-fold. First, the user interface is designed for ease of use enabling users to routinely apply the protection mechanisms. Second, the user's protection goals and his understanding of the protection mechanism must match the protection mechanism so that mistakes can be avoided. If the user has to translate a protection concept to the one implemented this may easily result in mistakes which may negatively influence data security.

9. *Work factor*: The work factor is defined in this context as the cost to circumvent security mechanisms. Giving an example, a 4-letter password consisting of alpha-numeric symbols (A-Z, 0-9) leads to 36^4 possibilities.

---

[2]The RAND project was a U.S. Air Force project developed by the RAND corporation. The memorandum cited here deals with the design of a digital data communication system based on a distributed, encrypted network concept.

The principle says that it is important to calculate the work necessary to circumvent protection mechanisms wherever possible. The problem is that especially in authorization mechanisms this factor can very often not be calculated. In military environments, tactical security is measured in the sense, that something is secure for a time period of x hours.

10. *Compromise recording*: This design factor suggests the recording of unauthorized access. When an unauthorized access is recorded on a file, this mechanism might help to detect (further) unauthorized access on the same file or on other files. An example is the tracking of the date and time of the most recent access of a file. If the time stamp does not match the last authorized access, a compromise is detected. The problem of this design principle is that thus a recording must be tamper-proof and may not be changed by a possible attacker. Furthermore, the mechanism must ensure that any compromise is detected and the detection cannot be circumvented.

The 10 design principles of Saltzer and Schroeder are in many aspects valuable for today's computer system security mechanisms. Especially, the principles *economy of mechanism, fail-safe defaults*, and *separation of privilege* are factors which can be found in many available software pieces.

The *open design principle* can be discussed controversially: A supporter of this principle may argue that security should only come from open, but strong mechanisms. In contrast, hidden mechanisms may provide additional security. A good example for the first group is the area of public-private key encryption, where algorithms like RSA, Diffie-Hellman or elliptic curve techniques are open, but nevertheless considered as safe (mostly dependent on the key length). Open mechanisms enable the calculation and discussion of the vulnerability of the mechanism by a broad (scientific) community. The option of hiding the mechanism is often exercised by private companies putting forward the argument if one does not know the mechanism an attacker has no obvious attack point. We were confronted with such a strategy when one of our students worked for a large energy and power company writing his master thesis. His task was to design a REST interface for a smart power-meter which included connectivity to the internet and intranet. Although working for the company and being a key issue for his work, he was not allowed to get knowledge about the security infrastructure and mechanisms related to internet/intranet connectivity making it impossible for him to adapt his code to the companies specific technical environment [Bur11].

In summary, we see the 10 design principles of Saltzer and Schroeder still as important guidelines which should be considered for any security mechanism.

2.2. Triple-A – Authentication, Authorization, Accounting

When talking about access control, the so-called "Triple-A" is a commonly used term. "Triple-A" or "AAA" is an acronym for authentication, authorization, and accounting. In RFC2989 [ZCH+00] the following definitions are used:

- Authentication: "The act of verifying a claimed identity, in the form of a pre-existing label from a mutually known name space" [ZCH+00, p.2]. Authentication ensures that a user is the one he claims to be. Common mechanisms are password identification or biometric methods.

- Authorization: "The act of determining if a particular right, such as access to some resource, can be granted to the presenter of a particular credential" [ZCH+00, p.2].

- Accounting: "The act of collecting information on resource usage for the purpose of trend analysis, auditing, billing, or cost allocation" [ZCH+00, p.2].

Similar definitions for these terms can be found in the literature.

An important standard concerning AAA is the RADIUS protocol. RADIUS (Remote Authentication Dial In User Service) is a standard of the IETF described in the RFCs 2865 [WRRS00] and 2866 [Rig00]. RADIUS development started in 1992 and was standardized by the IETF in 2000 [Vol06]. RADIUS is a client and server protocol on the application layer of the internet using UDP as transport protocol. It serves three purposes: (1) authenticate users and/or devices, (2) authorize users and/or devices, (3) provide accounting and logging for these services. The first two services are described in RFC 2865. As first step, the RADIUS protocol sends a request from the client to the server containing access credentials. This can be e.g. a user name and a password or a security certificate. The RADIUS server checks this information and decides on the request. This decision process is not part of the RADIUS protocol and provided by back-end functionality (e.g. LDAP, Active Directory, ...). The decision is then forwarded from the server to the client.

RFC 2866 describes the accounting part of the RADIUS protocol.

Generally, RADIUS is a widely-used AAA protocol. However, we already said that it is a protocol and relaying information. RADIUS is not dealing with the decision making on the server side, thus if authentication and authorization is granted or not.

2.3. Important Definitions and Concepts

Quite often the terms user, principal and subject are used indifferently and with the same meaning. Nevertheless, all terms have different definitions. We follow Benantar's definitions [Ben06]:

User.   A user is the human being interacting with a computer system. It is the natural person sitting in front of a PC or the one using a head-up display.

Account and Profile.   Information about a user (his ID, his name, address, password etc.) is stored in the user's profile, which sometimes is also called user account or simply account. A user may have several accounts: One might have several accounts in the micro-blogging service Twitter[3], e.g. a professional and a private account. Many users have two accounts on their private Microsoft Windows computer at home, a normal account and an administrative account.

Principal.   A principal is an internal representation of a user in a computer system. A user may have several principals representing him in a specific computer environment. E.g. Ann working for the company Comp Inc. may have two principals. One principal is related to the accounting system and the other principal, with different permissions, related to the project management system. Quite often, the phrase account is used instead of principal: "one has several accounts" instead of "one has several principals associated with accounts (the profile)".

Microsoft [Net03] gives another definition: "Security principals include the following: (a) Any entity that can be authenticated by the system, such as a user account, a computer account, or a thread or process that runs in the security context of a user or computer account. (b) Security groups of these accounts." [Net03]

Subject.   RFC3198 defines a subject as "an entity, or collection of entities, which originates a request, and is verified as authorized/not authorized to perform that request" [SHC$^+$01, p.16].

A different definition is provided by Benantar: "A subject is the term used to identify a running process, a program in execution. Each subject assumes

---

[3] http://www.twitter.com, last accessed 2013-04-26

the identity and the privileges of a single principal." [Ben06, p.9]. While a subject is related to a process (who is executing the process), a principal is the representation of a user in a system. Both are related: In many environments the privileges of the principal starting a program are inherited by the process executing the program. Nevertheless, a principal is not the same concept as a subject. For example, in UNIX-like systems, a program (exactly: a file) may be associated with a so-called sticky bit. If the bit is enabled, the program is executed with administrative rights independent of the rights of the executing principal/user. The subject of the task is then the administrator ("root"), while the executing principal may be a regular, non-administrative user.

Object.   Objects are entities/information which are accessed (or tried to be accessed) by a subject. Examples can be a file to be opened, a database table to be deleted, a printer to be used or a program which is executed.

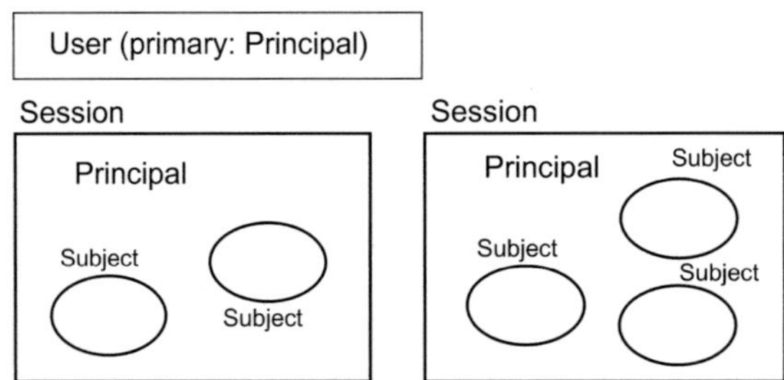

Figure 2.2.: Overview of the terms user, session, principal, and subject and their relationships following [Ben06, p.10].

An assembly of the terms user, principal, subject, and session are depicted in figure 2.2. We see that the user is placed outside of all boxes. Users are real-world entities and not part of a computer system. They are internally represented by principals (probably occurring in different sessions). A principal is associated with exactly one user (1-n relationship). When executing programs, subjects come into place. Subjects are the entities which execute the program. Normally, they inherit the access rights of the principal.

Sometimes the terms user - principal - subject are often used interchangeable representing the concept of "the one who is doing something".

Session.   A session is an encapsulated environment. It encapsulates one or a series of access control requests. Sessions are normally limited in time and related to authentication: Within a session, a principal is represented by one or more subjects. A session may consist of one or many transactions.

Transaction. A transaction is an atomic operation between one or more subjects requesting access to one or many objects. Access on a transaction maybe denied or granted.

Policies. Policies are defined as "a set of rules to administer, manage, and control access to network resources" [SHC+01, p.7]. The abstraction level of policies can be very different: "Ranging from business goals to device-specific configuration parameters" [SHC+01, p.8]. Following RFC 3198 a policy can contain policy conditions and actions.

In RFC 3198 we find some important definitions of architectural elements for authorization frameworks:

- "A Policy Enforcement Point PEP is a logical entity that enforces policy decisions" [SHC+01, p.9]. The component makes sure that before a service can be accessed a corresponding authorization request has to be issued and answered.

- "A Policy Decision Point PDP is a logical entity that makes policy decisions for itself or for other network elements that request such decisions" [SHC+01, p.9]. In other words, it is the component answering with yes or no.

A lot of effort has been put into the formalization of a policy and in designing an object-oriented information model of policies. RFC 3060 [ESMW01] describes the joint answer of the IETF Policy Framework Working Group and the Distributed Management Task Force. Without going too much into detail, policies (actually called policy rules here) can consist of conditions and actions. Conditions define logical expressions in conjunctive or disjunctive normal form which have to be full-filled to make the policy applicable. If so, the policy rule is executed. Policies can be grouped in hierarchic policy groups.

Please note, that the focus of the RFC 3060 is not (only) authorization. It is thought as a very generic approach, how policies can be modeled. Actually, the focus was more on quality of service (QoS) and IPSec issues. Nevertheless, it provides a formalized model of policies in the form of production rules: (1) the pre-condition (rule) as a logical expression, (2) the consequence (action) which has to be performed when the pre-condition is met.

2.4. A Short History of Access Control

The work on access control began in the 1960s with addressing security issues in early time-sharing computer systems and it developed rapidly in the 1970s [FKC07].

The earliest formal work on access control has been published by Lampson [Lam71] introducing the formal definitions of subjects and objects and the concept of the "access matrix". We describe this approach in section 2.5. It was his work that led later to the well-known HRU model from Harrison, Ruzzo, and Ullman (HRU) [HRU76, HR78] and their proof of the general safety problem of this model (see section 2.5 and, especially, 2.5.6).

A different idea developed from military security requirements is mandatory access control. While the access matrix related models – called discretionary access control models (DAC) – are based on the triple subject, object, and permission, military ways of handling protection start with security classes, e.g. confidential, secret, top secret. The latter models are referred to as mandatory access control models (MAC). A report from the RAND corporation from 1970 [War70] analyzed the requirements of the U.S. Department of Defense (DoD) concerning security in IT systems. Not surprisingly, the established approach of military security levels was re-introduced: While users are assigned clearance levels, objects are related to classification levels. A user may only access an object, if his clearance level is at least as high as the object's classification level. The work was extended to a multi-level security system including development plans for such a system by the U.S. Air Force [And72]. The formalization of this model lead to the famous Bell-LaPadula model [BL73] discussed in section 2.6.2.

In 1983 the DoD published its "Orange Book" (Defense Trusted Computer System Evaluation Criteria (TCSEC, for unknown reasons, the D is omitted) standard) [oD83]. In this publication the phrases discretionary access control (DAC) and mandatory access control (MAC) were introduced. The DAC models refer to the family of access matrix based models (e.g. the HRU model). In this model family, the user decides upon the security requirements and enforcements of security requirements on objects. In contrast, the MAC model family implements security levels like the Bell-LaPadula model, leaving the users almost no options about access control. Instead the security requirements are handled automatically, users cannot decide about access for an object.

Setting very high security standards and requirements the TCSEC standard was not accepted for business use. "Despite the efforts to promote TCSEC-compliant systems as commercial security solutions, most commercial firms recognized that DAC and MAC were not sufficient for their needs" [FKC07, p.9]. In a path-setting paper, Clark and Wilson [CW87] argued that for commercial applications integrity of data is more important than confidentiality. In other words, the way how data is modified by authorized users only is of the highest importance, while the prohibition of access to information is less important. The formalization of Clark and Wilson lead to the concept of "separation of duty": paying out money can be initiated by person A, but has to be acknowledged by person B, e.g. the head of the department. This concept cleared the way for the development of the role-based access control models (RBAC).

The idea behind role-based access control is simple and compelling – as many fundamental concepts are: In a firm a person fulfills several roles. One may be a project leader of project A, a project member in project B and head of department C. All these roles come with different obligations and privileges. This daily-life concept from organization theory was adapted by IT access control scientists in the 80s and 90s. The bridge between security models and enterprise models was built by Dobson and McDermid through introducing the term "functional roles" [DM89]. Before the term RBAC was established, Brewer and Nash introduced the Chinese Wall model [BN89]. It combined DAC with mandatory restrictions. We will go into details in section 2.8.

2.5. Discretionary Access Control Models (DAC)

"[Discretionary access control] is a means of restricting access to objects based on the identity of users or the groups to which they belong, or both. The controls are discretionary in the sense that a user or subject given discretionary access to a resource is capable of passing that information along to another subject" [FKC07, p.44f].

Historically, discretionary access control models (DAC) models are often seen as the only or at least most important access control models. The work of Lampson [Lam71, Lam74] was path-breaking for the development of DAC models. It was improved by Graham [GD71] and formalized by Harrison, Ruzzo, and Ullman (HRU) [HRU76, HR78]. Sometimes, the HRU-model, also called access matrix model, is even used as a synonym for DAC models. Strictly seen, this is not correct as the access matrix model applies to all access control models, not only DAC. Nevertheless, it lends itself well to discretionary policies [Ben06].

2.5.1. The Access Matrix Model

The access matrix model uses three basic abstractions: subjects, objects, and access rights. The definitions of subjects and objects match the definitions given in section 2.3.

	file1	file2	file3	subject1	subject2	subject3
subject1	read	read	read	–	–	–
subject2	read, write	read, write	read, write	–	–	–
subject3	–	read	write	–	–	–

Table 2.1.: Example of a protection state as access matrix

Let S be the set of subjects, O the set of objects, and P the set of permissions. The two-dimensional access matrix consists of $m \times (n + m)$, m rows and $n + m$ columns with $m = |S|$ and $n = |O|$. One row represents one subject. One column represents one object or a subject. The subjects are seen as objects, too, in order to be able to define access rights on subjects as well.

The permissions are modeled in the content of each matrix cell. An example of an access matrix can be found in table 2.1. The example shows an access matrix of three objects (file1-3) and three subjects (subject1-3). Subject1 may read file1, file2, and file3. Subject2 may read and write file1-3. Subject3 has no access to file1, may read file2 and may write file2.

We see that the columns include not only files1-3 but also the subjects. This allows the representation of access rights for one subject (represented as a row) for the subject "as an object" (represented as a column). Through this, we can express that subject1 might be able to modify subject2 (as an object) but not file3. Access rights not explicitly granted, thus not present in the table, have not been provided.

A snapshot from the access matrix at any point in time represents a so-called protection state. The protection-state defines for every object which subject can access it with which access rights. Then, formally a state is the triple (S, O, P). Therefore, the access matrix model corresponds to a (finite) state machine. A change on the matrix leads to a different state of the state machine. It is finite because for the system the number of possible states for the current set of subjects, objects and permissions is restricted to $|S| \times (|S| + |O|) \times |P|$.

Of course, the number of possible states can increase or decrease if subjects, objects or permissions are added or deleted.

State transitions transform the matrix. The HRU model supports the following primitive operations: add/delete a subject, add/delete an object, add/delete a permission.

However, implementations of access matrices share a problem: The matrix is far from dense and, if implemented as an array, huge amounts of memory/data storage have to be used representing mostly empty cells of the matrix. This

subject	object	permission
subject1	file1	read
subject1	file2	read
subject1	file3	read
subject2	file1	read
subject2	file1	write
subject2	file2	read
subject2	file2	write
subject2	file3	read
subject2	file3	write
subject3	file2	read
subject3	file3	write

Table 2.2.: Representation of the example protection state as authorization table

fact leads to different views on the access matrix: access control lists (ACL), capability lists (CL), and authorization tables (AT).

2.5.2. Authorization Tables

Authorization tables are a flat representation of protection states as a three column table. Any protection state represented as an access matrix can be transformed into an authorization table: All non-empty cells of the matrix are written into the table consisting of the columns subject, object, and permission. A representation of the example protection state – depicted as access matrix in table 2.1 – can be found in table 2.2. Representations of this type are used for storing a protection state in a database environment.

2.5.3. Access Control Lists

Access control lists (ACL) describe the state of the protection state from the perspective of objects. For each object in the system a list is generated and associated with the corresponding object. The list consists of all users and their permissions on the object. Figure 2.3 shows the ACL representation of the protection state shown in table 2.1.

We see that access control lists are the third variant for the representation of a protection state. The advantage of representing a protection state as ACL is

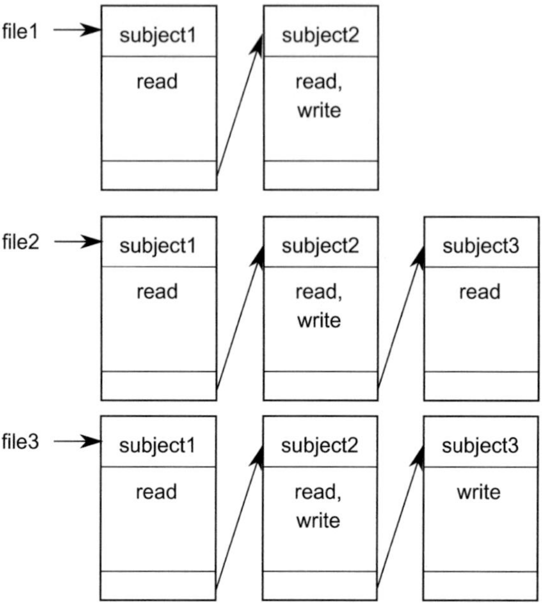

Figure 2.3.: Representation of the example protection state as access control list

the low number of calculation necessary to retrieve all access rights for a specific object. If the access rights of an object are queried, the necessary data can
directly be retrieved by iterating through the list of this object. For any user,
this leads to the complexity $O(m)$ with $m = |S|$ being the number of subjects.
Contrary, the evaluation of all access rights for a specific user requires more
computational effort: All lists of objects have to be searched for the specified
user leading to a search time of $O(m \times (n + m))$ with $m = |S|, n = |O|$ being
the number of subjects resp. objects. Adding objects leads to actually no computational effort ($O(1)$) in the ACL. Adding subjects is more complex as up to
n objects have to be adapted ($O(n)$). Adding permissions can be quite complex
($O(m \times n)$) as any subject/object combination might be changed.

In contrast, deleting subjects or permissions is complex as all ACL lists have
to be searched for the user (or permission) and his entries have to be removed
from the list. Deleting objects is fast ($O(1)$), as the complete list can be deleted.

Concerning expressive power, access control lists, access matrices, and authorization tables are equal: They are different representations of a protection
state.

2.5.4. Capability Lists

Capability lists are a reversed view of a protection state concerning access control lists. Instead of focusing on objects and describing each object's access list, capability lists describe the access rights (capabilities) of each user. For every user, a capability list is created. A capability list consists of all objects the user owns at least one permission with. An example can be found in figure 2.4 representing the same protection state example used in the last 3 subsections, here represented as a capability list.

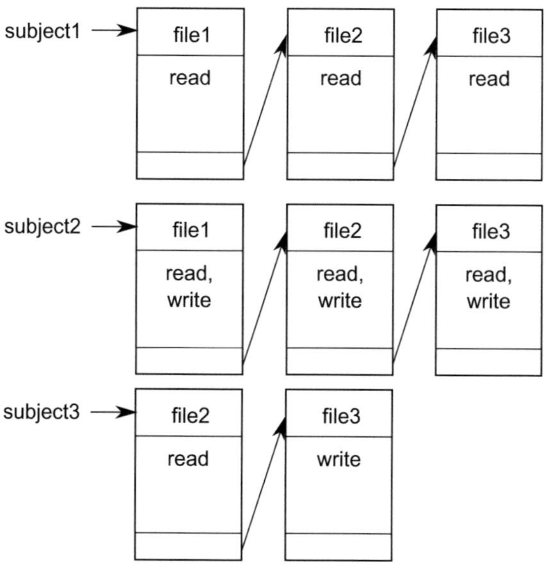

Figure 2.4.: Representation of the example protection state as capability list

Obviously, as capability lists are the inverse representation of a protection state compared to access control lists, the advantages of the ACL are the disadvantages of capability lists and vice versa. We immediately see that the deletion of a subject becomes very easy now as the corresponding list of the subject can be simply deleted. On the other hand, deletion of objects requires now more effort as all lists of the users have to be searched for the object and individually deleted in the list. However, the deletion of permissions has the same complexity as for ACLs.

Again, the expressive power of a capability list matches the ones of access control lists, authorization tables and access matrices. All are representations of a protection state.

2.5.5. Vulnerability of Discretionary Access Control Models

A general problem of DAC models is described by Samarati and de Capitani di Vimercati [SV01]: "discretionary policies do not enforce any control on the flow of information once this information is acquired by a process, makes it possible for processes to leak information to users not allowed to read it. All this can happen without the cognizance of the data administrator / owner, and despite the fact that each single access request is controlled against the authorizations" [SV01, p.146].

Samarati and de Capitani di Vimercati describe a scenario, where a user named "Vicky" creates a sensitive document. Another user "John" creates a Trojan horse and installs it on the computer of Vicky. When Vicky executes the Trojan horse, the Trojan horse runs with the access rights of Vicky (because the user Vicky and the subject in the system share the same rights). Therefore, the Trojan horse is able to copy the information of the sensitive document to a file John has previously created and given write permissions to Vicky.

The vulnerability is based on two assumptions of DAC models: (1) users and subjects are handled identically, (2) information is not protected when access has been given.

The first assumption is that any process started by Vicky inherits all access rights Vicky has. Actually, there is no differentiation between a user and a subject. Samarati and de Capitani di Vimercati argue that this is a fundamental weakness.

"While users are trusted to obey the access restrictions, subjects operating on their behalf are not. With reference to our example, Vicky is trusted not to release the sensitive information she knows to John, since, according to the authorizations, John cannot read it. However, the processes operating on behalf of Vicky cannot be given the same trust. Processes run programs which, unless properly certified, cannot be trusted for the operations they execute. For this reason, restrictions should be enforced on the operations that processes themselves can execute" [SV01, p.148].

Actually, we think that the weakness is not so much related to DAC models as to their implementation. It seems possible to implement a DAC model, where subjects and users are modeled differently and still follow the DAC approach. An example is the way, how Microsoft is dealing with administrative rights since Windows Vista: Whenever administrative rights (e.g. install a program, change system properties) are required, the subject asks the user through a pop-up, if it may continue or not. This example shows that the subject – also having the administrative rights of the user – double-checks with the user before executing sensible operations. Nevertheless, Microsoft Windows uses a DAC model.

The second assumption is that information is not protected as soon as access has been granted. In Samarati's and de Capitani di Vimercati's example, Vicky can gain access to the sensible document. As there are no further protection mechanisms Vicky's subject can now write this information to a different file giving John access. We think that the second argument indeed is a potentially dangerous vulnerability of DAC models. One way to protect the information is the Bell-LaPadula/Biba model (see section 2.6.2 and section 2.6.2): Subjects are assigned so-called security levels. Information can only be provided to subjects with a higher security level than the author of a document. This approach could avoid the described attack: Although Vicky can access the sensible data, she is not able to provide the information to John, because John has a lower security level than Vicky. The premise for this is that Vicky cannot remove the security level of the object by copying the content of the file to another file.

2.5.6. The General Safety Problem

Another problem of DAC models is described by Harrison, Ruzzo, Ullman in [HRU76, HR78]: It is undecidable if a protection system based on an access matrix model leaks a generic right r or not. The term "leaks" is defined in the following way: "Given a protection system, we say command a leaks generic right r from configuration $Q = (S, O, P)$ if a, when run on Q, can execute a primitive operation which enters r into a cell of the access matrix which did not previously contain r" [HRU76, p.467]. In other words, it cannot be decided for a HRU model, if a subject gains access to an object he did previously not have access to, or not. The HRU proof reduces this general safety problem to the well know halting problem of a Turing machine [Tur38].

2.6. Mandatory Access Control Models (MAC)

2.6.1. The Bell-LaPadula model

One of the first access control models later categorized as a mandatory access control model is the model suggested by David Bell and Leonard LaPadula in 1973 [BL73, McL88]. The model was created for military purposes and assumes clearance levels for persons and security levels for military documents. It suggests that each principal (user) is assigned a clearance level. The same is done for objects (documents) by assigning them a security level. The access of principals to objects can either be read access or write access. Here, "read" means, that the user can read the content of a document, but not edit it. The permission "write" means, that the user can file a document, but is not able to read its content later.

The Bell-LaPadula model makes use of two policies.

- Simple security property or read down: Subjects may only access objects by read, if the clearance level of the subject is at least as high as the security level of the object.

- Star-property (*-property) or write up: Subjects may access objects by write only, if the clearance level of the subject is at least as low as the security level of the object.

These two policies mainly have two effects: The simple security property prevents users from being able to read information that is above their clearance level. The star property disallows subjects to write information of a level x to containers (e.g. files) with a lower security level.

Ferraiolo and Kuhn [FKC07] describe how these policies solve the "Trojan horse" problem described by Samarati and de Capitani di Vimercati [SV01] (see section 2.5.5): Frank is cleared for the confidential level but wants to steal top secret documents. He makes use of a Trojan horse. Frank makes Chris execute Frank's Trojan horse as Chris is cleared for top secret documents. Frank's Trojan horse is able to read top secret documents as it is running with the privileges of Chris. However, the Trojan horse fails to write the information to a file / container which is accessible by Frank: this is prevented by the star property. Frank is still able to destroy the content of the top secret file, as nothing prevents him to write higher level information. But Frank can, in contrast to DAC models, not leak information.

2.6.2. Biba's Integrity Model

We have seen that the Bell-LaPadula model successfully prevents leaking of information. However, we also learned that is does not prevent unauthorized modification of information.

Some years after the introduction of Bell and LaPadula's model, K. Biba suggested an extension of the Bell-LaPadula model in 1977 [Bib77]. The Bell-LaPadula model exclusively pertains confidentiality issues while ignoring integrity issues. Created as an extension for the Bell-LaPadula model, the Biba model addresses only integrity issues leaving the confidentiality issues to the Bell-LaPadula model.

Like Bell-LaPadula, Biba's model is based on integrity levels assigned to subjects and objects. Biba's policies are similar to Bell-LaPadula's policies except that they are reversed:

- Simple integrity property: Subjects may only access objects by read, if the security level of the object dominates the clearance level of the subject.

- Integrity star-property: Subjects may access objects by write only, if the clearance level of the subject dominates the security level of the object.

We see, that read access is only permitted if the subject has a lower or equal security level as the object. Write access is permitted, if the subject's clearance level is at least as high as the object's security level.

2.7. The Clark-Wilson model

Clark and Wilson [CW87] were the first to recognize that the so far developed MAC models focused only on military usage. Clark and Wilson argued that major concerns for commercial usage are more about integrity than secrecy. In their work they suggest two major principles ensuring information integrity: well-formed transactions and separation of duty.

In contrast to Bell-LaPadula and Biba, control does not apply to basic operations (like read or write), but on an application or transactional level. Their "commercial integrity model" defines permissions of a transactional level, e.g. a saving deposit transaction or a bank wire transfer. Such transactions may include several low-level read and write permissions. Clark and Wilson argue that policies should apply to the transactional level for commercial usage and not to the low-level.

The second principle is the separation of duty: Each operation is divided into multiple subparts. Each subpart has to be executed by a different person. E.g. when purchasing an item, the recording of the arrival and the payment process have to be executed by at least two separate persons.

2.8. The Chinese Wall Policy

The Chinese Wall policy was suggested by Brewer and Nash in 1989 [BN89].
It picked up the observation of Clark and Wilson [CW87] that the security requirements of military and commerce are different. Taking this into account,
the Chinese Wall policy extends the discretionary access control with parts of
the Bell-LaPadula model. The set of objects are divided into so-called "conflict-
of-interests classes". These classes are sub-divided into "company data sets"
grouping the individual objects (e.g. files). Company data sets belong, as the
name suggests, to one company or organizational unit. The classification is
depicted in figure 2.5.

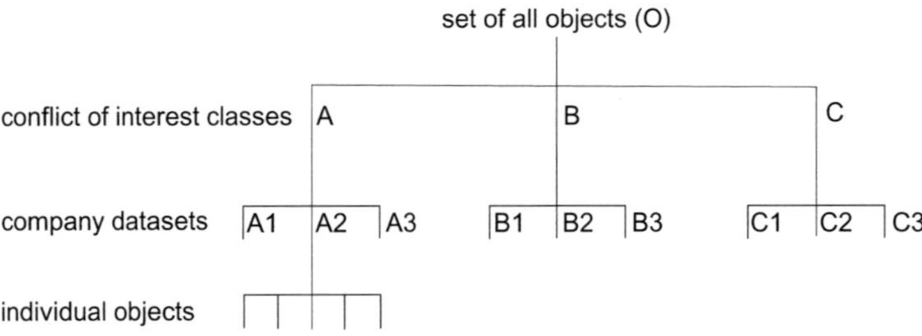

Figure 2.5.: Composition of objects in the Chinese Wall policy following [BN89,
p.208]

As a result, the Chinese Wall policy works like a "scattered Bell-LaPadula"
model. In each conflict of interest class, the Bell-LaPadula clearance and security levels of subjects, respectively, objects apply. However, the conflict of
interest classes are completely separated from each other.

2.9. Role Based Access Control

In 1992 Ferraiolo and Kuhn [FK92] suggested the family of role-based access
control models (RBAC). The authors argue that while mandatory access control models are mainly designed for military usage, discretionary access control
models are perceived to be the choice for industry and civilian government.
However, so Ferraiolo and Kuhn, "reliance on DAC as the principal method
of access control is unfounded and inappropriate" [FK92, p.554]. Instead the
authors suggest a new access control model named role-based access control
model.

The Core RBAC model [FKC07] recognizes five basic elements (see figure 2.6): (1) users, (2) roles, (3) permissions. Permissions consist of (4) operations applied to (5) objects. Roles are a new, intermediate element between users and permissions: Permissions are associated with roles. Roles can be assigned to users.

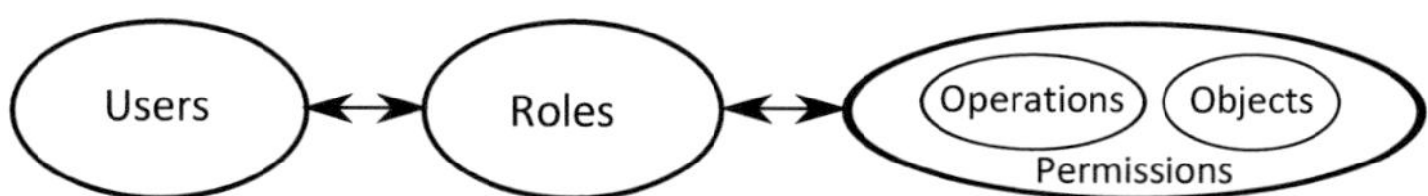

Figure 2.6.: Elements of the Core RBAC model [FKC07, p.64]

The introduction of the new abstraction "role" has some significant advantages: It supports both ideas of Clark and Wilson, the separation of duty and the formulation of access rights on a transactional level. The access rights necessary to perform a certain business activity (e.g. pay an invoice) can be pooled in one role. The necessary low-level operations (read invoice, create a wire transfer, create entries for accounting, ...) can be pooled in a corresponding role. Each company employee can then be assigned the role allowing him to perform the task. We see that roles are an intermediate object pooling low-level operations to business operations, following the idea of Clark of Wilson. Also the separation of duty is supported by roles: A business process can be split into several sub-processes. Each sub-process is authorized by a corresponding role. To ensure the separation of duty, it has to be made sure that one person does not own all roles necessary for a complete process.

RBAC was standardized by the US National Institute of Standards and Technology (NIST) [SFK00] and became an ANSI standard (359-2004) in 2004.

Several extensions of the core RBAC model have been suggested: Sandhu et al. [SCFY96] suggest a hierarchy of RBAC models. "$RBAC_0$ as the base model at the bottom, is the minimum requirement for an RBAC system. Advanced models $RBAC_1$, and $RBAC_2$, include $RBAC_0$, but $RBAC_1$, adds role hierarchies (situations where roles can inherit permissions from other roles), whereas $RBAC_2$, adds constraints (which impose restrictions on acceptable configurations of the different components of RBAC). $RBAC_1$, and $RBAC_2$, are incomparable to one another. The consolidated model, $RBAC_3$, includes $RBAC_1$, and $RBAC_2$ and, by transitivity, $RBAC_0$." [SCFY96, p.40].

We provide the definitions of Sandhu et al. [SCFY96, p.42-44] in the following:

The $RBAC_0$ consists of:

- U, R, P, and S (users, roles, permissions, and sessions)

- $PA \subseteq P \times R$, a many-to-many permission-to-role assignment relation

- $UA \subseteq U \times R$, a many-to-many user-to-role assignment relation

- $user : S \rightarrow U$, a function mapping each session s_i to the single user $user(s_i)$ (constant for the session's lifetime)

- $roles : S \rightarrow 2^R$, a function mapping each session s_i to a set of roles $roles(s_i) \subseteq \{r \mid (user(s_i), r) \in UA\}$ (which can change in time) and session s_i has the permissions $\cup_{r \in roles(s_i)} \{p \mid (p, r) \in PA\}$.

In $RBAC_0$ sessions are controlled by the user: Concerning the model a user can create a session and activate some subset of the user's roles. The role activation can be changed by the users as necessary. A session can also be ended by the user.

$RBAC_1$ is an hierarchical extension of $RBAC_0$:

- U, R, P, S, PA, UA, and $user$ are unchanged from RBAC

- $RH \subseteq R \times R$ is a partial order on R called the role hierarchy or role dominance relation, also written as $\geq$

- $roles : S \rightarrow 2^R$ is modified from $RBAC_0$, to require $roles(s_i) \subseteq \{r \mid (\exists r' \geq r)[(user(s_i), r') \in UA]\}$ (which can change with time) and session s_i has the permissions $\cup_{r \in roles(s_i)} \{p \mid (\exists r'' \leq r)[(p, r'') \in PA)]\}$.
  The symbols $\leq$ and $\geq$ refer to the partial order RH.

Roles can be organized in hierarchies creating senior and junior roles. The permissions in a session are those directly assigned to the roles activated in the session plus those assigned to junior (inherited) roles.

$RBAC_2$ is defined in the following way: "$RBAC_2$ is unchanged from $RBAC_0$ except for requiring that there are constraints to determine the acceptability of various components of $RBAC_0$. Only acceptable values will be permitted." [SCFY96, p.44].

Examples for such constraints are mutually exclusive roles. These constraints enable the separation of duty: If a user U is assigned the role $role(s_i)$ he might not be assigned role $role(s_j)$. E.g. if a user may transfer money from the company's bank account he is not allowed to audit the transfers.

Other examples for constraints are cardinality (a role can only be assigned to exclusively one user) or prerequisites (a role can only be assigned if the user has already been assigned another role).

$RBAC_3$ is a combination of $RBAC_1$ and $RBAC_2$ combining hierarchical roles and role constraints.

2.9.1. Derived Role Based Access Control Models

The influence of role based access control models was so strong that several extensions and modifications have been suggested. We describe a selection of these derived RBAC models below.

Ubi-RBAC Sejong Oh [Oh10] suggests the Ubi-RBAC model. According to the authors, the development of ubiquitous computing led to new requirements. These requirements are (following [Oh10, p.608]):

- Subjects do not explicitly log on but simply use machines/devices.

- Objects are not only traditional files or tables, but also devices like copy machines, telephones, and so on.

- Permissions like read, write, and execute are insufficient. More activities like on/off, touch, push, connect-to and so on, are required.

- User's authority may change dynamically depending on location, time, and environment.

- Location (space) is an important variable. A user might be allowed to use a device in one space (at work) but not at another (at home).

Consequently, Oh extended the original RBAC model family by spaces, context-constraints and user-role-space assignments. Spaces are introduced as locations where user access might occur. Spaces can be organized in hierarchies, called space hierarchies. Context constraints are special conditions that allow or disallow permissions, e.g. (open-room216,OPEN) is only allowed during office hours. The user-role-space assignment is a 3-ary relation between $(users, roles, space)$ which must be satisfied to grant access.

We see that Ubi-RBAC basically introduces the concept of spaces and some specific conditions related to these locations.

GRBAC Covington et al. [CMA00] suggest the generalized role-based access control (GRBAC).

Besides the traditional roles in RBAC, which Convington et al. call "subject roles", the authors introduce "environment roles" and "object roles". "Environment roles" are conditions that must apply to grant access related to the environment. E.g. "managers may edit salary data for their employees only on the first Monday of each month" [CMA00, p.6] is an environment role. "Object roles" allow policies to be defined on properties on the object itself, e.g. a security level of a file, the creator of an object and so on.

We see that GRBAC actually extends RBAC by additional conditions. Depending on the conditions which apply to an object or depending on the environment, Covington et al. call them object roles or environmental roles.

However, the authors do not provide information how these conditions are formally represented or checked.

TRBAC   Bertino et al. [BBF01] suggest a temporal extension of RBAC models. The assignment of roles to a user becomes time-dependent, thus the role assignment maybe available at certain time periods and unavailable at other time periods (e.g. during weekdays but not during weekends).

The temporal role-based access control model (TRBAC) supports periodic role enabling and disabling and temporal dependencies expressed by so-called role triggers.

Bertino et al. provide an example implementation making use of database triggers of the Oracle database management system.

Location-aware Access Control Models   Ray, Kumar, and Yu [RKY06] extend the Core RBAC model by location-based information and location-based constraints. Objects and subjects (named "users" by the authors) can be assigned to locations. Also, locations can be assigned to roles. The assignment of locations to roles can be used to restrict the locations in which a role can be assigned to a user. Furthermore, the activation of a role by a user can be restricted to certain locations. Additionally, tuples of permissions and objects can be limited to locations restricting the access to such a tuple.

A similar approach is suggested by M. Decker [Dec10]. In contrast to Ray et al., Decker bases his access control model not on RBAC models but on discretionary access control models. However, his approach is similar compared with the approach of Ray et al., he extends a standard DAC with location-based constraints. His approach "forbid[s] the access to computer resources when the mobile user stays at a place where it is not reasonable or not safe enough to access the respective resources. For example, using this approach a policy could be enforced that demands that a confidential document (resource) can only be read (operation) while staying on the premises of a particular company." [Dec10, p.26].

Technically, the introduction of location-aware access control models is the introduction of one or more constraints (e.g., subject and location, object and location, permission and location).

However, the question remains open why those specialized constraints are modeled in specific ways and not generalized as a generic constraint independent from its meaning: Instead of introducing specialized models for location-aware or time-aware access control, a generalized approach would allow to introduce any additional constraints. One of these generic constraints can then deal with location, another with time, and so on.

2.10. Standards in Authorization

In this section we provide a short overview of standards in authorization. We start with RFC 2753 which is the first document in which todays typical definitions, like policy definition point (PDP), have been introduced. We identify further standards extending and developing important terms in the field of access control. Besides the foundations of the terminology we search for goals and requirements of access control and how they are represented in standards.

2.10.1. RFC 2753 Framework for Policy-Based Admission Control

Yavatkar et al. describe in IETF's RFC 2753 [PYG00] a framework for policy-based admission control. Although the standard focuses on the resource reservation protocol (RSVP), the authors outline that the policy mechanisms described in the standard may and should apply to other contexts. The standard provides definitions for the typical concepts in policy-based authorization environments (see section 2.3), e.g. policy, policy decision point, policy enforcement point and so on. Actually, RFC 2753 is partially a predecessor of RFC 3198 [SHC$^+$01]. The latter was issued about a year after RFC2753 when the IETF decided that policy-based terminology is of such importance that its definitions should be externalized in a separate document.

Besides laying the foundations of terminology for policy-based access control, RFC 2753 defined goals and requirements. We will discuss them below, omitting specific RSVP-related goals (which are not related to access control).

- *Policies vs. mechanisms:* The framework specified in RFC 2753 deals only with architectural elements and mechanisms, abstracting this from specific policy behavior.

- *Support for many styles of policies:* The mechanisms should support many policies and policy configurations including priority systems.

- *Provision for monitoring and account information:* It must be possible to monitor policy states and resource usage, e.g. for accounting and billing purposes. This goal has been later adopted by XACML's obligation and monitoring abilities (see section 2.11).

- *Fault tolerance and recovery:* The mechanisms of the framework are designed to be fault tolerant in a way that they may recover from failures, e.g. failure of sub-components, disruption in communication and so on. We see here one origin for the design decision of XACML to let (sub-)policies return "indeterminate", thus neither permit nor deny and the problems that arise from it (see section 2.11).

- *Scalability, distinctiveness when merging policies:* Scalability and distinctiveness when merging policies are seen as a key success factor. "In particular, scalability must be considered when specifying default behavior for merging policy data objects and merging should not result in duplicate policy elements or objects" [PYG00, p.4]. Scalability here is related to local processing time per node and local memory consumption in nodes.

- *Security and denial of service considerations:* The threat of theft and denial of service attacks should be minimized and the involved identities can verify each other's identity.

Besides defining requirements, RFC 2753 also provides two important architectural elements: the policy enforcement point (PEP) and the policy decision point. As in RFC 3198, the PEP runs on one or many nodes which are policy aware. It ensures that certain operations are legitimated before they are executed.

In contrast, the Policy Decision Point (PDP) is located on a central instance. The PEP requests policy decision from the PDP. The PDP evaluates facts and policies and returns its decision back to the PEP. The interaction necessary between PEP and PDP is described by the protocol requirements in the RFC although no protocol itself is defined. Requirements are, for example, message reliability, small delays, asynchronous notification.

RFC 2753 can be seen as a starting point for the meanwhile well-established architecture of authorization frameworks. Although targeting a specific problem of RSVP – which itself has nothing to do with access control – the central elements PEP and PDP and their interaction are defined and described. RFC 2753 focuses on architectural elements of a security system without going too much into details (like policy formulation, exact message protocols and so on.)

2.10.2. RFC 2904-2906 AAA Authorization Framework

RFC 2904 [FHdL+00] describes a quasi-standard for an authorization frame-work. Authentication is explicitly excluded from the document's scope. It is assumed that authentication is handled by a different component. The framework makes use of four conceptional basic entities:

1. *Users* interested in gaining access to resources.

2. The user's *home organization* being responsible to decide whether the user may gain access to a service/resource.

3. The *service* of a service provider the user wants to gain access to.

4. The *AAA server* of the service provider containing general service agreements with the user's home organization on a general level – without knowing the individual user.

The document describes several message sequences between user, user home organization and service providers to be able to decide on the requested access. It deals with roaming users and distributed services as well. It provides basic information where which parts of authorization decisions can be made in the framework.

The subsequent RFC 2905 [HdBG+00] describes several examples of services making use of the authorization framework in RFC 2904. PPP dial-in, Mobile IP, Bandwith Broker, Internet Printing, Electronic Commerce, and Computer Based Education and Distance Learning are the examples provided. For each example, a message sequence is given, describing how the authorization process has to be modeled.

RFC 2906 [FLG00] is the third document in this series. Its content consists of the requirements which lead to the framework design of RFC 2904.

2.10.3. RFC 3198 Terminology for Policy-Based Management

Westerinen et al. [SHC+01] provide today's definitions for many access control related terms. The RFC 3198 is a melting-pot of terms already introduced in previous RFCs (e.g. RFC 2026, RFC 2828, RFC 2753) and aims to be a "clear, concise, and easily understood documentation" [SHC+01, p.1]. We already introduced the relevant terms for our work in section 2.3 and omit them here.

2.11. XACML - The eXtensible Access Control Markup Language

The extensible access control markup language (XACML) [Ris10] is an XML based language. It allows policy definitions and defines an underlying architectural framework to model an access control mechanism. It also includes a processing model, how access control requests are handled by the components. XACML is standardized by the OASIS consortium. The Organization for the Advancement of Structured Information Standards (OASIS)[4] maintains several standards, e.g. DocBook and OpenDocument, two file formats representing text documents. OpenDocument is used in LibreOffice/OpenOffice, an open-source alternative to the Microsoft Office products.

XACML wants to be "a common language for expressing security policy. If implemented throughout an enterprise, a common policy language allows the enterprise to manage the enforcement of all the elements of its security policy in all the components of its information systems" [Mos05, p.11]. It aims to unify many policy enforcement points an organization has. Therefore, XACML is split mainly into three components:

1. the XACML language definition (see section 2.11.1)

2. a definition of the architectural elements and components (see section 2.11.2)

3. a processing model how the components are invoked (see section 2.11.3).

2.11.1. XACML Language Definition

XACML defines the following requirements which are seen to be solved within XACML. Thus, we say that concerning language definition, XACMLs functionality is as follows:

- "To provide a method for combining individual rules and policies into a single policy set that applies to a particular decision request." [Mos05, p.11]

- "To provide a method for flexible definition of the procedure by which rules and policies are combined." [Mos05, p.11]

- "To provide a method for basing an authorization decision on attributes of the subject and resource." [Mos05, p.12]

---

[4]`http://www.oasis-open.org`, last accessed 2012-11-28

- "To provide a set of logical and mathematical operators on attributes of the subject, resource and environment." [Mos05, p.12]

- "To provide a method for handling a distributed set of policy components, while abstracting the method for locating, retrieving and authenticating the policy components." [Mos05, p.12]

We cited not all requirements but chose the ones we see as important. XACML aims to combine policies to policy sets. This includes mechanisms which decide on a combined policy result, if not all sub-policies could be evaluated or return conflicting results. E.g. one sub-policy allows access, another denies. Another functionality XACML aims to provide is to offer attributes for certain subjects or resources. However, this functionality is not provided by XACML in a sense that it offers APIs or functionality to determine an attribute. Instead, XACML allows defining attributes in XML's syntax.

This functionality is expressed in XML making the XACML expressions machine-readable. Unfortunately, XML expressions become easily very large and thus unreadable for human beings.

2.11.2. XACMLs Architectural Elements

XACML provides definitions of its architectural elements. We cite them from the XACML standard ([Ris10]). However, some definitions of elements have been omitted in the XACML standard.

- Access requestor: This architectural element is present in the data flow diagram but not explained in the standard. We assume, it is an entity which wants to get a decision upon an access request, e.g. a user program.

- PEP (policy enforcement point): "The system entity that performs access control, by making decision requests and enforcing authorization decisions" [Ris10, p.11].

- Context Handler: The system entity that converts decision requests in the native request format to the XACML canonical form and converts authorization decisions in the XACML canonical form to the native response format" [Ris10, p.10].

- PDP (policy decision point): "The system entity that evaluates applicable policy and renders an authorization decision" [Ris10, p.10].

- PAP (policy administration point): "The system entity that creates a policy or policy set" [Ris10, p.11].

- PIP (policy information point): "The system entity that acts as a source of attribute values" [Ris10, p.11].

- Subjects: "An actor who's attributes may be referenced by a predicate" [Ris10, p.11].

- Obligation Service: The term is not defined in the XACML standard. The term "obligation" is defined as "an operation specified in a policy or policy set that should be performed in conjunction with the enforcement of an authorization decision" [Ris10, p.11]. So we assume that an obligation service is taking care of the execution of obligations.

- Resource: "Data, service or system component" [Ris10, p.11].

- Environment: "The set of attributes that are relevant to an authorization decision and are independent of a particular subject, resource or action" [Ris10, p.10].

After introducing the major architectural elements of XACML we go on describing the data flow between those elements.

2.11.3. XACMLs Data Flow

Besides its language definition, XACML also provides the data flow between XACMLs architectural elements.

Figure 2.7 depicts relevant XACML architectural components and the data flow connecting the components. Both, picture and explanation of the data flow are explained in the official XACML standard [Mos05, p.17f], which we cite here.

1. The policy administration point (PAP) creates policies or policy sets. It is made available for the policy decision point (PDP). The PDP is responsible for evaluating the policies and return an authorization decision.

2. An access requester sends a query to the policy enforcement point (PEP). It is the task of a PEP to receive access queries, make decision requests and enforce authorization decisions. PDP and PEP are originally defined in RFC3198 [SHC+01].

3. The PEP transmits a request to the context handler. It may be enriched with attributes.

4. The context handler builds an XACML request and transmits it to the PDP.

5. If necessary, the PDP requests additional attributes (from subject, resource, action or environment) from the context handler.

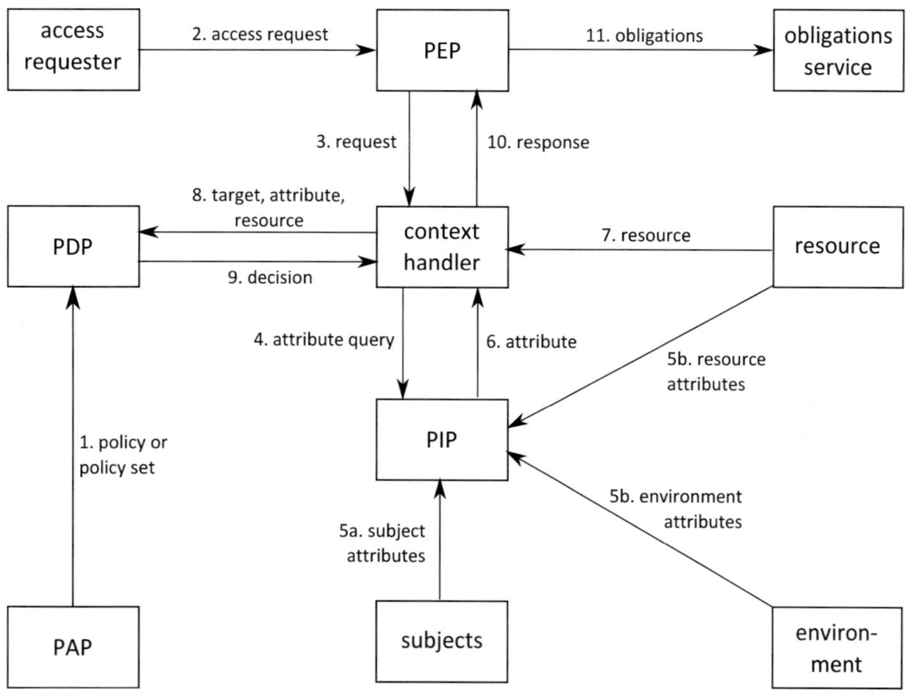

Figure 2.7.: Architecture and data flow of XACML. Taken from [Mos05, p.17].

6. Those attribute requests are delegated from the context handler to the policy information point (PIP). A PIP is defined as a source of attributes. In contrast to the terms PDP and PAP, the term PIP has to our knowledge not been defined outside of XACML.

7. The PIP obtains the request's attributes. XACML does not specify, how.

8. The PIP returns the obtained attributes to the context handler.

9. The context handler includes the resource in the context.

10. The requests attribute and resource are sent to the PDP. The PDP then evaluates the policy.

11. The PDP returns the authorization decision to the context handler.

12. The context handler returns the response to the PEP.

13. The PEP fulfills obligations that might come along with the policy. Obligations are, e.g. logging entries, changing the state of a variable, and so on.

We see that XACML introduces a standardized way, how access requests are handled. Besides the already standardized PDP and PEP, a new component is introduced, the policy information point.

2.11.4. Problems of XACML

Attribute retrieval   XACML does not explain how attributes of subjects, objects, and the environment can be evaluated and which attributes or attribute types are supported.

Obligations   XACML introduces so-called obligations. Obligations are functions that are performed by the PEP when a policy linked with the obligation grants access. An example is logging or the need to change one's password. However, it does not become clear what kind of obligations are exactly supported and how the obligation service is implemented.

Implementation   To our knowledge, it took several years until the first implementation of a XACML framework was created. Sun's XACML implementation[5] is based on the XACML release from February 2003 and was released in 2006. Although in 2012 OASIS is in the process of releasing version 3 of XACML, there is no implementation available for version 2. Version 2 was already released by OASIS in 2005.

Weaknesses in policy strategy combination   Li et al. [LWQ+09] state that XACML has a very flexible approach for policy strategies, namely deny-overrides, permit-overrides, first-applicable, and only-one-applicable. However, XACML lacks very common strategies like logical combinations of policies. E.g. a permit may only be granted, if two sub-policies allow it. In addition, Li et al. list common strategies not supported by XACML:

- *Weak-consensus:* A request is only permitted, if at least one sub-policy allows access and no other sub-policy denies it. The request is denied, if at least one sub-policy denies access and none permits it. A conflict has to be raised, if some sub-policies deny and others permit access.

- *Strong-consensus:* All sub-policies must either permit or deny a request. A conflict is indicated if at least one sub-policy differs in its conclusion. This strategy differs from the weak-consensus strategy as a sub-policy may neither return a permit nor deny, thus is indifferent for a request.

---

[5] `http://sunxacml.sourceforge.net`, last accessed 2013-01-17

In such a case, the strong-consensus will yield a conflict while the weak-consensus does not.

- *Weak-majority:* A request is granted access, if the majority of all sub-policies grant access and only a minority denies access. Sub-policies being indifferent are not counted for the votes.

- *Strong-majority:* Permission is granted, if over half of all sub-policies permit request and denied, if over half of all sub-policies deny. If no majority can be gained, the policy is indifferent or in conflict. The strong-majority handles indifferent sub-polices stricter than the weak-majority strategy. Li et al. do not define, how indifferent sub-policies count towards the majority.

Generally, Li et al. criticize the lack of strategies allowing the combination of policies of XACML. "XACML has become the de facto standard for specifying access control policies for various applications, especially web services. Extensibility and flexibility of policy combining are thus desirable to meet the needs of these applications. XACML explicitly allows additional user-defined combining algorithms. However, it does not provide a standard approach (or a specification language) for doing so." [LWQ+09, p.135f]. Consequently, they suggest a Policy Combination Language (PCL) which allows a flexible combination and definition of strategies.

Ambiguity of indeterminate policies   Ni et al. [NBL09] criticize the ambiguity of the policy result "indeterminate" of XACML. They provide an example making use of a two sub-policy XACML policy: The first sub-policy r_1 returns "permit" while the second sub-policy r_2 returns "indeterminate". Although the expected overall result is expected to be "permit", so Ni et al., XACML returns "deny" for the policy ps_1 being counter-intuitive. "If there is no error or no missing information r_2 can only evaluate to either "permit" or "not applicable". If r_2 evaluates to "permit", the final effect is "permit", and if r_2 evaluates to "not applicable", the final effect is "permit" too. However, based on the standard policy combining algorithm provided in XACML 2.0 and 3.0 WD 6, ps_1 returns "deny". The reason for such an unintended result is that the meaning of "indeterminate" is overloaded, which indeed may represent different access decisions. XACML policy combining algorithms cannot distinguish these different meanings and are "indeterminate", thus may generate such an unintended result." [NBL09, p.298]

From this we see, why XACML is criticized to be complex and sometimes counter-intuitive in its semantics and behavior.

2.12. Access Control and the Semantic Web

"The Semantic Web will bring structure to the meaningful content of web pages, creating an environment where software agents roaming from page to page can readily carry out sophisticated tasks for users." [BLHL+01, p.34]

"Most of the web's content today is designed for humans to read, not for computer programs to manipulate meaningfully." [BLHL+01, p.34]

These two quotes from Berners-Lee et al. in their pioneering paper "The Semantic Web" [BLHL+01] explain the motivation and aim of the semantic web. The general approach was to use ontologies to represent knowledge in different domains. The knowledge is represented by specific formal languages (e.g. OWL, RDF). Reasoning engines support logic inference and queries about the modeled facts. In a recent article Shadbolt, Hall, and Berners-Lee [SLH06] mainly see five areas of ongoing development concerning the semantic web: universal resource identifiers (URIs) as resource identifiers, triple stores as knowledge database, RDF translation as data exchange format, web ontology languages as powerful alternative to RDF and rules and inference engines to reason on the data.

The idea is not far to use the results of the semantic web development as a base for access control. An attempt in this direction is made by Finin et al. [FJK+08]. They model a standard RBAC model in the web ontology language OWL.

Kagal et al. [KBCW06] suggest a framework to manage policies using semantic web technologies. Their framework "Rein" is designed to support many possible policy languages. Rein stores the data in ontologies (expressed in OWL and RDF). It is able to reason on them by standard ontology mechanisms, e.g. the RDF-S or OWL reasoner. The Rein model has the fixed entities requester, resource and access (type). It supports additional environmental conditions which must be expressed in the model of the ontology.

Kagal et al. do not provide any runtime times and answer times of their implementation. Bock et al. did a benchmarking for OWL reasoners [BHJV08] recently. They compared six OWL reasoners (Sesame, OWLIM, KAON2, HermiT, RacerPro, Pellet) based on some standard data sets. E.g. the VICODI dataset was compared in five flavors ranging from 50k to 250k axioms. The response time for a query was between 0.2 seconds up to 3 seconds (best OWL reasoner on the VICODI dataset was RacerPro with 0.2 seconds, worst KAON2 with 3s). These answer times are a serious issue, when using OWL standard reasoners as query engines, as Kagal et al. [KBCW06] did. Answer times are crucial for access control systems. Being able to perform about one access check request per second (assuming an average answer time of 1s) is at least two orders of magnitudes too slow. Think of the case that a list of 30 entries, e.g. books, must be checked for access. This would mean a response time of 30s for the user. Obviously, this is orders of magnitudes too slow.

Having a look at the sample data sets used in the experiment of Bock (about 250k at most) we see that this is actually a very small data set for access right queries. A typical notebook's file system today may have roundabout 200k files, independently of other conditions like access rights, users and so on. The used data sets, therefore, can be seen to be representative for a single user environment and not by far for larger web systems with millions of entities. We did find no information about the scaling of inference engines used by Bock et al. Nevertheless, more entities will lead to longer response times. Therefore, we hold these approaches for unusable for practical, real world access control problems.

2.13. Logic-Based Authorization Models

In [SV01] P. Samarati and de Capitani di Vimercati criticize that "several authorization models have been formalized and access control mechanisms enforcing them implemented. However, each model, and its corresponding enforcement mechanism, implements a single specified policy, which is in fact built into the mechanism. As a consequence, although different policy choices are possible in theory, each access control system is in practice bound to a specific policy. The major drawback of this approach is that a single policy simply cannot capture all the protection requirements that may arise over time" [SV01, p.184].

They argue, "that different users may have different protection requirements" [SV01, p.184], "a single user may have different protection requirements on different objects" [SV01, p.184], and "protection requirements may change over time" [SV01, p.184]. This is an argumentation that we used to motivate our own work. We refer to a current use case supporting this argument [Son13].

One solution for this problem is the usage of logic-based languages. Logic-based languages have a large expressive power and a formal representation. We provide two examples for this kind of access control models below.

2.13.1. Woo and Lam's approach

Woo and Lam [WL92] describe such an approach, actually the first one we could find. The model of Woo and Lam is depicted in figure 2.8.

Before a subject s can perform access r on object o, a request in the form $req(r, s, o)$ is submitted to the authorization module. The module responds

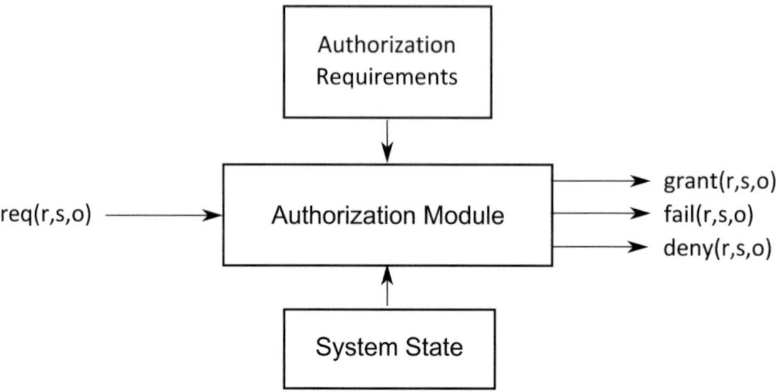

Figure 2.8.: Authorization model of Woo and Lam [WL92, p.38].

either with a $grant(r, s, o)$ or a $deny(r, s, o)$. It might also return a $fail(r, s, o)$, if the authorization module fails to establish a grant or deny.

The authorization module is described as an interpreter. As input the interpreter takes a set of policy bases $\{B_i\}$ and the current system state.

Woo and Lam [WL92] define an authorization policy as "over a set of subjects S, a set of objects O and a set of access rights R as a 4-tuple (P^+, P^-, N^+, N^-) where each component is a subset of $\{(r, s, o) \mid r \in R, s \in S, o \in O\}$" [WL92, p.39]. P^+ is the set of explicitly granted rights, i.e. $(r, s, o) \in P^+$ explicitly allows access of subject s on object o with right r. N^+ are the rights explicitly denied. P^- and N^- are the rights that should not explicitly be granted (denied, respectively) under this policy.

The policy language of Woo and Lam is a many-sorted first-order logic with a rule construct. The rule construct is similar to rule constructs used in default logic [Rei80]. Woo and Lam name two restrictions of their language:

- The semantics of the language should be computable and valid. As an infinitary theory is in many cases semi-decidable, Woo and Lam restrict their language to a finitary theory: they do not allow function symbols and use only finite sets. By this, the authors also omit quantifications.

- Disjunction is limited in a very restricted way only. By this restriction, the language is not able to express requirements like "subject A is allowed to read file A or file B". Like the authors, we see this second limitation not too restrictive. It is a rare case that in policies access is restricted by such an OR-combination. More often statements like "subject is allowed to read file A and file B" will occur.

Woo and Lam [WL92] express a rule in the form $\frac{f:f'}{g}$. f is the prerequisite of the rule, f' is the assumption, and g is the consequence. When no assumption is required, $f \Rightarrow g$ is an abbreviation for $\frac{f:T}{g}$ with T being the symbol for *true*.

We provide an example rule (see [WL92]):
$execute^+(x, P.exe) \Rightarrow read^+(x, P.doc)$

This rule says that any user x who is explicitly $(+)$ authorized to execute a program *P.exe* is also authorized to read the associated document *P.doc*.

Woo and Lam [WL92] provide as a real-world example the policy base of the Bell-LaPadula model. One problem of the Bell-LaPadula model expressed in Woo and Lam's language is, that Woo and Lam show the example only for two clearance / security levels, *low* and *high*. If more than these two security level have to be modeled, the necessary policy expressions explode. With 2 levels, 4 expressions are necessary, with 3 levels already 9 policies are required, 4 levels require 16 policies and so on.

Besides this, Woo and Lam [WL92] do not provide an implementation of their language. The authors only refer to Prolog as an interpreter of their language.

Another critic is put forward by Samarati and de Capitani di Vimercati [SV01]. "As a drawback, authorization specifications may result difficult to understand and manage. Also, the trade-off between expressiveness and efficiency seems to be strongly unbalanced: the lack of restrictions on the language results in the specification of models which may not even be decidable and therefore will not be implementable. (...) Woo and Lam's approach is based on truth in extensions of arbitrary default theories, which is known, even in the propositional case to be NP-complete, and in the first order case, is worse than undecidable" [SV01, p.185]. In other words, Woo and Lam's approach is too complex to compute.

2.13.2. Jajodia et al.

Another suggestion comes from Jajodia et al. [JSSS01]. They propose a "flexible authorization framework" (FAF). The FAF is, like Woo and Lam's approach, a logic-based language trying to balance flexibility, expressive power, ease of management, and performance. Jajodia et al. claim that any model expressed in their language can be "computed in quadratic time data complexity" [JSSS01, p.239], which is better than the NP-hard run time of Woo and Lam's approach.

The language of Jajodia et al. makes use of 5 predicates, we introduce the two most important. Let o be an object, s be a subject, and a an "action term" or permission type, and $+$ or $-$ a sign representing allowance or denial for a policy.

- $cando(o, s, \langle sign \rangle a)$
  Is an explicit allowance or denial. E.g. $cando(o, john, +read)$ allows (+) user *john* to *read* object o.

- $dercando(o, s, \langle sign \rangle a)$
  dercando represents an authorization derived by the usage of logical rule inference.

- $do(o, s, \langle sign \rangle a)$ *do* is an access enforcement, thus access must be granted or must be denied. The expression is used to solve conflict resolution in case both "permit" and "deny" can be inferred by application of logical rules. It is a kind of default decision.

Besides these predicates, the language supports hierarchies, e.g. memberships in hierarchical user groups. Furthermore, relationships between entities are supported, e.g. an owner relationship in the form $owner(user, object)$.

However, Jajodia et al. do not provide an implementation for their suggested language. The authors do not proof (1) if their language can be implemented in any kind of logic interpreter, like Prolog. And if so, (2) how fast access decisions can be made using real-world examples. In their paper, the authors do not even provide a theoretical use case like implementing a standard access control model, like Bell-LaPadula, to show, how complex the expressions are which are necessary to mimic the example access control model.

2.14. Summary

In this chapter we selected several access control models and approaches suggested by different authors during the last 50 years. We started with important general design principles and continued with the famous HRU-model and its derivations. Further, we introduced the differentiation between mandatory and discretionary access control models as it was first mentioned in DoD's Orange Book. Besides the military access control models we introduced commercially important models like the Clark/Wilson model, the Brewer/Nash model, and the RBAC model family. Furthermore, we cited important standards and RFCs introducing important and relevant terms. Hereby, we mentioned RADIUS as relevant communication protocol. We laid out the basics of the extensible access control language XACML together with its architecture and protocol. We finished the chapter by giving examples how access control models can be realized making use of the semantic web and, as one of the latest developments in access control models, how these models can be expressed by logic-based languages.

3. Motivating Example

In this chapter we present an informal introduction of the Access Definition and Query Language (ADQL) thought as a motivating example. It aims to give the reader a first impression about ADQL, its structure, goal, and concepts.

ADQL is a formal language utilizing different mathematical concepts and interpreted by a software service. Without going into details we present a usage example for an access control model. We show how this example is described in ADQL concerning the access control model definition, facts, policies, and access queries. With the facts we explain the underlying concepts, again in an informal manner.

The complete language is explained in chapter 5. We provide a definition and usage of all concepts in chapter 4. Further, in-depth usage examples are presented in chapter 6.

3.1. Components of ADQL

One of the first questions to be answered when designing an access control system is: What are the components required to fulfill the task? An access control system decides on access checks: it either grants or denies access.

We illustrate these considerations with an example: User "Ann" wants to access a file "file1.jpg". She wants to read the file. It is Friday, 31.8.2012. She requests access from her home computer through a VPN connection to a server in her company.

How can we decide if the access request should be granted? To enable this decision basically four components are required:

System State. First, a system state is required. A system state is a description of the environment necessary to be able to decide on access checks. E.g. Who is the user requesting access? What is the operation the user wants to apply? On which object is access requested?

3. Motivating Example

In our example, "Ann" wants to access "file1.jpg" with a read operation. Maybe, even the current system time or the network the user sends the request from are also necessary system states. In our example, it is Friday, 31.8.2012 and the used network is a VPN. All in all, we need 5 variables to represent the system state of our example: the user, the requested file, the requested operation, the system date, and the network.

The concept ADQL uses to represent a system state is called *scope*.

An ADQL scope consists of a collection of *variables*. Each variable describes one facet of the current system state, e.g. who is the current user or which object is accessed? Within a scope, a variable is bound to a specific value. E.g. the variable user is bound to Ann. We write $\triangleright user = \{Ann\}$ with $\triangleright$ being an ADQL symbol marking variables.

Our example represents one system state represented by 5 variable bindings: The user is "Ann", the object is "file1.jpg", the requested permission is "read", the date is 2012-08-31, and the network is VPN.

ADQL provides no mechanisms to detect the current system state, i.e. it is out of scope of ADQL to define, how it can be determined that the user is "Ann" and bind "Ann" to a variable. We assume that the binding of variables to values is done before querying ADQL.

Policies. A policy describes conditions when access is granted or denied. Policies granting access are called positive access rights, policies denying access are called negative access rights. In the current version, ADQL supports the formulation of positive access rights.

ADQL models policies as sets of conditions. If all conditions of a policy p are met, then p grants access. We say, that the conditions of policy p are logically AND-concatenated. ADQL refers to these conditions as *tests*. We model tests as boolean functions.

Example for a test: "Is the current user 'Ann'?". Example for a policy: "Grant access, if (a) the current user is "Ann" and (b) the currently requested object is "file1.jpg".

Model. The model is the very basic description of the space an access control system is modeled in. Without defining, that e.g. a concept "users" exists, no policies, no facts, and no system states can be described for the concept "users". Therefore, the access control model describes all these basic concepts and how the concepts are related.

To describe the concept, ADQL introduces the concepts entity, container, relation, and filtered 1-projection. All concepts will be described in-depth in chapter 5. For now, we introduce the above concepts briefly:

- Entities represent "things" within ADQL. E.g. the user "Ann" is an entity. The permission "read" is an entity.

- Containers are used to group entities. E.g. a container can be used to group all user entities. Containers can be organized in hierarchies and networks.

- Relations represent properties of entities. E.g. a user may have assigned attributes, like a supervisor or a proxy.

- Filtered 1-projections are a concatenation of a filter operation and a projection. ADQL utilizes filtered 1-projections to query on relations and relation structures. With the help of filtered 1-projections queries like "return all proxies of the user Ann" can be answered.

Facts   Facts describe the reality and create the framework, ADQL makes its decisions on. E.g. it is a fact, that "Ann" exists. It is another fact that "Ann" is a "user".

Facts are based on the model. They describe the reality making use of the concepts defined in the model. A model describes the "layout" of the access control model. E.g. a model says, things like "users" exist. In contrast, the facts describe the details about the concepts of the model layer. E.g. which users do actually exist? While the model describes the availability of certain concepts, the facts describe the population of this space.

This "population of the space" is used by policies and the system state. In order to issue a policy, that "the user must be Ann", (1) the concept "user" must be introduced in the model, and (2) the fact that "Ann" is a "user" must be defined. The same is true for the system states: The variable "user" can be assigned to the value "Ann" only, if both, model and fact, exist.

3.2. Motivating Example

We demonstrate the usage of the Access Definition and Query Language with a small usage scenario. The scenario will not explain all concepts in-depth, but tries to give an overview on ADQL's structure and usage.

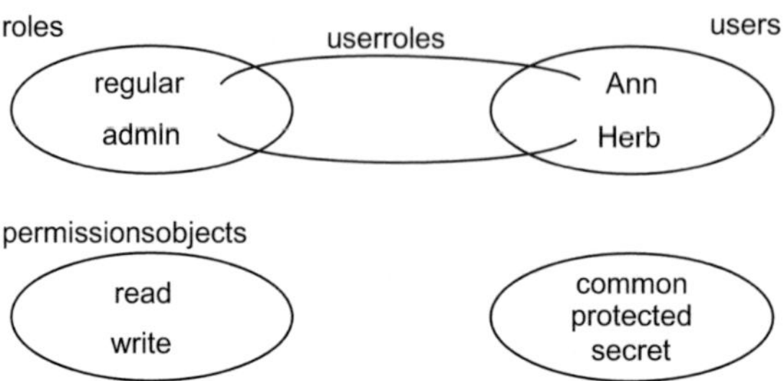

Figure 3.1.: Graphical illustration of the simple RBAC example.

Our example is the simple Role-Based Access Control Model (RBAC) depicted in figure 3.1.

In our simple RBAC example `users` can be assigned to `roles`. A `role` itself consists of tuples of `permissions` and `objects`, e.g. (`read`, `common`) allowing "read" access to object "common". Our goal is to model this basic RBAC model in ADQL. Furthermore, we want to describe the facts, that "Ann" and "Herb" are users, "Ann" is a "regular" user while "Herb" is an "administrator". Our model supports the operations "read" and "write" and distinguishes three objects, "common", "protected", and "secret". We define three policies:

1. Any regular user may read and write object "common".

2. Any regular user may read object "protected". They must not access object "secret".

3. Administrators have full access to all objects.

We start by defining the access control model. An access control model provides a framework, how policies, access rights and facts are described. In this example our model consists of the following parts:

A concept "users" is required. It is modeled as a container. We describe this in ADQL:

$$\underbrace{users}_{symbol} = \underbrace{\triangle}_{definition} \underbrace{c}_{container} \underbrace{()}_{arguments} \; ; \tag{3.1}$$

We define ("$\triangle$") a new container ("c"). Containers are objects which are used to collect entities. Currently it is empty ("$()$"). The new container is assigned the symbol "users", we say the "container is named 'users' ". Every ADQL statement is finished by a semicolon.

Ann and Herb are users. ADQL says that the entities "Ann" and "Herb" exist:

$$Ann = \triangle e(); \tag{3.2}$$
$$Herb = \triangle e(); \tag{3.3}$$

The symbol "Ann" is assigned a newly defined ("$\triangle$") entity ("e"). The same applies to Herb. Each statement is ended by a semicolon.

We assign both entities, "Ann" and "Herb" to the container "users".

$$users = \triangle c(Ann, Herb); \tag{3.4}$$

We define a new container ("$\triangle c$"). This container is assigned the entities referenced by the symbols "Ann" and "Herb". The new container is assigned to the symbol "users". Please note, that the container defined in our very first command ($users = \triangle c();$) is no longer referenced by the symbol "users". A new container has been defined and was assigned the symbol "users". The "old" and empty container is not referenced by any symbol anymore.

Side note: Our current implementation of ADQL does not support automatic garbage collection. However, as we will see later, all defined ADQL concepts (like entities and containers) can be referenced by internal ids and therefore deleted or modified, although no symbol is referencing the item.

Next, we introduce the two roles "regular" and "admin":

$$roles = \triangle c(regular = \triangle e(), admin = \triangle e()); \tag{3.5}$$

A "container" ("c") is defined ("$\triangle$") and assigned to the symbol $roles$. It consists of two entities "regular" and "admin". Both entities "regular" and "admin" are defined within the same command and assigned its respective symbol. This statement is an example for nesting commands: Three definitions, two for entities and one for a container, are written down in one statement.

We model the fact, that Ann is a regular user and Herb is an administrator:

$$\underbrace{userroles}_{symbol} = \underbrace{\triangle r(users, roles)}_{relation\ definition} : \underbrace{\{(Ann, regular), (Herb, admin)\}}_{values}; \tag{3.6}$$

The above ADQL expression defines a new relation ("$\triangle r$") on the containers "users" and "roles". A relation allows to *link* entities of the containers with each other. In this case, we link the entities "Ann" and "regular". This fact says that "Ann" is a "regular" user. Consequently, "Herb" is an "administrator". The relation is assigned the symbol "userroles".

3. Motivating Example

Let us now turn to permissions (called "operations" in some RBAC models).
We introduce a container for all modeled permissions and assign "read" and
"write" to it.

$$permissions = \triangle c(read = \triangle e(), write = \triangle e()); \tag{3.7}$$

The command is syntactically comparable to the definition of the roles: Two
entities and an embracing container are defined in one statement.

Next, we introduce the three objects "common", "protected", and "secret".

$$objects = \triangle c(common = \triangle e(), protected = \triangle e(), secret = \triangle e()); \tag{3.8}$$

As we have introduced the access control model and all facts, we are now
able to define the access control policies which state when access should be
granted.

Let us repeat the required policies:

1. Any regular user may read and write "common".

2. Any regular user may read "protected". They must not access "secret".

3. Administrators have full access to all objects.

The first policy can be expressed saying that "regular users may read and write
the common object". This policy can be divided into smaller "sub-policies":

1. The current user has to own the role regular,

2. the requested access has to be either read or write,

3. the object has to be "common".

ADQL refers to sub-policies as "tests".

We start modeling in ADQL with the third test, as it is the simplest to explain.
The condition "the object has to be 'common'" can be re-formulated as a question: "Is the current object common?". The current object is represented in
ADQL as a variable which can be assigned any entity belonging to the container "objects".

$$\underbrace{\triangleright}_{variable} \underbrace{objects}_{symbol} \tag{3.9}$$

This expression refers to the variable $\triangleright objects$. In ADQL, variables are predefined: A variable of the same symbol as a container is automatically defined in ADQL when a container is defined. We already defined the container "objects" before, consequently, the variable $\triangleright objects$ has already been defined.

We want to check if the value of the current object is "common". ADQL formulates this test in the following way: "Does the value of the variable object match at least one element in a single-entity container with the element "common"?

$$\underbrace{objIsCommon}_{symbol} = \triangle t(\underbrace{\triangleright objects}_{left\ side}, \underbrace{\triangle c(common)}_{right\ side}, \underbrace{\theta}_{test\ operator}); \qquad (3.10)$$

This expression defines a new test ("$\triangle t$"). ADQL tests consist of three arguments, two containers or variables ("left side" and "right side") and an operator. The operator is a boolean function. In the above example, the "left" argument is the variable "objects" ("$\triangleright objects$"). (If you wonder: ADQL expects as left and right side arguments of the type container. The value of a variable in ADQL is of the type container.) The "right" argument is a newly defined container with one entity assigned: "objects" ("$\triangle c(common)$"). This container is not assigned a symbol, we say, it is "anonymous". The third argument of the test is a boolean function, here θ (theta). *theta* returns true if both containers share at least one entity.

We summarize: The test "objIsCommon" checks whether the variable object and a container holding the entity "common" share at least one entity. As variables are used to express certain system states, we can call the value of a variable the "current value" for a specific point in time. In other words: Is the "current object" the entity "common"? This is exactly what we wanted to express.

Let us continue with the second test of our first policy, (2) the requested access has to be either read or write. This test is similar to the above test: "Is the currently requested access either read or write?".

$$permRW = \triangle t(\triangleright permissions, \triangle c(read, write), \theta); \qquad (3.11)$$

The test *permRW* checks whether the current permission has at least one element in common with a newly defined container holding the entities "read" and "write". Or, is the current permission read or write?

We go on with the first test for our policy "(1) the current user has to own the role regular". We can re-formulate this problem by asking "does the current user own the role regular?". ADQL formulates the test in this way: "Does the set of roles assigned to the current user match at least the set containing the role regular"? This expression requires the following concepts to be used: (A) Who is the current user? (B) Which roles is this user assigned to? (C) Do these roles contain the role regular?

The current user (part A) is, as we already know, represented in ADQL as variable "$\triangleright users$". Part B "which roles is this user assigned to?" requires a so-called filtered 1-projection:

$$\underbrace{assignedroles}_{symbol} = \triangle pr(\ \underbrace{userroles}_{relation\ symbol}\ )(\underbrace{\triangleright users,.}_{parameters}\ ); \tag{3.12}$$

We define a new filtered 1-projection ("$\triangle pr$") on the relation "userroles". The first input parameter for the filtered 1-projection is the value of the variable users ("$\triangleright users$"), thus the current user. This is the filter applied in the operation: all tuple elements of the relation not matching this filter are ignored. The second input parameter, denoted by the dot ("."), marks the argument of the relation the filtered 1-projection projects to. This is the projection applied on the relation. As the result is always one-dimensional, we refer to it as "1-projection". In other words, if a relation is interpreted as table with each column being a "link", the dot marks the remaining column when the filtered 1-projection is applied. The concatenation of the filter operation and 1-projection is referred to as "filtered 1-projection" or "1F-projection". The example filtered 1-projection is assigned to the symbol "assignedroles".

Please recall the definition of the relation "userroles": It is defined on the containers *users* $\times$ *roles*. As the "dot" is at position 2, the result of the filtered 1-projection are the second part of each "link" (element of the relation), in this case an entity of the container "roles".

The above definition of the filtered 1-projection "assignedroles" needs to be evaluated. ADQL calls the evaluation of definitions an "application". The symbol for an application is ∇. Consequently, the application of the above filtered 1-projection is denoted by

$$\nabla(assignedroles)() == \nabla(\triangle pr(userroles)(\triangleright users,.))(); \tag{3.13}$$

Side note: The symbol "=" or ":=" is used in ADQL as an assignment operator, assigning the right side of the equal sign to the left side. To differentiate assignments from the statement "is equal to" we denote the latter with the symbol "==".

The result of the above application $"\nabla(assignedroles)()"$ is depending on the second argument $"()"$ of the application, which has been omitted so far. The second argument is a scope representing a certain system state with variable bindings. Within a scope, variables can be bound to values. Scopes do not interfere with each other. Only variable bindings are scope dependent. Definitions of the access control model, facts, and policies are global definitions valid for any scope.

$$
\begin{aligned}
s_1 &= \triangle s(\triangleright users = \triangle c(Ann)); & (3.14)\\
s_2 &= \triangle s(\triangleright users = \triangle c(Herb)); & (3.15)\\
s_3 &= \triangle s(\triangleright users = \triangle c()); & (3.16)\\
s_4 &= \triangle s(\triangleright users = \triangle c(Ann, Herb)); & (3.17)
\end{aligned}
$$

The above statement defines four scopes $("\triangle s")$. The scopes are assigned to the symbols s_1, s_2, s_3, and s_4. Each scope binds the variable $\triangleright users$ to a container. s_1 assigns the variable $\triangleright users$ to the container $\triangle c(Ann)$ with the entity "Ann".

The variable $\triangleright users$ can be bound to any container.

We show the results of the applications for every scope $s_1, ..., s_4$, respectively.

$$
\begin{aligned}
\nabla(assignedroles)(s_1) &== \triangle c(regular) & (3.18)\\
\nabla(assignedroles)(s_2) &== \triangle c(admin) & (3.19)\\
\nabla(assignedroles)(s_3) &== \triangle c() & (3.20)\\
\nabla(assignedroles)(s_4) &== \triangle c(regular, admin) & (3.21)
\end{aligned}
$$

In scope s_1, the variable $\triangleright users$ is assigned to an anonymous container including "Ann". In scope s_1 $\triangleright users$ is assigned to an anonymous container with "Herb", in scope s_3 to an empty anonymous container, and in scope s_4 to an anonymous container with "Ann" and "Herb".

The filtered 1-projection is executed (or applied) on all four cases. They use the definition of the relation "userroles" which links "Ann" with the role "regular" and "Herb" with the role "admin".

We immediately see that the application of the filtered 1-projection "assignedroles" returns exactly what we wanted to know for part B of our test: "which roles is this user assigned to?".

This leaves the third part C: "do these roles contain the role regular?". We already modeled a question like this before. We re-formulate the question to "do the roles match at least one element in a single-entity container with the element "regular?".

Putting together the parts A-C we end up with the test:

$$roleIsRegular = \triangle t(\nabla(\triangle pr(userroles)(\triangleright users, .)(), \triangle c(regular), \theta); \quad (3.22)$$

We define a new test ("$\triangle t$") which is assigned the symbol "roleIsRegular". It consists of the application ("∇") of a newly defined filtered 1-projection ("$\triangle pr$") on the relation "userroles". The filtered 1-projection uses as input parameters the variable users ("$\triangleright users$") and the filtered 1-projection target. It returns the assigned roles (based on the relation "userroles"). The test compares the result of this application of the filtered 1-projection with the newly defined container ("$\triangle c$") containing the entity "regular". The operator of the test is theta ("θ"), returning true if both operands share at least one element. This is true, if one role of the current user is regular. We see that we modeled the sub-policy "the current user has to own the role regular".

So far, we modeled all three sub-policies of the first policy "regular users may read and write the common object". We combine the sub-policies, ADQL calls them "tests", to a "policy":

$$regUsersMayRWCommon =$$
$$\triangle p(roleIsRegular, permRW, objIsCommon); \quad (3.23)$$

A policy is defined ("$\triangle p$"). It consists of the above defined tests "roleIsRegular", "permRW", and "objIsCommon". The policy is assigned the symbol "regUsersMayRWCommon".

Alternatively, we could have defined the policy and the three tests in one statement:

$$RegRWCommon = \triangle p($$
$$roleIsRegular = \triangle t($$
$$\nabla(\triangle pr(userroles)(\triangleright users, .))(),$$
$$\triangle c(regular),$$
$$\theta),$$
$$permRW = \triangle t(\triangleright permissions, \triangle c(read, write), \theta),$$
$$objIsCommon = \triangle t(\triangleright objects, \triangle c(common), \theta)$$
$$); \quad (3.24)$$

Let us continue with the third policy, we want to represent ("administrators have full access to all objects"). The third policy is represented by a quite short ADQL statement:

$$adminFullAccess = \triangle p(\triangle t(assignedroles, \triangle c(admin), \theta)); \qquad (3.25)$$

We define a new policy ("$\triangle p$") and assign it the symbol *adminFullAccess*. The policy consists of only one test ("$\triangle t$"). The test compares the previously defined filtered 1-projection *assignedroles* with a new container ("$\triangle c$") holding only the previously defined entity *admin*. The operator for the test is θ which becomes true, if the left and the right side share at least one common entity. So, the test is true, if one of the assigned roles of the current user is "admin". The policy becomes true, if the test becomes true. No further conditions apply. In other words, whatever object the user wants to access or which permission he may require, it is sufficient to be assigned the user role "admin". This is exactly, what we want to express.

We leave the definition of the second policy to the reader.

Let us quickly summarize what we have defined so far. First, we defined the access control model, thus the containers and relations necessary to represent the simple RBAC model we want to use. Second, we created the sample facts in the model, e.g. that "Ann" and "Herb" are users, "common" is an object and so on. Third, we created two policies which defined conditions when access is granted. With these three steps we defined the access control model, facts, and policies.

We finish our introduction in ADQL by showing how access queries are defined. Before being able to ask queries we must be able to represent the current system state. We have already seen that this can be done using ADQL "scopes". Within a scope, variables can be bound to values.

$$
\begin{aligned}
s_1 = \triangle s(\\
\triangleright users = \triangle c(Ann), \\
\triangleright permission = \triangle c(read), \\
\triangleright objects = \triangle c(common) \\
);
\end{aligned}
\qquad (3.26)
$$

The above statement defines a new scope ("$\triangle s$") and assigns it to the symbol s_1. The scope includes three explicit variable bindings: The variable $\triangleright users$

is assigned to a new container definition including "Ann" ("$\triangle c(Ann)$"). The variable $\triangleright permissions$ is assigned to a container holding "read", the variable $\triangleright objects$ to a container holding "common".

To find out, if the defined policies grant access for this scope, it is sufficient, to define an application on this scope:

$$\nabla(s_1)(); \tag{3.27}$$

For evaluating the return value of this application, all policies defined are evaluated using the evaluated scope. We immediately see that the policy "RegRW-Common" evaluates true: "Ann" has the role "regular", the requested permission is "read" and the requested object is "common". Subsequently, the result of the application of s_1 is:

$$\nabla(s_1)() == true \tag{3.28}$$

We end this section here. It was our target to give a short introduction into ADQL. We have shown how ADQL represents a simple RBAC model, models facts, policies, system states, and queries.

4. The Access Definition and Query Language (ADQL)

The aim of this chapter is to present syntax and semantic of the Access Definition and Query Language.

We continue this chapter with an in-depth explanation of ADQL's syntax.

4.1. The Syntax of ADQL

The complete extended Backus-Naur-Form (BNF) of ADQL – named after the scientists John Backus and Peter Naur [Knu64] – can be found in appendix A. As BNF defines the syntax but not the meaning of a formal language, we will iterate through all language elements in this section. One by one we will discuss the element, explain its meaning, explain its relation to the concepts of ADQL, and provide examples.

The ADQL language version explained in this chapter is technically referred to as version 3.0. Earlier versions of the language followed a different syntax paradigm more related to standard SQL. We will not explain the differences between the language versions here. Readers interested in this detail, can find them e.g. in [SGS12].

Generally, a well-formed ADQL expression consists of a list of terms. Each term is either a definition or an application. This basic approach may remind the reader to the well-known Lambda calculus (e.g. [Bar85]): A Lambda term consists of either a variable, an abstraction (definition) or an application. Although we think that syntax, semantic, and purpose of ADQL is quite different to that of the famous Lambda calculus, we decided to follow the Lambda calculus concerning our syntax.

4.2. Expression

An ADQL expression consists of one term or a list of terms separated by a semicolon ";".

BNF notation:

$$\langle \text{Expression} \rangle \models \langle \text{Term} \rangle \text{ ";" } | \langle \text{Term} \rangle \text{ ";" } \langle \text{Expression} \rangle$$

We see in the BNF notation, that an expression consists of a term or a concatenation of terms. An empty ADQL term is sufficient for a well-formed expression.

4.3. Term

An ADQL term is defined either as empty, a definition or an application.

BNF notation:

$$\langle \text{Term} \rangle \models \epsilon | \langle \text{Definition} \rangle | \langle \text{Application} \rangle$$

We see that a term can either be a definition or an application. Definitions introduce new facts (which can be related to all ADQL layers, see section 5.1), while applications evaluate definitions, in other words do calculations with them. We use the terms "application" and "evaluation" synonymically, there is no difference between an ADQL application and an ADQL evaluation.

Empty terms are valid. They are expressed by ϵ.

Terms can be put into a comma-separated list. Term lists will be used by non-terminals introduced later in this chapter.

Example:
"$Ann = \triangle e();$" is the definition of an entity.
The smallest well-formed ADQL expression is ";".

4.4. Symbols and Identifier

4.4.1. Symbols

Before we explain definitions and applications, we want to introduce symbols and identifiers.

ADQL supports two global symbol tables: The first is the internal symbol table. Each definition is automatically and ADQL-internally referenced by a symbol from the internal symbol table. As already said, this symbol table is global for all definitions. Direct assignments or changes to the internal symbol table are not possible; the administration is ADQL-internal. Nevertheless, the internal symbols can be looked up and used in ADQL expressions.

The second global symbol table is the external symbol table. Each definition can be assigned an external symbol. Symbols are assigned with the equal "=" operator. The external symbol can be chosen externally by an ADQL user. If an external symbol already in use is assigned to another definition, the symbol assignment is overwritten. No error or warning is raised in this case. In contrast, internal symbols cannot be overwritten.

Example:
$\triangle e()$;
This is a well-formed entity definition without an assignment of an external symbol. Only an internal symbol is assigned to this definition automatically.

$Ann = \triangle e()$;
This is also a well-formed entity definition with an assignment of an external symbol. In this latter case, an internal and an external symbol reference this definition.

BNF notation:

$$\langle\text{Symbol}\rangle \models \langle\text{ExtSymbol}\rangle \mid \langle\text{IntSymbol}\rangle$$
$$\langle\text{ExtSymbol}\rangle \models \langle\text{ExtIdentifier}\rangle$$
$$\langle\text{IntSymbol}\rangle \models \langle\text{IntIdentifier}\rangle$$

The BNF notation shows that symbols can either be chosen from the external symbol table *ExtSymbol* or from the internal symbol table *IntSymbol*. External symbols can be assembled according the naming rules of an external identifier, internal symbols by the rules of an internal identifier.

4.4.2. Identifiers

Identifiers are the name of symbols. They are defined by the following syntactic name building rules.

BNF notation:

$$\langle\text{ExtIdentifier}\rangle \models \langle\text{RegularId}\rangle \mid \langle\text{EscapedId}\rangle$$
$$\langle\text{IntIdentifier}\rangle \models \langle\text{InternalId}\rangle$$

$$\langle\text{RegularId}\rangle \models \langle\text{letter}\rangle \mid \langle\text{digit}\rangle$$
$$\mid \langle\text{RegularId}\rangle\langle\text{letter}\rangle \mid \langle\text{RegularId}\rangle\langle\text{digit}\rangle$$
$$\langle\text{EscapedId}\rangle \models \text{'''} \langle\text{anychar}\rangle \text{'''}$$
$$\langle\text{InternalId}\rangle \models \text{"\$"} \langle\text{digit}\rangle$$

$$\langle\text{letter}\rangle \models A \dots Z a \dots z$$
$$\langle\text{digit}\rangle \models 0 \dots 9$$
$$\langle\text{anychar}\rangle \models any\ UTF\text{-}8\ symbol\ but\ ' \mid any\ UTF\text{-}8\ symbol\ but\ ' \langle\text{anychar}\rangle$$

An identifier can either be an external identifier $ExtIdentifier$ or an internal identifier $IntIdentifier$.

An external identifier $ExtIdentifier$ can be a regular identifier $RegularId$ or an escaped identifier $EscapedId$. A $RegularId$ can contain any permutation of Latin letter symbols a-z and A-Z and digits 0-9, e.g. Ann, MyUser1234, 625Z1H.

To be able to use white spaces and other UNICODE characters in identifiers, the $EscapedId$ can be used. Starting with a single quotation mark any UTF-8 can follow except another quotation mark. Escaping is currently not supported but can easily be introduced. The $EscapedId$ is finished by a closing parenthesis, e.g. 'my_user', 'my user 1'.

An internal identifier $IntIdentifier$ is represented by an internal id $InternalId$. An internal id consists of a leading dollar sign "\$" and subsequent digits, e.g. \$1234.

4.5. Definitions

We will first introduce definitions in detail and deal with applications later. As some concepts and syntax variants are based on a combination of definitions and applications we will refer in these cases to the corresponding sections in the application part.

The aim of definitions is to define entities, containers, relations, filtered 1-projections, tests, policies and scopes. Definitions are prefixed by the symbol $\triangle$. As this symbol is hard to type in a standard ASCII or UNICODE environment on a computer, an alternative notation is DEFINE.

Definition 1 (ADQL definition). *An ADQL definition is a polymorphic function. It is used to define the ADQL data types entities, containers, relations, filtered 1-projections, tests, policies, and scopes. The function returns an internal representation of the defined data type. The execution of the definition function leads to changes in the internal system state which are documented in section 7.1.*

A definition defines one of the seven basic concepts of ADQL: entities, containers, relations, filtered 1-projections, tests, policies, and scopes.

BNF notation:

$$\langle \text{Definition} \rangle \quad \models \quad \langle \text{Entity} \rangle \mid \langle \text{Container} \rangle \mid \langle \text{Relation} \rangle \mid \langle \text{Projection} \rangle$$
$$\mid \langle \text{Test} \rangle \mid \langle \text{Policy} \rangle \mid \langle \text{Scope} \rangle$$

A definition is a function. The function is prefixed by the definition symbol $\triangle$ and the type of the definition: entities ($\triangle e$), containers ($\triangle c$), relations ($\triangle r$), filtered 1-projections ($\triangle pr$), tests ($\triangle t$), policies ($\triangle p$), and scopes ($\triangle s$). The definition function is followed by the required arguments, embraced by brackets ("()"). The number of arguments is dependent on the type of the definition, e.g. entity definitions have no arguments, container definitions include a list of entities, ... (see sections below).

If well-formed, ADQL's system state changes when the definition is stored in an internal symbol table. Additionally, the result of the function can be assigned to an externally referenced symbol by the assignment sign "=", e.g. "$x = \triangle e()$". Please note, that any definition is stored in ADQL's internal symbol table. The external symbol table is optional.

E.g. $\triangle e()$;
The command is a well-formed definition of an ADQL entity. This statement changes the internal symbol table of ADQL by creating an anonymous entity. Technically, it is assigned to an internal symbol. Nevertheless, as no external symbol is assigned to the entity, it cannot be referenced by an external symbol.

In contrast, $"Ann = \triangle e();"$ is a well-formed definition of an ADQL entity with an external symbol assignment. The statement changes the internal symbol table of ADQL by creating an internal symbol for this definition. Additionally, an external symbol – "Ann" – is assigned to the definition. We see the latter definition is assigned to two symbols, an external symbol and an internal symbol.

If a syntax error occurs ADQL's system state does not change: Neither an external nor an internal symbol is assigned. An error message explaining the mistake is returned.

4.5.1. Definition of Entities

For the concept of an entity (and all following ADQL concepts), we refer to chapter 5. An entity is the most basic concept of ADQL representing anything to be modeled in ADQL, e.g. users, objects, permissions, facts, ...

BNF notation:

$$\langle \text{Entity} \rangle \quad \models \quad \langle \text{ExtSymbol} \rangle \mid \langle \text{EntityDef} \rangle \mid \langle \text{ExtSymbol} \rangle "=" \langle \text{EntityDef} \rangle$$
$$\langle \text{EntityDef} \rangle \quad \models \quad \triangle e \; "(" \; ")"$$

A new entity definition $EntityDef$ consists of the fixed pre-fix $\triangle e$ and empty brackets enclosed. After their definition, entities can be referenced by their assigned symbol (or identifier). Entities (as any other definition and application) can be assigned to a symbol.

Example:
$"Herb = \triangle e();"$ defines ("$\triangle$") a new entity ("e"). The definition function $\triangle e$ has no argument ("()"). The entity is assigned the external symbol "Herb".

4.5.2. Definitions of Containers

A container is, as the name says, an object which can contain other objects. Technically, a container is a set of ADQL terms. Please note, a container is not defined as a set of entities but as a set of terms. This allows recursive definition of containers: A term can be a container, thus a container can become a part of another container. We will deal with this important detail later.

BNF notation:

$$\langle \text{Container} \rangle \quad \models \quad \langle \text{Symbol} \rangle \mid \langle \text{ContainerDef} \rangle$$
$$\mid \langle \text{ExtSymbol} \rangle "=" \langle \text{ContainerDef} \rangle$$
$$\langle \text{ContainerDef} \rangle \quad \models \quad \triangle c \; "(" \; \langle \text{Terms} \rangle \; ")"$$

A container definition $ContainerDef$ consists of the fixed literal $\triangle c$ with an ADQL expression embraced by round brackets. Within the brackets a comma-separated list of ADQL $Terms$ can be provided.

When used in a referencing context (this means, a container is required as a nonterminal), either a previously defined container symbol or a new container definition can be used.

We said that a container can contain any valid term as an element of itself. This detail is important, as it is part of the expressive power of ADQL. Containers hold as elements any valid ADQL term. We have seen that terms consist of definitions and applications. Definitions allow the user to define entities, containers, relations, filtered 1-projections, tests, policies and scopes. We have not yet introduced the definition of relations, filtered 1-projections, tests, policies, and scopes, as well as applications. Therefore, we will continue the discussion of containers later in this section. For now, we focus on two important properties of containers: (1) containers serve as collectors for ADQL terms, (2) any ADQL term can be decomposed to ADQL entities by the iterative application of the Value-Function (see section 5.4). The result of this iterative application is the decomposed container.

Example:
$users = \triangle c(Ann = \triangle e(), Herb = \triangle e(), Jim = \triangle e());$
$permissions = \triangle c(read = \triangle e(), write = \triangle e());$
$objects = \triangle c(fileA = \triangle e(), fileB = \triangle e());$

The above example illustrates one ADQL expression consisting of three ADQL terms. The first term defines three entities and assigns them to the symbols Ann, Herb, and Jim. The three entities are assigned to a new container. The container is assigned to the symbol "users".

The second term defines a container named "permissions" with the entities "read" and "write".

The third term does the same for the container "objects" with the entities "fileA" and "fileB".

Example 2:
$Ann = \triangle e(); Herb = \triangle e(); Jim = \triangle e();$
$groupA = \triangle c(Ann, Herb);$
$groups = \triangle c(\nabla(groupA)(), \nabla(\triangle c(Herb, Jim))());$

The second example is illustrated in figure 4.1. In the first line, it defines three entities referenced by the external symbols Ann, Herb, and Jim. The second line defines a container with "Ann" and "Herb". The container is assigned to the symbol "groupA". The next term defines additional containers and assigns external symbols: one "inner" container and one "outer" container. The

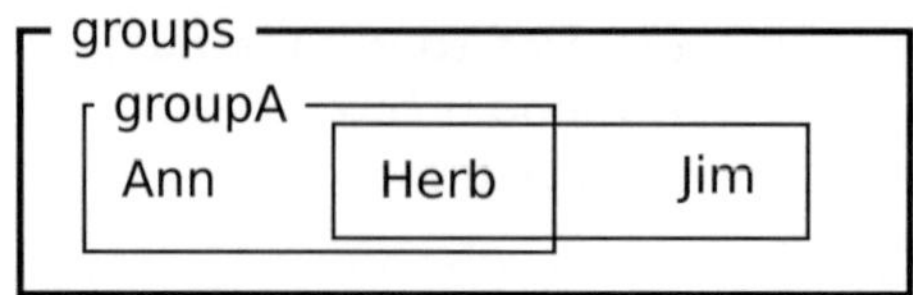

Figure 4.1.: Illustration of the container example 2

inner container $\triangle c(Herb, Jim)$ is anonymous, thus has no assigned symbol, and contains the entities "Herb" and "Jim". The outer container referenced by the external symbol *groups* contains the container *groupA* and the anonymous container.

We omit the explanation of the application ("∇") here and refer to the explanation of applications.

Extensions   Please note, that the suggested ADQL syntax does not allow to incrementaly add or remove elements to/from containers. It is not possible to incrementaly add the entity "Charly" to container "groupA". Instead, the container has to be re-defined. However, we not really see this as a problem for ADQL as a language. It would be simple to introduce a new statement like $\triangle groupA + = \triangle c(Charly)$ allowing to add "Charly" to the already existing definition of the container groupA.

4.5.3. Usage of Variables

For the next subsections a concept named "variable" is going to be used. Therefore, we introduce it here.

Generally, variables are symbols which can be assigned a value. In ADQL, a variable is not explicitly defined. Instead, for each defined container implicitly a corresponding variable is defined automatically. The symbol of this implicit variable is the container symbol prefixed by "$\triangleright$".

In case the symbol $\triangleright$ is not available, instead the literal `BIND` can be used.

BNF notation:

$$\langle\text{Variable}\rangle \ \models\ \triangleright\langle\text{Symbol}\rangle$$

Example:
By defining a container "$users = \triangle c();$" automatically a variable "$\triangleright users$" is defined as well.

A variable can be assigned to a value within so-called scopes (see below).

Side note:
We are aware that in some use cases two variables are required to express certain policies. A good example is laid out in [Mir12]. Mironov provides an access control model for a generic health care services model, the latter suggested by Silverston (cf. [Sil01a, Sil01b]).

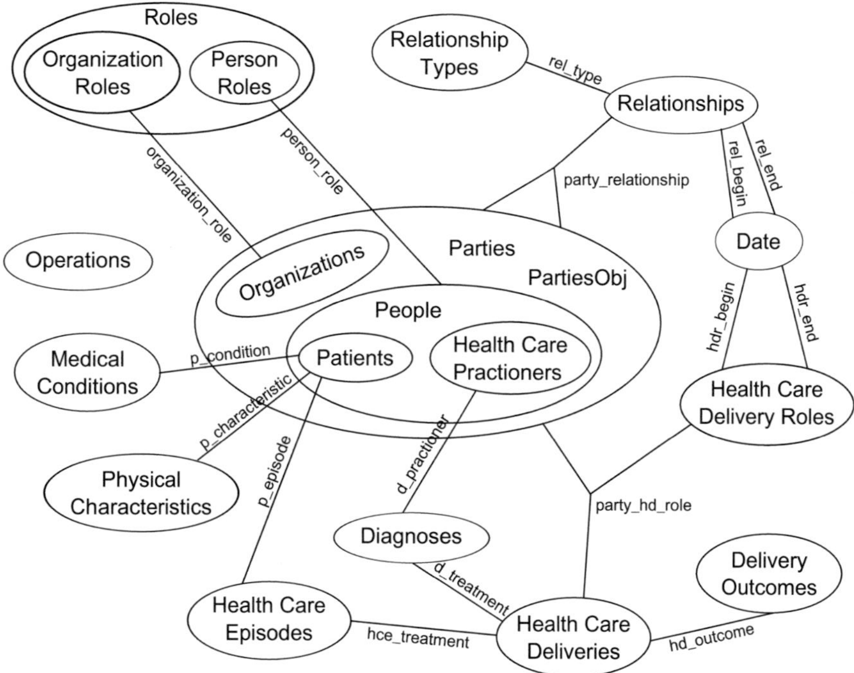

Figure 4.2.: Access control model defined by Mironov [Mir12, p.10] demonstrating a use case scenario for the requirement of two variables for a container.

For his access control model, Mironov models health-care parties. Parties can either deliver or receive health care services. We refer to figure 4.2. Ellpises represent ADQL containers, lines between containers relations (see later in this chapter).

Mironov's policies want to ensure that a relationship between the delivering and receiving party has not yet ended. This condition requires that the variable ▷*Parties* must be bound to two values at the same time, namely the receiving and the delivering entity, which is not possible by the straight forward use of the implicit variable definition schema of ADQL.

As ADQL does not support freely defined variables, the common way to handle such a requirement is to define an "artificial" container holding the container requiring another variable. In the above example a container *"PartiesObj* $= \triangle c(\nabla (Parties)())"$ is defined. With this trick, a second variable is available and it is ensured that both containers include the same entities (we refer to applications of containers below, as we did not introduce this syntax yet).

Extension A general solution for the problem is that ADQL allows the definition of explicit variables. In this case one variable would be assigned to the value of the receiving party, the other variable to the value of the delivering party.

The syntax could look like this:

$$receiving\_party = \triangle v(Parties);$$
$$delivering\_party = \triangle v(Parties);$$

This extension is currently not part of ADQL. We argue, that allowing new symbols for variables can make it difficult for the person defining the policies to recall the correct names and types (here: "Parties") of a variable. With the current restriction to implicit definitions, the name and type of a variable is always clear as it is strictly related to the container. However, we may introduce free variables in ADQL at a later point of time.

So, for our current work, variables are implicitly defined for each container definition. We will explain how values are assigned to values in section 4.5.8.

4.5.4. Definition of Relations

Relations are sets of n-ary links between n decomposed containers (see section 5.5). Let C_1, C_2, C_3 be containers. Then $R_1 \subseteq Val(C_1) \times Val(C_2) \times Val(C_3)$ is a 3-ary relation on the decomposed containers C_1, C_2, C_3. The decomposition of a container, denoted by Val, is explained in section 5.4. The result of $Val(C_i)$ is a "flat" container, that is a list of entities it contains.

BNF notation:

$$
\begin{aligned}
\langle\text{Relation}\rangle &\models \langle\text{Symbol}\rangle \mid \langle\text{RelationDef}\rangle \\
&\quad \mid \langle\text{ExtSymbol}\rangle\text{"="}\langle\text{RelationDef}\rangle \\
\langle\text{RelationDef}\rangle &\models \langle\text{RelationHead}\rangle \mid \langle\text{RelationHead}\rangle \text{":"} \langle\text{RelationBody}\rangle \\
\langle\text{RelationHead}\rangle &\models \triangle\text{r "("} \langle\text{Containers}\rangle \text{")"} \\
\langle\text{Containers}\rangle &\models \langle\text{Container}\rangle \mid \langle\text{Container}\rangle \text{","} \langle\text{Containers}\rangle \\
\langle\text{RelationBody}\rangle &\models \text{"\{"} \langle\text{Tuples}\rangle \text{"\}"} \\
\langle\text{Tuples}\rangle &\models \langle\text{Tuple}\rangle \mid \langle\text{Tuples}\rangle \text{","} \langle\text{Tuple}\rangle \\
\langle\text{Tuple}\rangle &\models \text{"("} \langle\text{SymbolList}\rangle \text{")"} \\
\langle\text{SymbolList}\rangle &\models \langle\text{Symbol}\rangle \mid \langle\text{Symbol}\rangle \text{","} \langle\text{SymbolList}\rangle
\end{aligned}
$$

A relation is either referred to by a previously defined symbol representing a relation or a new relation definition. A relation definition $RelationDef$ consists of a $RelationHead$ and an optional $RelationBody$. We first explain the header and come back to the body below.

$RelationHead$s follow the syntactical structure of entities and containers. The relation head is built by the fixed literal $"\triangle r"$ and the nonterminal $Containers$ embraced by round brackets. $Containers$ is a simple concatenation of $1..n$ $Container$, defined above when introducing container definitions.

Example:

$$
\underbrace{isowned}_{symbol} = \triangle r \underbrace{(objects, users)}_{relation\ head}
$$

The example defines the relation named $isowned$ by defining a named relation on the containers $objects$ and $users$. We assume, that the symbols $objects$ and $users$ are defined symbols as in the above examples of the last sections.

We continue with the second part of a $Relation$ definition, the $RelationBody$. While the header describes the structure of the relation, namely the containers the relation is defined on, the body is an enumeration of all links of the relation. These links are n-tuples and have to be listed explicitly. The $RelationBody$ consists of $Tuples$ embraced by curly braces. $Tuples$ is an enumeration of the nonterminal $Tuple$ separated by commas. A $Tuple$ is a $SymbolList$ embraced by round brackets. The $SymbolList$ is a comma-separated list of entities, containers, relations, filtered 1-projections, tests, policies, and scopes.

Example:

$$
\underbrace{isowned}_{symbol} = \triangle r \underbrace{(objects, users)}_{relation\ head} : \underbrace{\{(fileA, Alice), (fileB, Bob), (fileB, Charly)\}}_{relation\ body/links};
$$

The above example defines a 2-ary relation upon the containers "objects" and "users". It is identified with the external symbol "isowned".

Furthermore, the relation "isowned" contains three 2-tuple links. Semantically, the owner of "fileA" is "Alice". "fileB" has two assigned owners, "Bob" and "Charly".

We see that ADQL supports explicitly defined relations. Implicitly defined relations, e.g. expressed by a boolean term are not part of ADQL for now.

Extensions Currently, ADQL supports only explicitly defined relations, thus all elements of a relation have to be enumerated.

We suggest two extensions:

- *Implicit relations*: Implicit relations are defined by a boolean condition as a filter. SQL provides examples for this. In SQL we can write statements like `SELECT * FROM table WHERE variable < 100;`. This is an implicit relation definition.

- *External relations*: ADQL can be extended to support externally defined relations. E.g. the assignment of users to roles is defined not within ADQL but can be retrieved from external data resources (like LDAP, databases, UNIX groups, etc.).

4.5.5. Definition of Filtered 1-Projections

In ADQL, we define a "filtered 1-projection" (short: F1-projection) as the concatenation of a filter operation and a one-dimensional projection. In this chapter, we provide only syntactical definitions, for details about the mathematical definition we refer to section 5.5). A filtered 1-projection transforms a n-dimensional relation to a 1-dimensional list. We say, when executing a filtered 1-projection, that $n - 1$ dimensions are bound, while the remaining dimension is called unbound.

BNF notation:

$$\begin{aligned}
\langle\text{Projection}\rangle &\models \langle\text{Symbol}\rangle \mid \langle\text{ProjDef}\rangle \mid \langle\text{ExtSymbol}\rangle "="\langle\text{ProjDef}\rangle \\
\langle\text{ProjDef}\rangle &\models \triangle\text{pr } "(" \langle\text{Relation}\rangle ")" "(" \langle\text{ProjTuple}\rangle ")" \\
\langle\text{ProjTuple}\rangle &\models "." "," \langle\text{VarContApps}\rangle \mid \langle\text{VarContApps}\rangle "," "." \mid \\
&\quad \langle\text{VarContApps}\rangle "," "." "," \langle\text{VarContApps}\rangle \\
\langle\text{VarContApps}\rangle &\models \langle\text{VarContApp}\rangle \mid \langle\text{VarContApp}\rangle "," \langle\text{VarContApps}\rangle \\
\langle\text{VarContApp}\rangle &\models \langle\text{Variable}\rangle \mid \langle\text{Container}\rangle \mid \langle\text{Application}\rangle
\end{aligned}$$

Again, the definition of a filtered 1-projection follows the structure of the other concepts. A filtered 1-projection definition *ProjDef* consists of a fixed literal $"\triangle pr"$ followed by the nonterminal *Relation* the filtered 1-projection is defined on embraced in brackets. The *Relation* can be a pre-defined relation referenced by a symbol or be a relation definition. It is followed by the filtered 1-projection tuple *ProjTuple* embraced in brackets. A filtered 1-projection tuple *ProjTuple* is built of a comma-separated list. This list consists exactly of one dot and several variables, applications or containers, named *VarContApp*. The dot marks the position of the unbound dimension which is the projection target.

Two side notes, although we did not yet introduce applications:

1. At a first glance, the construct *VarContApp* may seem arbitrary. Nevertheless, we will see below, when an application is evaluated that the result type is always a container. Furthermore, a variable can be assigned a container within a scope. This being said, it becomes obvious that *VarContApp* is a language construct referencing the "data type" container.

2. Relations and F1-projections are inter-related: F1-projections are defined on relations. Although the BNF-syntax does not enforce the same number of arguments for a relation and a related F1-projection, the ADQL implementation cross-checks this fact and returns an error if the number of arguments of a F1-projection differs from the number of arguments of its related relation.

   Example:
   Let r be a 2-ary relation. Syntactically, a F1-projection p may be defined on r by $"\triangle pr(r)(., A, B)"$ being A, B some containers. ADQLs implementation will raise an error, as the F1-projection is 3-ary $(., A, B)$ while the relation is 2-ary.

Examples:

$$
\begin{aligned}
isowned \quad &= \quad \triangle r(objects, users): \\
&\qquad \{(fileA, Alice), (fileB, Bob), (fileB, Charly)\}; \\
ownedbyAlice \quad &= \quad \triangle pr(isowned)(., \triangle c(Alice)); \\
ownerOffileB \quad &= \quad \triangle pr(isowned)(\triangle c(fileB), .);
\end{aligned}
$$

The first line is, again, the definition of the relation *isowned*. The second line in the example defines a F1-projection on the relation *isowned*. The tuple consists of the unbound container – here *objects* – and the bound F1-projection element *Alice*. If evaluated, all *objects* which link to *Alice* will be returned. We come back to this later, when we discuss applications of F1-projections.

We see that a F1-projection consists of bound and unbound elements. In an n-ary relation, $n - 1$ elements must be bound, thus fixed. The one unbound element is flagged by the point and is the target of the F1-projection.

Definition 2 (Validity of F1-projections). *A F1-projection of an n-ary relation is called valid if*

- *it has $n - 1$ bound and 1 unbound tuple elements and*

- *all bound tuple elements are subsets of the corresponding Value function (see chapter 5)*

Examples:
$\triangle pr(isowned)(.,.)$ is invalid, as it has two unbound tuple elements,
$\triangle pr(isowned)(\triangle c(fileA), \triangle c(Alice))$ is invalid, as it has no unbound elements,
$\triangle pr(isowned)(\triangle c(Alice),.)$ is invalid as $\triangle c(Alice) \nsubseteq Val(objects)$.

ADQL's implementation raises an error if an invalid F1-projection is used.

Extensions The current definition of projections (as F1-projections) is very strict. It follows from the fact, that any application (see below) must return a container. However, we can think of cases where projections are nested. It can enhance the expressive power of ADQL if projections are not limited to F1-projections, thus allows not only one unbound dimensions but more.

4.5.6. Definition of Tests

ADQL tests are defined as 2-ary boolean expressions which evaluate to `true` or `false`. In ADQL, a test has three parameters, two containers and a boolean operator. Operators are explained in chapter 5.9. An operator compares the two containers of a test with its inner logic and returns either true or false. A typical operator is θ returning true, if both containers share at least one entity.

As for all ADQL syntax elements, tests can be referenced by symbols sharing the global ADQL namespace.

BNF notation:

$$
\begin{aligned}
\langle \text{Test} \rangle &\models \langle \text{Symbol} \rangle \mid \langle \text{TestDef} \rangle \mid \langle \text{ExtSymbol} \rangle \text{"="} \langle \text{TestDef} \rangle \\
\langle \text{TestDef} \rangle &\models \triangle t \text{ "("} \langle \text{TestBody} \rangle \text{ ")"} \\
\langle \text{TestBody} \rangle &\models \langle \text{VarContApp} \rangle \text{ ","} \langle \text{VarContApp} \rangle \text{ ","} \langle \text{Operator} \rangle
\end{aligned}
$$

A test $Test$ consists either of an already defined test $Symbol$ or a new test definition $TestDef$. The latter $TestDef$ includes the fixed literal $\triangle t$ followed by the test body $TestBody$ embraced by round braces.

The test body $TestBody$ is built of two nonterminals $VarContApp$ and an boolean operator $Operator$, all separated by a comma. $VarContApp$ is a variable, a container, or an application.

Example 1:
$$\underbrace{userIsAlice}_{symbol} = \triangle t(\underbrace{\triangleright users}_{left\ side}, \underbrace{\triangle c(Alice)}_{right\ side}, \underbrace{\theta}_{operator});$$

The test definition ($"\triangle t"$) is assigned to the external symbol $userIsAlice$. Its first argument is the variable $\triangleright users$. The second argument is an on-the-fly defined anonymous container holding the entity referenced by the external symbol "Alice", this is the user "Alice". The used operator is θ which is defined as "intersection of both decomposed containers is not empty". We will deal with operators and the evaluation of this test later. It checks whether the current value of the variable "users" is Alice, in other words: "Is the current user Alice?".

Example 2:
$$userIsValid = \triangle t(\triangleright users, users, \theta);$$

The second example test is slightly different. The variable $\triangleright users$ is compared with the container "users". The operator is again θ. In other words: Is the current user part of the container "users", or: "Is the current user a valid user?".

In ADQL tests are used to model (atomic) conditions. These conditions can be combined to policies allowing defining complex conditions when access should be granted.

4.5.7. Definition of Policies

An ADQL policy is a set of n ADQL tests.

BNF notation:

$$\begin{aligned}
\langle \text{Policy} \rangle &\models \langle \text{Symbol} \rangle \mid \langle \text{PolicyDef} \rangle \mid \langle \text{ExtSymbol} \rangle "=" \langle \text{PolicyDef} \rangle \\
\langle \text{PolicyDef} \rangle &\models \triangle p\ "("\ \langle \text{Tests} \rangle\ ")" \\
\langle \text{Tests} \rangle &\models \langle \text{Test} \rangle \mid \langle \text{Test} \rangle "," \langle \text{Tests} \rangle
\end{aligned}$$

A policy definition $PolicyDef$ is created by the fixed literal $\triangle p$ and an enumeration of tests $Tests$ embraced by brackets.

A policy is a logical AND-concatenation of tests. To become true, all tests of a policy have to evaluate to true.

Example:
$$p1 = \triangle p($$
$$\qquad userIsAlice,$$
$$\qquad permIsRead = \triangle t(\triangleright permissions, \triangle c(read), \theta),$$
$$\qquad \triangle t(\triangleright objects, objects, \theta)$$
$$\qquad);$$

The above example policy $p1$ consists of three tests.

1. The first test is referencing the symbol $userIsAlice$ and is defined as in the previous example.

2. The second test is defined on-the-fly and assigned the symbol $permIsRead$. We see that the variable $\triangleright permissions$ must match the defined fixed container $\triangle c(read)$: The currently requested permission must be "read".

3. The third test is anonymous (i.e. not assigned to an external symbol). It compares the currently requested object (variable $\triangleright object$) with all possible objects. In other words, the object must exist and be an object.

Although we did not yet introduce applications, the complete policy $p1$ will evaluate true if the three conditions are met: (1) The user is Alice, (2) the permission is read, (3) the object is valid. Or: Alice can read all valid objects.

4.5.8. Definition of Scopes

Within scopes, variables can be bound to values. Therefore, we say that ADQL scopes are sets of variable assignments. The variable binding is only valid within a scope. Of course, several scopes with different variable bindings may exist.

Scopes can be assigned themselves to an external symbol sharing the name space with all other ADQL symbols.

BNF notation:

$$
\begin{aligned}
\langle\text{Scope}\rangle &\models \langle\text{Symbol}\rangle \mid \langle\text{ScopeDef}\rangle \mid \langle\text{ExtSymbol}\rangle''=''\langle\text{ScopeDef}\rangle \\
\langle\text{ScopeDef}\rangle &\models \triangle s\ ''(''\ \langle\text{VarAssignments}\rangle\ '')'' \\
\langle\text{VarAssignments}\rangle &\models \langle\text{VarAssignment}\rangle \\
&\quad \mid \langle\text{VarAssignment}\rangle\ '',''\ \langle\text{VarAssignments}\rangle \\
\langle\text{VarAssignment}\rangle &\models \langle\text{Variable}\rangle\ ''=''\ \langle\text{Container}\rangle
\end{aligned}
$$

A scope definition *ScopeDef* consists of the literal $\triangle s$ and a list of variable assignments *VarAssignments* embraced by brackets. We see that a scope can consist of $0..n$ variable assignments. Therefore, *VarAssignments* is a list of *VarAssignment*-s, separated by commas. Each variable assignment *VarAssignment* assigns a variable *Variable* to a container *Container*. Please note that the value which is assigned to a variable is of the type container (and not entity).

Example:
$s1 = \triangle s($
$\qquad \triangleright users = \triangle c(Alice),$
$\qquad \triangleright perm = \triangle c(read),$
$\qquad \triangleright objects = \triangle c(fileA)$
$);$

The scope $s1$ includes three variable assignments. The variable $\triangleright users$ is bound to an anonymous container holding the entity *Alice*. Variable $\triangleright permission$ is assigned to an anonymous container with entity *read*. The variable $\triangleright objects$ is assigned to an anonymous container including entity *fileA*.

We see that a scope is a set of variable assignments.

4.6. Applications

So far, we have introduced all ADQL syntax elements concerning definitions. Definitions are used to inform the ADQL engine about the authorization model, policies, and facts. Besides definitions, applications are the second important construct of ADQL. Applications are the "logic part" of ADQL, the "inference mechanism".

Definition 3 (ADQL application). *An ADQL application is a polymorphic function. It can be applied to entities, containers, relations, F1-projections, tests, policies, and scopes; thus all ADQL data types. The result of an application is a container.*

Let $ECRPrTPS$ be the united space of all ADQL entities E, containers C, F1-projections Pr, tests T, policies P, and scopes S.

$$\nabla : ECRPrTPS \times S \to C$$

An application is prefixed by the symbol ∇. An alternative notation is `APP`, if the symbol ∇ cannot be used.

BNF notation:

$$\langle \text{Application} \rangle \models \nabla \ ''('' \ \langle \text{Term} \rangle \ '')'' \ ''('' \ \langle \text{Scope} \rangle \ '')''$$

An *Application* is formed by the literal "∇", a term *Term* embraced by round brackets, and a scope *Scope* embraced by round brackets.

We see that applications can be applied on definitions (and other applications) by using a scope as an argument. An application corresponds to the *Val*-function introduced in chapter 5.

As a definition *Definition* can either be an entity, a container, a relation, a F1-projection, a test, a policy, or a scope, we will explain the application of every concept one by one.

4.6.1. Application of Entities

The execution of an application of an entity results simply in the one-entity container containing the entity itself, thus the identity function wrapped by a container. The scope argument "$(\langle Scope \rangle)$" is ignored for the evaluation of the application of an entity.

Example:
Let $Alice = \triangle e()$;
Then:
$\nabla(Alice)() == \triangle c(Alice)$

Please note, that we use "$=$" as assignment symbol and "$==$" as symbol for "is equal to". The execution of the application of the entity *Alice* results in a single-entity container holding the entity *Alice*.

The syntax of ADQL allows assigning external symbols to applications.

Example:
$AliceApp = \nabla(Alice = \triangle e())()$;

The example shows a valid ADQL expression. An entity "Alice" is defined. This definition is used in an application. The application is then assigned the symbol *AliceApp*.

Please note, that the symbol *AliceApp* references the application on an entity and not the result value! When executing the term $\nabla(AliceApp)()$, the result of this application is, of course, $\triangle c(Alice)$. In the next section we will show how this detail can be used.

4.6.2. Application of Containers

We continue with the application of containers. A container is defined as a set of ADQL terms. Again, a term may consist of an ADQL definition or an ADQL application. In the first case the term is a definition. An element of a container can be an entity, a container, a relation, a F1-projection, a test, a policy, or a scope. These kinds of elements we refer to as "definition element" of the container. In the second case, the element is an application. If the latter case, we call it an "application element" of the container.

In this section we explain how the execution of an application deals with flat containers, hierarchical containers, and symbol assignments of the applications.

Flat Container Applications *Examples:*
Let some containers be defined the following way:

$$
\begin{aligned}
users &= \triangle c(Alice, Bob, Charly); \\
groupA &= \triangle c(Alice, Bob); \\
groupB &= \triangle c(Bob, Charly); \\
groups1 &= \triangle c(groupA, groupB); \\
cont &= \triangle c(Alice, groupA, owners, p1);
\end{aligned}
$$

Then, the following is true:
$\nabla(users)() == \nabla(\triangle c(Alice, Bob, Charly))() == \triangle c(Alice, Bob, Charly) == users$

The application of a flat container – consisting of definition elements only – is the identity of the container, thus the container itself.

We repeat this for the other examples:

1. $\nabla(groupA)() == \nabla(\triangle c(Alice, Bob))() == \triangle c(Alice, Bob) == groupA$

2. $\nabla(groupB)() == \nabla(\triangle c(Bob, Charly)() == \triangle c(Bob, Charly)$
   $== groupB$

3. $\nabla(groups1)() == \nabla(\triangle c(groupA, groupB))() == \triangle c(groupA, groupB)$
   $== groups1$

4. $\nabla(cont)() == \nabla(\triangle c(Alice, groupA, owners, p1))() ==$
   $\triangle c(Alice, groupA, owners, p1) == cont$

Hierarchical Container Applications   This behavior changes, when a container includes application elements. We showed above, that a container consists of terms. A term can be a definition or an application. If an element of a container is an application, we say it is an "application element". The application of an application element applies the Val-function, defined in chapter 5 on the element. The result is a container. The application of a whole container is the repeated application on all application and definition elements and returns the set union of all results.

Example:
Let $groups2 = \triangle c(\nabla groupA, \nabla groupB)$;
On the next pages we use $"\nabla groupA"$ as a short-cut for $"\nabla(groupA)()"$.

Then:
$$\nabla groups2 == \nabla \triangle c(\nabla groupA, \nabla groupB) ==$$
$$\triangle c(\nabla \nabla groupA, \nabla \nabla groupB) ==$$
$$\triangle c(Alice, Bob, \nabla \nabla groupB) ==$$
$$\triangle c(Alice, Bob, Bob, Charly) ==$$
$$\triangle c(Alice, Bob, Charly)$$

We see that the usage of application definitions of containers ($\nabla container$) can be used to create hierarchies of containers. Let $A, B_1, B_2, C_{11}, C_{12}, C_2$ be containers. Then the following commands define a container hierarchy:

Example:
$$B_1 = \triangle c($$
$$\nabla(C_{11} = \triangle c()),$$
$$\nabla(C_{12} = \triangle c())$$
$$);$$

C_1 and C_2 are defined as empty containers and assigned their corresponding symbols. The application of the containers C_1 and C_2 is assigned to the set linked to the symbol $B1$. The result of ∇B_1 would therefore be $\nabla c()$, thus an empty container.

Proof:

$$\nabla B_1 == \nabla \triangle c(\nabla \triangle c(), \nabla \triangle c()) == \triangle c(\nabla \nabla \triangle c(), \nabla \nabla \triangle c()) == \triangle c()$$

The equality is compared on the level of resulting values not on structural identity. We define $B_2 = \triangle c()$. It follows: $\nabla B_1 == \nabla B_2$. However, the equality is related to the result value only. The structures of B_1 and B_2 are not equal. Currently, ADQL does not provide an operator to compare equality of (hierarchical) structures.

We provide a more complex example illustrated in figure 4.3.

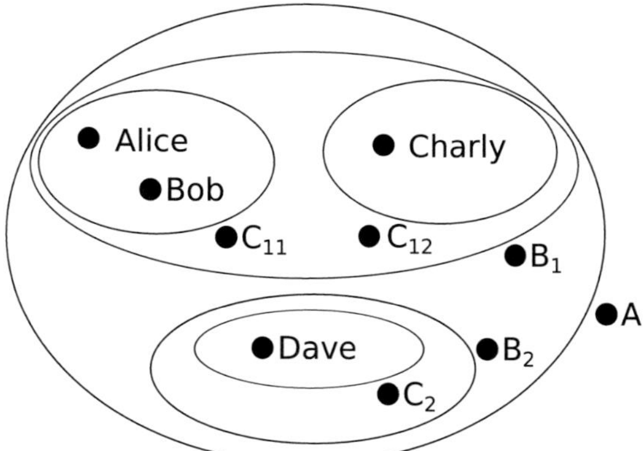

Figure 4.3.: Example of a container hierarchy built through indirect entity structures

Example of container hierarchies:
$$A = \triangle c($$
$$\quad \nabla(B_1 = \triangle c($$
$$\quad\quad \nabla(C_{11} = \triangle c(Alice, Bob)),$$
$$\quad\quad \nabla(C_{12} = \triangle c(Charly))$$
$$\quad)),$$
$$\quad \nabla(B_2 = \triangle c($$
$$\quad\quad \nabla(C_2 = \triangle c(Dave))$$
$$\quad))$$
$$);$$

Let us do some sample evaluations:

$$\nabla C_{11} == \nabla \triangle c(Alice, Bob) == \triangle(Alice, Bob)$$
$$\nabla C_{12} == \nabla \triangle c(Charly) == \triangle(Charly)$$
$$\nabla C_2 == \nabla \triangle c(Dave) == \triangle(Dave)$$

The examples show the simple rule that definition elements of a container evaluate to their identity.

$$\nabla B_1 == \nabla \triangle c(\nabla C_{11}, \nabla C_{12}) ==$$
$$\quad \triangle c(\nabla \nabla C_{11}, \nabla \nabla C_{12}) ==$$
$$\quad \triangle c(Alice, Bob, \nabla \nabla C_{12}) ==$$
$$\quad \triangle c(Alice, Bob, Charly)$$

$$\nabla C_2 == \nabla \triangle c(\nabla C_2) ==$$
$$\quad \triangle c(\nabla \nabla C_2) ==$$
$$\quad \triangle c(Dave)$$

We see here, how application elements are resolved. The application is executed on all elements of the container. The result is the set union of the results of these applications.

$$\nabla A == \nabla \triangle c(\nabla B_1, \nabla B_2) == \triangle c(Alice, Bob, Charly, Dave)$$

The last example applies the application rule iteratively twice. We avoid all single steps in the example, as we already proofed it for all container elements of A, namely B_1 and B_2.

We have shown how application elements of a container can be used to define container hierarchies of any depth. If the symbol ∇ is present within a container definition, the sub-elements are included in the container of the higher level. It can be seen as inheritance behavior. We therefore call the assignment of such container elements "indirect". The elements are not assigned directly, but resolved to their contents recursively.

Differently, when avoiding the symbol ∇ in a container definition, the elements of the container are not further decomposed. We speak of a "direct" assignment, as the sub-container is not assigned as a container to the father container, but as a kind of entity.

What we did not show is that this concept works for all possible combinations. We can think of the standard example, where we assign container A indirectly to container B while at the same time assigning container B indirectly to container A. Actually, this is not a question of the ADQL language itself, but a question how this cycle is resolved. We will discuss this in section 5.4.

Symbol Assignments of Applications   An important fact about ADQL applications is that assignments of applications to symbols do not store the result of the execution of the application, but the syntactical definition of the application.

We provide a simple example:
$users = \triangle c(Alice, Bob, Charly)$;
$userApp = \nabla users$.

When executed, $\nabla userApp$ returns $\triangle c(Alice, Bob, Charly)$.

However, when we change the definition of $users$ (and do not touch the symbol $userApp$), the execution of $userApp$ also changes:
$users = \triangle c(Herb)$;

After this re-definition of $users$, the execution of the application of $userApp$ returns $\nabla userApp == \triangle c(Herb)$.

We see that not the result of the execution of $\nabla users$ is assigned to the symbol *userApp*. If this were the case, the result value of the second execution of $\nabla users$ would not have changed compared to its first execution. Instead, the symbol *userApp* is assigned the "syntactical definition of the application", which is $\nabla users$. This leads, as we have shown, to a change in the result value, if the nested concepts are changed.

We summarize: Symbols which are assigned to an ADQL term do not store the result values but the definition itself. If nested elements change during time, the application of the symbol also changes. This is true for all symbol assignments; it is not limited to containers.

We illustrate this behavior with another example.

Example 2:
We have shown above, that $\nabla A == \triangle c(Alice, Bob, Charly, Dave)$.

We change C_{12}: $C_{12} = \triangle c()$;
When executing ∇A we receive as new result $\triangle c(Alice, Bob, Dave)$.

Resolving Cycles in Nested Containers   ADQL's syntax allows cyclic definitions of containers. A container A can be assigned to container B. Container B is assigned to container C. Container C is assigned to container A. A cycle is created.

Example:
$A = \triangle c(Alice, \nabla C)$;
$B = \triangle c(Bob, \nabla A)$;
$C = \triangle c(Charly, \nabla B)$;

When executing an application on container A, the cycle is correctly resolved by enumerating all entities of the nested containers:
$\nabla A == \triangle c(Alice, Bob, Charly)$;

Both ADQL's definition and its implementation will resolve nested and cyclic container applications correctly and avoid never ending loops.

4.6.3. Applications of Relations

The application of a relation is defined in the same way as an application of entities: the result is an anonymous container containing the relation itself.

Example:
$owners = \triangle r(objects, users) : ((fileA, Alice), (fileB, Bob), (fileB, Charly))$;

Then:
$$\nabla owners() == \triangle c(owners)$$

Practically, we are not aware of any usage scenario for a relation application.

4.6.4. Applications of F1-Projections

The application of a F1-projection of a n-ary relation results in a container of 1-ary elements.

We repeat the previous example and extend it:
$$owners = \triangle r(objects, users) : ((fileA, Alice), (fileB, Bob), (fileB, Charly));$$
$$pr_1 = \nabla(owners(., \triangle c(Alice)))();$$
$$pr_2 = \nabla(owners(\triangle c(fileB), .))();$$

The first line is the definition of the relation $owners$:
The expression $\nabla(owners(., \triangle c(Alice)))()$ is an ADQL application on the F1-projection $owners(., \triangle c(Alice))$. The latter is a F1-projection with the unbound dimension $objects$ and the bound dimension $users$ fixed with a container holding the entity $Alice$.

$$\nabla(pr_1)() == \nabla(owners(., \triangle c(Alice)))() == \triangle c(fileA)$$

The result of the application pr_1 is a container of all files having $Alice$ as assigned user.

Similarly, the the term ∇pr_2 is evaluated:
$$\nabla(pr_2) == \nabla(owners(\triangle(fileB), .))() == \triangle c(Bob, Charly).$$

Relation $owners$ links $fileB$ to "Bob" and "Charly". Consequently, the result of the application of the F1-projection pr_2 is a container with Bob and Charly.

4.6.5. Application of Tests

We come to the application of ADQL tests.

The result of an application of a test is a container with either the fixed entity TRUE or the fixed entity FALSE. Thus, the result value of a test application is $\triangle c(true)$ or $\triangle c(false)$.

The syntax of an application includes a scope argument. We recall the syntax definition of an application:

$$\langle\text{Application}\rangle \;\models\; \nabla\;''(''\;\langle\text{Term}\rangle\;'')''\;''(''\;\langle\text{Scope}\rangle\;'')''$$

Applications of entities, containers, relations, F1-projections, and scopes ignore scope arguments when executed. In contrast, the execution of applications on tests and policies utilize the scope argument: Test definitions consist of a "left", "right side", and an operator. Each of these two "sides" consists of a variable, a container, or an application.

When applications of tests (and policies and scopes) are evaluated, the variable assignment is taken from the scope argument specified in the application.

Example:
We repeat the examples from the test definitions:
$userIsAlice = \triangle t(\triangleright users, \triangle c(Alice), \theta);$

We evaluate the test with different scopes:
$scope = \triangle s(users = \triangle c(Alice));$
$eval_1 = \nabla(userIsAlice)(scope);$

$\nabla(eval_1)() ==$
$\qquad \nabla(userIsAlice)(scope) ==$
$\qquad \nabla(\triangle t(\triangleright users, \triangle c(Alice), \theta))(scope) ==$
$\qquad \nabla(\triangle t(\triangleright users, \triangle c(Alice), \theta))(\triangle s(users = \triangle c(Alice))) ==$
$\qquad \nabla \triangle t(\triangle c(Alice), \triangle c(Alice), \theta) ==$
$\qquad \triangle c(\triangle c(Alice) \cap \triangle c(Alice) \neq \emptyset) ==$
$\qquad \triangle c(true)$

The result of the application of test $userIsAlice$ with the scope argument $scope$ returns a container with the entity $true$. As described, the test $userIsAlice$ checks if the scope binding of the variable user is Alice.

Like any other application assignment to symbols, the application result may change when a related definition changes. We show this by changing the definition of the scope and repeat the evaluation of the test application.

Scope re-definition:
$scope = \triangle s(users = \triangle c(Bob));$

The variable $\triangleright users$ is now bound to Bob.

$\nabla(eval_1)() ==$
$\qquad \nabla(userIsAlice)(scope) ==$
$\qquad \nabla(\triangle t(\triangleright users, \triangle c(Alice), \theta))(scope) ==$
$\qquad \nabla(\triangle t(\triangleright users, \triangle c(Alice), \theta))(\triangle s(users = \triangle c(Bob))) ==$
$\qquad \nabla \triangle t(\triangle c(Bob), \triangle c(Alice), \theta) ==$

$$\triangle c(\triangle c(Bob) \cap \triangle c(Alice) \neq \emptyset) ==$$
$$\triangle c(false)$$

The example shows, that with a differently defined scope *scope* (the variable ▷*user* is now bound to Bob), the same test application results in a container with the entity false. This is logically correct, as the test should become true only, if the current user is Alice, which is obviously not the case.

What happens, if the scope argument is omitted, the scope argument is empty or a scope without a binding for the container *users* is provided?

$$\nabla(userIsAlice)() =$$
$$\nabla(\triangle t(\triangleright users, \triangle c(Alice), \theta))() =$$
$$\triangle c(\triangle c() \cap \triangle c(Alice) \neq \emptyset) =$$
$$\triangle c(false)$$

No binding for the variable ▷*users* is provided with the (empty) scope in the above example. If not present, implicitly a binding of the variable to an empty container is assumed. The result of the application is then the container $\triangle c(false)$.

Order Operators in Tests   The pre-defined order operators interpret symbols as values. This are namely the operators smaller, smaller-equal, greater, and greater-than.

Example:
$$t = \triangle t($$
$$\triangle c(1 = \triangle e()),$$
$$\triangle c(2 = \triangle e()),$$
$$<);$$

The test t defines as "left side" a container with entity "1". "1" is the symbol of the entity, as entities do not have assigned values. The "right side" consists of a container holding an entity with the symbol "2".

When evaluating the application ∇t, the symbol names are interpreted as values. The operator "$<$" checks: $1 < 2$? The result of this test application is $\triangle c(true)$.

4.6.6. Application of Policies

Policies are sets of containers. Like the application of a test, the application of a policy returns either $\triangle c(true)$ or $\triangle c(false)$. These values can be interpreted as `true` or `false`.

The return value of an application of a policy is $\triangle c(true)$, if all applications of tests of the policy evaluate to $\triangle c(true)$.

Like applications of tests, applications of policies utilize scope arguments.

Formally:
Let $t_1, t_2, ..., t_n \in \mathcal{T}$ be ADQL tests.

$$\nabla(\triangle p(t_1, t_2, ..., t_n))(S) = \begin{cases} \triangle c(true), & \text{if } \forall t_i : \nabla(t_i)(S) = \triangle c(true) \\ \triangle c(false), & \text{else} \end{cases}$$

A policy can be interpreted as a logical AND-concatenation of all assigned tests.

Example:
$AliceMayReadAnyObject = \triangle p($
    $userIsAlice = \triangle t(\triangleright users, c(Alice), \theta),$
    $permIsRead = \triangle t(\triangleright permissions, c(read), \theta),$
    $validObject = \triangle t(\triangleright objects, objects, \theta),$
  $);$

$scope1 = \triangle s($
    $\triangleright users = \triangle c(Alice),$
    $\triangleright permissions = \triangle c(read),$
    $\triangleright objects = \triangle c(fileA)$
$);$

$scope2 = \triangle s($
    $\triangleright users = \triangle c(Bob),$
    $\triangleright permissions = \triangle c(read),$
    $\triangleright objects = \triangle c(fileA)$
$);$

We calculate the results of the policy, first with the argument $scope1$, then $scope2$:

$\nabla(AliceMayReadAnyObject)(scope1) == \triangle c(true)$
$\nabla(AliceMayReadAnyObject)(scope2) == \triangle c(false)$

The above policy application becomes true if all three tests applications evaluate true. The application of test $userIsAlice$ is true, if the scope definition of $users$ is $Alice$. The application of the second test $userIsRead$ evaluates true, if the scope definition of $permissions$ is $read$. The application of the third test becomes true, if the current object is part of the container objects.

Summarized, the policy is true, if the current scope user is Alice, the permission is read and the object a valid object. In other words: Alice may access all objects with read access.

4.6.7. Application of Scopes

The last construct for applications is the application of scopes. The application of a scope returns either $\triangle c(true)$ or $\triangle c(false)$. An application of a scope s returns $\triangle c(true)$, if all defined policies in the system, which are applied using the scope s, return $\triangle c(true)$.

Formally:
Let $S \in \mathcal{S}$ be a scope and $\mathcal{P}$ be the set of all policies.
Then $\nabla(S)() : \mathcal{S} \rightarrow \triangle c(true|false)$.

$$\nabla S = \begin{cases} \triangle c(true), & \text{if } \exists P \in \mathcal{P} : \nabla(P)(S) = \triangle c(true) \\ \triangle c(false), & \text{else} \end{cases}$$

A scope is evaluated true, if a policy $P \in \mathcal{P}$ exists which can be evaluated true for the scope S. If no such policy exists, the result is $\triangle c(false)$.

Applications of scopes are used to test all policies in the system. Usually this is the case if an access check is performed. A scope is used to represent a current system state by binding the variables to specific values. Then all policies are checked, if access can be granted or not. If a policy evaluates true for the given scope, access is granted. If no policy can be found, the access is denied.

Please note, that syntactically a scope s application may have a scope *argument* $sarg$: $\nabla(s)(sarg)$. However, the evaluation of a scope application considers only scope s itself, ignoring the scope argument $sarg$. Thus, scope arguments can be omitted when using scope applications.

4.7. Summary

In this chapter, we presented and discussed all syntax elements of the ADQL language. The syntax definition reminds us of the famous Lamda calculus: A valid ADQL term consists either of a definition or an application. Both can be used with entities, containers, relations, F1-projections, tests, policies and scopes.

The access control model consists of the model layer. Here, the access control model is defined: What is relevant for access control, e.g. users, objects, permissions, and how are these concepts interrelated with each other. The definitions of the model correspond to container and relation definitions and, in some parts, to entity definitions. Containers are bags for entities. They can be used to represent container hierarchies and container networks by indirect container definitions (container A may be part of container B). These are indirect entity structures. On the other side, containers can be used within access control by assigning them directly to other containers. In the latter case, statements about containers can be realized. The same is true for relations. Relations link together two or more containers. The definition of a relation can consist of an explicit enumeration of their elements. Implicitly relation definitions can be realized by using boolean expressions. The latter is not yet part of ADQL.

The facts layer definitions are represented by entity definitions. Here, all facts, e.g. *Alice* is a *user*, *pic1* is an *object*, ... are defined. It relies on the definitions of the model layer.

The policy layer includes tests and policies. While tests are boolean operations on exactly two containers, policies are logical AND-combinations of tests. A policy becomes true, if all its tests evaluate true. A test consists of two containers and an operator. The operator maps the test to a boolean value, thus $true$ or $false$.

This leads to the so-called applications. While ADQL definitions only define things, applications evaluate things. Entities simply evaluate to their identity. This becomes more complex for containers.

Applications of containers may be used to decompose or flatten container hierarchies and/or container networks.

In contrast, applications of relations are used for so-called projections. F1-projections of n-ary relations define $(n-1)$ bound and one unbound container. The latter is the target for the F1-projection. The result is a container with all elements of the relation including the unbound values in their tuple, projected to the space of the variable entity. It is used for complex queries used in tests.

The application of tests results in a simple $true$ or $false$. The current scope is used to evaluate the test. The result is boolean. The same is true for the application of policies. If all tests become $true$, the policy is also $true$.

Finally, scopes can be evaluated. This corresponds to a typical access check. All defined policies are evaluated. If one is found returning $true$, the scope application becomes $true$, too. If none is found, the scope, and with it the access query, is denied.

We have laid out the complete ADQL syntax in this chapter and provided examples.

5. The Concepts of the Access Definition and Query Language

In this section, we describe all concepts of the Access Definition and Query Language. We provide a description of every concept and explain how the concept is going to be used in ADQL. We start with basic concepts which are not interrelated with other concepts and continue with derived concepts, which are interrelated with other ADQL concepts. The ADQL language itself is not part of this chapter. The language is described in chapter 4. We advise to read at least the motivational example to learn about the language basics in chapter 3.

5.1. Overview of ADQL's Concepts

ADQL relies on a relatively small number of concepts. These are: entities, containers, relations, filtered 1-projections, tests, policies, variables, and scopes.

Entities are the "things" in ADQL. Anything modeled in ADQL is an entity. This can be e.g. a user, a group of users, a permission, a file, an attribute of a user or an object. An entity is represented by a symbol (an identifier).

Containers are used to group entities. E.g. users may be grouped in certain user groups like "administrators" or "guests". Containers need not to be flat but may be organized in hierarchies or graphs. A container can be assigned to another container allowing topologies like trees, lattices, or graphs. "Alice" maybe a part of the container "administrators". This container is a part of the container "users", making "Alice" not only a part of "administrators" but also of "users".

Relations are used to describe properties of entities and model associations between entities. Relations link entities of two or more containers. E.g. the container "users" can be associated with the container "files" by the relation "owner". This allows linking a file from the container "files" to one or more owners from the container "owner". As relations can be defined not only between two containers, but n, complex situations can be described. E.g. the user

"Alice" is in the role "project leader" within the project "SAP migration". This fact requires at least a 3-ary relation, as Alice may be a regular member of a project team in another project and only leads the project "SAP migration".

Filtered 1-projections are used to query relations. This concept is used to answer questions like "who is the owner of file1.jpg". The relation "owner" is defined between "users" and "files". The relation "owner" explicitly defines, which user is the owner of a file. ADQL refers to an element of a relation as "link". To answer the above question, we need to filter the relation "owner" for all links containing "file1.jpg". After applying the filter on the links, the tuple element "files" is masked out leaving only the tuple element "users". In this example, "Ann". This is called a projection. In this case, the relation "owner" is projected towards "users". ADQL currently only supports projections to one tuple element of the relation. To reflect this, we refer to filtered 1-projections and not to general filters or projections.

Tests are used to represent boolean expressions. In ADQL a test consists of two expressions which are combined by a boolean operator. A common operator in ADQL is the θ-operator. θ returns true if both expressions share at least one entity. Tests are used to represent logical queries. E.g. a test can check whether the current "user" is "Alice" and if the "owner" of a "file" is the current user.

Policies allow combining tests to complex logical expressions. ADQL describes a policy as collection of tests, which must all be true to let the policy become true. A policy can, therefore, be interpreted as conjunctive normal form.

Variables represent certain aspects of the system state which will be checked by the access control system. E.g. the variable user is bound to "Alice" representing the current user. Variables are dependent on the scope they are defined in. In each scope, a variable can be assigned to a different value. Variables can be used in tests, to check for certain system conditions, e.g. "is the current user Alice?".

Scopes are used to represent specific system states. A scope is a collection of variable bindings. E.g. for scope s_1 the variable "users" is bound to "Ann", the "permission" is "read", and the "object" is "file1.jpg". Policies, tests, filtered 1-projections and other expressions of ADQL can be resolved based on scopes.

5.2. The Logical Layers of ADQL

Before going into details, we want to provide an overview of the logical layers of ADQL. ADQL has been designed to be able to implement different access control models, e.g. RBAC, Bell-LaPadula, Chinese Wall, ... Therefore, we argue that ADQL is a meta model of an access control model.

To be able to implement an access control model, ADQL makes use of its concepts. We have informally introduced these concepts in the last section. In this section, we want to provide an overview which concepts are combined to define the four layers necessary for access control: the access control model, the facts, the policies, and the access rights. We depict these layers in figure 5.1.

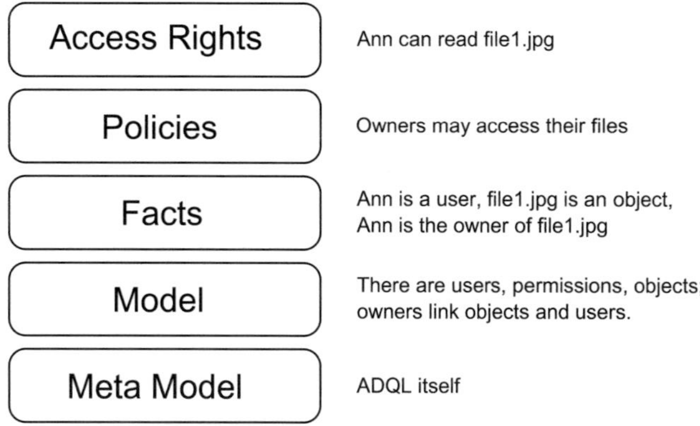

Figure 5.1.: Structure of the logical layers of ADQL

The Meta Model Layer. ADQL acts as a meta access control model. It can be used to define an access control model. The concepts of the meta-model layer are described in this chapter. The syntax of the formal language to define and calculate expressions is explained in chapter 4.

The Model Layer. In the model layer the access control model to be used in facts, policies and logic inference is specified. The access control model defines how the access control system acts. E.g. the model layer can be defined to act as a HRU-model, as a Bell-LaPadula model, as an RBAC model ... The model layer makes use of the concepts containers, relations, and entities. The example provided in figure 5.1, defines an access control model with users, permissions, and objects (like files). Furthermore, a relation between users and objects, the owner, is defined: Each object may be assigned to one or more users, defined as owner of the object.

The Facts Layer. The layer defines the facts for logical reasoning. The facts represent all possible system states of the access control system: Which users exist, which objects exist, which permissions are supported, and so on. The provided example establishes the facts that "Ann is a user", "file1.jpg" is an object, and

"Ann is the owner of file1.jpg". Conceptually, ADQL uses the concepts entities, assignment to containers, and relations.

The Policy Layer. The policy layer introduces the policies which are used to decide upon access checks. It depends on the model and facts layer. An example is, that "Ann may access all files". Before being able to formulate such a policy, we need to introduce the underlying model ("we use users, permissions, and objects") and some facts ("Ann is a users"). The ADQL concepts tests and policies belong to this layer. Any ADQL test and any ADQL policy belongs to the policy layer.

The Access Rights Layer. The last layer is the access rights layer. For example, "Ann can read file1.jpg". Access rights are not explicitly defined anywhere, but can be calculated from the other layers, namely the model, the facts and the policies. If users can access files they own, and Ann is the owner of "file1.jpg", then Ann, of course, may access "file1.jpg". The access rights are not explicitly expressed, but can be derived by applying the policies on the facts and the model. The access rights can even be pre-calculated for a given model, fact base, and policy collection, so that a query is a simple lookup on the pre-calculated access rights. The latter topics are discussed in section 7.2 and section 8.

Variables and scopes are not represented in ADQL's logical layers. Both are used for reasoning and to answer access check queries. For this task, all the above layers are required so that variables and scopes can be seen to be located in a separate layer orthogonal to the described layers.

We have provided a short overview of the ADQL concepts. Next, we will describe each concept. The language syntax and the usage of the concepts is explained in chapter 4.

5.3. Entities

The very basic concept of ADQL is an entity. We define an entity as any "object in reality" modeled in the system. Generally, everything modeled in ADQL is an entity: e.g. users, files, containers, relations, policies, tests, objects, permissions, Ann, Herb, read, write, file1, ...

An entity in ADQL is an object which is identified by a symbol. Technically, each symbol corresponds to a unique ID/key.

To be able to distinguish more advanced entity types which we will introduce subsequently in this chapter, we define basic entities.

Definition 4 (Basic entities and entities). *We introduce basic entities $e_1, e_2, \ldots, e_n$. We define the set E_G of all basic entities. Furthermore, we define the set of all entities E.*

$$E_G = \{e_1, e_2, \ldots, e_n\} \tag{5.1}$$
$$E = E_G \tag{5.2}$$

Letter E refers to the term *entity*, the letter G to the German term *Grundmenge* (engl. "base set"). E is the set of all entities in the system. For now, $E = E_G$. We will extend E subsequently on the following pages by adding more concepts to its definition.

To represent facts on an information system in ADQL we establish a mapping between facts in an information system and the ADQL environment. We depict an example in figure 5.2.

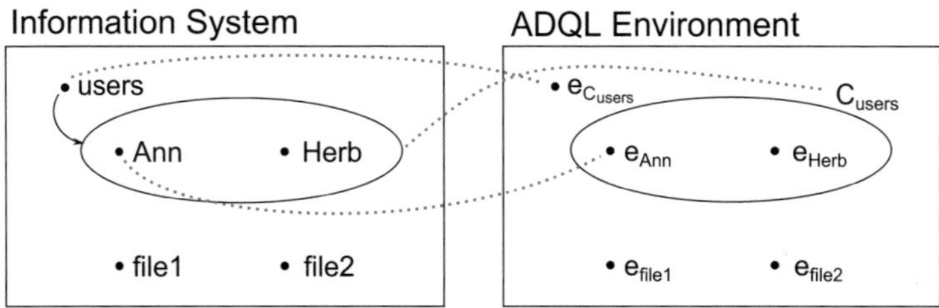

Figure 5.2.: Example showing the mapping of facts in an information system to the ADQL environment.

In the information system two users are present, "Ann" and "Herb". Ann and Herb are assigned to a set of "users". Furthermore, "file1" and "file2" are defined in the information system.

A mapping of this state of the information system is represented in the ADQL environment depicted in the right box.

- Ann is mapped to an entity with the symbol e_{Ann}.

- Herb is mapped to an entity with the symbol e_{Herb}, the objects $file1$ and $file2$ are mapped to the symbols e_{file1} and e_{file2}, respectively. (These mappings are not depicted in figure 5.2 for better readaility.)

- The concept "users" in the information system is mapped to the ADQL symbol $e_{C_{users}}$. $e_{C_{users}}$ is the symbol representing the concept "users".

- The "content of users" (Ann and Herb) in the information system is mapped to the ADQL symbol C_{users}.

We see, that we differentiate between mapping the *name* of an entity and mapping the *content* of an entity. The name of the concept "users" in the information system is mapped to the ADQL symbol $e_{C_{users}}$, while the content of "users" in the information system is mapped to the symbol C_{users}.

To distinguish between the name and the content of a symbol we introduce a concept named "entity structure". The phrase "structure" reminds us to the concept of "struct" in ANSI-C.

Definition 5 (Entity structures). *We define an entity structure as tuple $B = E \times \{d, \bar{d}\}$. We denote a tuple of B as $b_i = (e_i, d_i)$ where $d_i \in \{d, \bar{d}\}$. $D = \{d, \bar{d}\}$ is a boolean value. d is said to be "direct" referring to the name of e_i, $\bar{d}$ is said to be indirect or referring to the content of e_i.*

A tuple $b_i \in B$ is built from an entity $e_i \in E$ and the boolean value $\tilde{d} \in D$. We will use b_i to distinguish between the name of an entity and the content of an entity. Letter B refers to the term *basic set*.

- (e_i, d) is called a direct entity structure and refers to the name of the entity e_i.

- $(e_i, \bar{d})$ is called an indirect entity structure and refers to the content of the entity e_i.

In the example depicted in figure 5.2, the tuple (e_{users}, d) refers to e_{users}, the tuple $(e_{users}, \bar{d})$ to the content of e_{users}, which is the set $C_{users} = \{e_{Ann}, e_{Herb}\}$.

When we write "refers to", we need to define this term formally:

Definition 6 (Value function). *We introduce a transformation, the value function. The value-function is used for ADQL applications (∇).*

Let $b = (e_i, \tilde{d}) \in B$.

$$val : B \to \mathcal{P}(E)$$

$$val(b) = val((e_i, \tilde{d})) = \begin{cases} \{e_i\}, & \text{if } \tilde{d} = d, \\ \{\}, & \text{if } \tilde{d} = \bar{d}, \\ \{\}, & \text{if } b = \{\} \end{cases} \tag{5.3}$$

The *val*-transformation assigns a 2-tuple $(e_i, \tilde{d})$ to its so-called "value". For basic entities the value is a single-element set $\{e_i\}$ for direct entity structures, or the empty set for indirect entity structures.

We said that a direct entity structure refers to the name of the entity while an indirect entity structure refers to the content of the entity. Consequently, for basic entities, the name of an entity is the entity itself while the content of a basic entity is empty. There is simply no content. Of course, the latter will change, when we work with containers in the next section.

Definition 7 (Value function on sets). *We further define the value function on sets of entity structures.*

Let $X = \{b_1, \ldots, b_k\} \in B$.

$$Val : \mathcal{P}(B) \to \mathcal{P}(E)$$

$$Val(X) = \begin{cases} \cup_{i \in X} val(b_i), & \text{if } X \neq \{\}, \\ \{\}, & \text{if } X = \{\} \end{cases} \tag{5.4}$$

The value of a set of entity structures can be calculated by the union of the values of all single-element subsets. Thus, the value of the set X is the union of the values of all its elements. If the set X is the empty set, the value of it is the empty set, too.

Please note, that the *val*-function with a small "v" is defined on B, while the *Val*-function with a capitalized "V" is defined on $\mathcal{P}(B)$.

Summary of Entities

Let us shortly wrap up:

- E_G is the set of all basic entities.

- E is the set of all entities. Currently we defined only basic entities, $E = E_G$.

- B is an the set of entity structures. It contains 2-tuples with an entity and a boolean value named $\tilde{d} \in D$. Direct entity structures refer to the name of an entity. Indirect entity structures refer to the content of an entity.

- The value function *val* transforms entity structures to entities. Direct entity structures are mapped to the corresponding entity itself (its "name"), indirect entity structures are mapped to an empty set (the content of a basic entity is defined to be empty).

- *Val* is the corresponding function for sets of entity structures.

5.4. Containers

The next concept we introduce is the concept of containers. Containers are sets of entity structures.

Definition 8 (Container). *We define a container A as the finite set of entity structures. Let $b_i \in B$ be an entity structure with i an arbitrary index to enumerate entity structures.*

$$A = \{\ldots b_i \ldots\}$$

In case, more than one container is defined, we add an arbitrary index to the container symbol, e.g. C_i (instead of A). An element of the container C_i is then denoted by c_{ij} where the first index refers to the container and the second to the entity structure in the container.

$$C_i = \{c_{i1}, c_{i2}, \ldots, c_{im}\}$$

We know from the definition of entity structures (see definition 5): Each element c_{ij} of a container is an entity structure $(e_{ij}, \tilde{d})$, with e_{ij} being an entity from E and $\tilde{d}$ being a boolean value, direct ($\tilde{d} = d$) or indirect ($\tilde{d} = \bar{d}$).

We use containers to collect entities. E.g. we want to group the user entities "Ann", "Herb", "Jim", ... into the container "users".

Definition 9 (Container set). *Let C be the set of all containers C_i with $i = 1, \ldots, n$.*

We see, C is then a set of containers:

$$C = \{C_1, C_2, \ldots, C_n\} = \{\{c_{11}, c_{12}, \ldots, c_{1m}\}, \{c_{21}, c_{22}, \ldots, c_{2o}\}, \ldots\} \qquad (5.5)$$

The symbol C_i refers to a container in the set of containers C.

Symbols are used as substitution, in other words, the symbol C_1 is identical with $\{c_{11}, c_{12}, \ldots, c_{1m}\}$. Symbols are the "name" of an entity, here a container. In ADQL, we want to refer to a container not only as the name of a container (representing the container) but also to its content. Obviously, we need to introduce another symbol for the latter: For each container C_i we introduce the symbol e_{C_i}. It reflects, that each container C_i has a corresponding entity e_{C_i}.

Definition 10 (Container entities and entities). *Let C be the set of all containers C_i with $i = 1 \ldots m$. We define, that for each C_i there is an entity e_{C_i} and vice versa. We call e_{C_i} a container entity. The set of container entities is called E_C.*

$$E_C = \{e_{C_1}, e_{C_2}, \ldots, e_{C_m}\} \tag{5.6}$$

The set of all entities E is extended to consist of all basic and container entities.

$$E = E_G \cup E_C = \{e_1, e_2, \ldots, e_n, e_{C_1}, e_{C_2}, \ldots, e_{C_m}\} \tag{5.7}$$

Please note the difference between C and E_C. While C is a set of sets, E_C is a set of (container) entities.

We have introduced two new concepts in the last paragraphs:

- Containers are sets of entity structures.

- The symbol C_i represents a container as a set, thus, the content of a container.

- The symbol e_{C_i} refers to the container as an entity, thus, the name of a container.

The first allows us to build "flat" groups of entities, the latter allows us, combined with direct and indirect entity structures to build "deep" container hierarchies. To allow this, we extend the value-function. The definition looks complex at the first glance and we will explain it subsequently.

Definition 11 (Value function (extended version 2)). *Let $b = (e, \tilde{d}) \in B, e \in E, \tilde{d} \in D, S \subseteq E_C$, initially $S = \{\}$:*

$$val(b) = val_r(b, \{\}) \tag{5.8}$$

$$val_r : B \times E_C \to \mathcal{P}(E)$$

$$
val_r(b, S) = \begin{cases}
\{e\}, & \text{case (1), if } \tilde{d} = d, \\
\{\}, & \text{case (2), if } \tilde{d} = \bar{d} \wedge e \in E_G, \\
\{\}, & \text{case (3), if } b = \{\}, \\
\left.\begin{array}{l} R : \text{for } c_{ij} \in C_i \text{ do:} \\ \quad R = R \cup \\ \quad val_r(e_{c_{ij}}, S \cup e_{C_i}) \\ \text{end} \end{array}\right\} & \text{case (4), if } \begin{cases} \tilde{d} = \bar{d} \wedge e \in E_C \\ \wedge e_{C_i} \notin S, \end{cases} \\
\{\}, & \text{case (5), if } \begin{cases} \tilde{d} = \bar{d} \wedge e \in E_C \\ \wedge e_{C_i} \in S, \end{cases}
\end{cases} \tag{5.9}
$$

where C_i is the corresponding container to e, if $e \in E_C$. c_{ij} are the elements of C_i.

The value function val is extended and replaces definition 6. It makes use of a new transformation, the *recursive value function* val_r. The recursive value function is defined on $B \times S$ with S being a subset of E_C. E_C is the set of container entities. S is initially empty.

val_r distinguishes five cases:

1. If the entity structure $b = (e, \tilde{d})$ is direct ($\tilde{d} = d$), a set with the entity e is returned. This is the "name" of an entity.

2. If the entity structure is indirect ($\tilde{d} = \bar{d}$) and the entity is a basic entity ($e \in E_G$), then the empty set is returned. The content of a basic entity is empty.

3. If the entity structure b is null, an empty set is returned. So far, the three cases match definition 6 of the value function.

4. If the entity structure is indirect and the entity is a container entity ($e \in E_C$), a recursive function is applied. As the entity is a container entity there must exist a corresponding container C_i. The recursion is done for each element c_{ij} of this container C_i. c_{ij} is an entity structure from B, as c_{ij} is a container element and all container elements are from B. The recursive value function val_r is called again with the arguments c_{ij} and $S \cup e_{C_i}$. We call this the decomposition of container C_i. The set S is used to avoid never ending loops in the recursion: If a container is processed by a recursive step of this case, its corresponding container entity e_{C_i} is added to set S. Case (4) is applied only, if the container entity e_{C_i} is not part of set S, thus the related container C_i has not been processed by the recursion before. If e_{C_i} is in S, case 5 (see next bullet point) applies, stopping the recursion and avoiding never-ending loops.

5. If an indirect entity structure with container C_i has already been decomposed earlier in a recursive step (case 4), its corresponding container entity e_{C_i} has been added to the set S. In this case, it is not decomposed again, but an empty set is returned. This case is used to avoid neverending loops of case 4.

We see, that this definition allows recursive container arrangements.

Example

We illustrate this with the example depicted in figure 5.3.

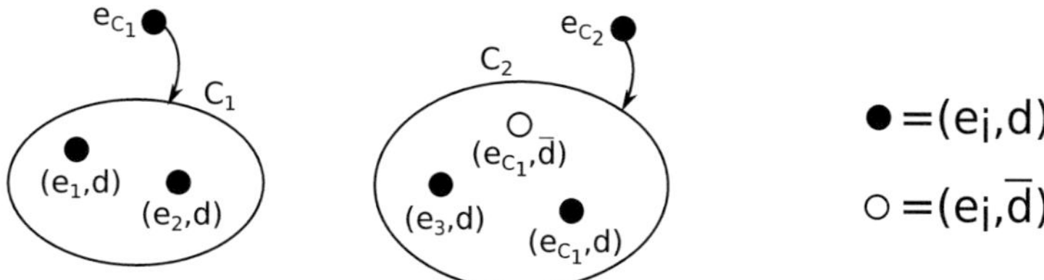

Figure 5.3.: Example of a recursive container definition. Full circles represent a tuple in the form $b_i = (e_i, d)$, empty circles $b_i = (e_i, \bar{d})$.

Depicted are two containers, C_1 and C_2. Container C_1 consists of two entity structures, b_1 and b_2. b_1 is defined as 2-tuple $b_1 = (e_1, d)$, $b_2 = (e_2, d)$. We denote 2-tuples $b \in B$ in the form of $b_i = (e_i, d)$, thus direct entity structures, by full circles and use empty circles for indirect entity structures in the form of $b_i = (e_i, \bar{d})$.

The second container is defined in the following way:
$C_2 = \{(e_3, d), (e_{C_1}, d), (e_{C_1}, \bar{d})\}$. Correspondingly, the container entity e_{C_2} exists. We see, that the container entity e_{C_1} is assigned to the container C_2.

Please note, that entity e_{C_1} is actually assigned twice to the container C_2: (e_{C_1}, d) assigns C_1 directly to C_2, while $(e_{C_1}, \bar{d})$ assigns C_1 indirectly to C_2.

We now evaluate some example expressions:

$$
\begin{aligned}
Val(C_1) &= Val(\{(e_1, d), (e_2, d)\}) \\
&= val((e_1, d)) \cup val((e_2, d)) \\
&= val_r((e_1, d), \{\}) \cup val_r((e_2, d), \{\}) \\
&= \{e_1\} \cup \{e_2\} \\
&= \{e_1, e_2\}
\end{aligned}
$$

The example $Val(C_1)$ is straight forward: The value of a container is the union of its entities (definition value function on sets, definition 7). On each entity structure, the value function is applied. As all entities are assigned directly, their value is the set of the entity. Obviously, the union is the set $\{e_1, e_2\}$.

Second example:

$$
\begin{aligned}
Val(C_2) &= Val(\{(e_3, d), (e_{C_1}, d), (e_{C_1}, \bar{d})\}) \\
&= val((e_3, d)) \cup val((e_{C_1}, d)) \cup val((e_{C_1}, \bar{d})) \\
&= val_r((e_3, d), \{\}) \cup val_r((e_{C_1}, d), \{\}) \cup val_r((e_{C_1}, \bar{d}), \{\}) \\
&= \{e_3\} \cup \{e_{C_1}\} \cup val_r((e_{C_1}, \bar{d}), \{\}) \\
&= \{e_3\} \cup \{e_{C_1}\} \cup \{e_1, e_2\} \\
&= \{e_1, e_2, e_3, e_{C_1}\}
\end{aligned}
$$

The second example makes use of indirect entity structures. Container C_2 consists of the entity structures (e_3, d), (e_{C_1}, d), and $(e_{C_1}, \bar{d})$. The first two entity structures are direct and are resolved by the value function to a set with entity e_3 and a set with entity e_{C_1}. For the third entity structure, $(e_{C_1}, \bar{d})$ the recursion of val_r is used. In this second recursion step, the val_r function is applied on the contents of the first recursion of the entity structure $(e_{C_1}, \bar{d})$. Container C_1 consists of the entity structures (e_1, d) and (e_2, d). The val_r applied on both returns the sets $\{e_1\}$ and $\{e_2\}$. The resulting set of the second recursion step is, therefore, $R = \{e_1, e_2\}$.

Completing the evaluation of val, we see that the decomposed container consists of $\{e_3, e_{C_1}, e_1, e_2\}$.

The concept of the boolean value $\tilde{d} \in \{d, \bar{d}\} = D$ became obvious: The value function is defined in such a way, that further evaluation is stopped if a direct entity structure $b_i = (e_i, d)$ is found. In contrast, the value function continues to evaluate on indirect entity structures of the form of $b_i = (e_i, \bar{d})$, if e_i is a container entity and has not been evaluated in the same decomposition before.

This mechanism enables ADQL to implement recursive container definitions. This is useful if containers modeling entities/containers in a security system are refined over time. For example, think about the introduction of new roles in an organization.

Assume a container *user* consists of the sub-containers *admins, regulars, guests*. We illustrate this in figure 5.4.

Liz is an administrator, Herb and Jim are regulars, while Ann and Tom are guests. All belong through indirect entity structure to the container "users".

We see that indirect entity structures can be used to build hierarchies of containers. By assigning a container indirectly to another container, a hierarchy is created. The value function recursively decomposes the container hierarchy.

In order to be able to "flatten" deeper hierarchies, we need to apply the value function recursively.

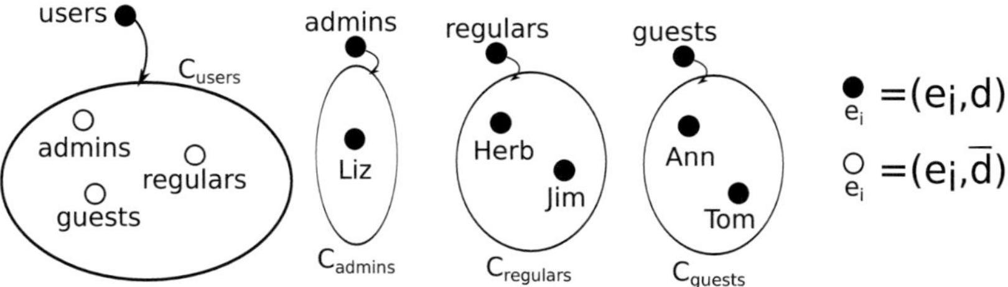

Figure 5.4.: Use case of a recursive container definition for user groups.

We will now proof that any container can be *decomposed* or *flattened*.

Proof. Let C_i be a container and C be the set of all containers. C is finite, thus $C_1 \ldots C_n$ are all containers in a current state of the ADQL system with $n < \infty$. Let c_{ij} be the entity structures of container C_i. The assignments of one container C_i are also finite, thus $\mid c_{ij} \mid < \infty$ for any fixed i.

$Val(C_i) = \cup_{k=1..j} val(c_{ik})$. If all $val(c_{ik})$ can be calculated and are finite, $Val(C_i)$ can also be calculated and is finite. $val(c_{ik}) = val_r(c_{ik}, \{\})$. Referring to definition 11 we immediately see that the latter is defined and finite for all cases but the case $\tilde{d} = \bar{d} \wedge e \in E_C \wedge E_{C_i} \notin S$.

We have to show it for this case. Definition 11 says for this case:
R : for $c_{ij} \in C_i$ do: $R = R \cup val_r(e_{c_{ij}}, S \cup e_{C_i})$ end

The loop will terminate, if (1) there are finite elements to iterate, thus C_i contains a finite number of elements c_{ij}. This is true as $\mid c_{ij} \mid < \infty$ for any fixed i. (2) if $val_r(e_{c_{ij}}, S \cup e_{C_i})$ terminates and is finite. For $val_r(e_{c_{ij}}, S \cup e_{C_i})$ the same cases apply as for $val(c_{ik})$. It will iterate again, if (1) another indirect entity structure is part of the container and (2) this indirect entity structure has not been evaluated in an iteration step before, thus its corresponding container entity $e_{C_i} \notin S$. We immediately see, that a maximum of $\mid C \mid$ iteration steps can occur, as there are maximallyhg $\mid C \mid$ containers in the system. Therefore, the iteration terminates. Each iteration step returns a finite set of elements, therefore, the union of finite sets is also a finite set. $\square$

Summary of Containers

Let us wrap up again:

- Containers C_i are used to store directly (e_{ij}, d) or indirectly $(e_{ij}, \bar{d})$ assigned entity structures. For the sake of shortness, we sometimes call this "direct" or "indirect entity assignments to containsers", although formally not an entity is assigned to a container but always an entity structure.

- The assignment of an indirect entity structures with a containers to another container enables ADQL to create container hierarchies.

- The Val-function is used to decompose or flatten container hierarchies.

5.5. Relations

We introduce the concept of a relation in ADQL.

Definition 12 (Relation). *Let $C_1, C_2, \ldots, C_n$ be containers in C. $J = \{1, \ldots, n\}$ is the index set of the containers. Let $Dom_{C_{1\ldots n}} = \times_{j \in J} Val(C_j) \cup \{\}$ be the domain including the empty set.*

We define a relation $R^n \subseteq Dom_{C_{1\ldots n}}$ as a table with n columns. A line r_i of the table represents a single relation point in the n-dimensional space $Dom_{C_{1\ldots n}}$ with $r_i^n = (c_{i1}, \ldots, c_{in})$ where $c_{ij} \in Val(C_j)$.

$$R^n \subseteq Dom_{C_{1\ldots n}}$$
$$R^n = \{r_1, r_2, \ldots, r_m | \forall p = 1, \ldots, m : \tag{5.10}$$
$$r_p = (c_{p1}, c_{p2}, \ldots, c_{pn}) \text{ with } \forall q = 1, \ldots, n : c_{pq} \in Val(C_q)\}$$

The definition of a relation follows the common mathematical definition.

The p-th row in the relation table corresponds with one n-tuple $r_p = (c_{p1}, c_{p2}, .., c_{pn})$. Each c_{pi} is an element of the decomposed container C_i, that is $Val(C_i)$.

We call one n-tuple $r_p \in R^n$ a *link* of R^n. For the sake of shortness we sometimes omit the n as part of a relation symbol.

In the case, that more than one relation is defined, we use an index symbol to differentiate between relations. E.g. $R_1, R_2, \ldots$ are relations.

Definition 13 (Set of all relations). *We define the finite set R of all relations*

$$R := \{R_1, R_2, \ldots, R_m\} \tag{5.11}$$

with R_i being a relation.

Like with containers, a relation symbol R_i refers to the relation itself. Again, we want to be able to refer to a relation "as an entity". Therefore, we introduce a symbol for the relation as an entity. As we want to have a symbol referring to the relation as an entity we define e_{R_i}.

Definition 14 (Relation entity). *For each relation R_i we define a relation entity e_{R_i}. The set E_R is the set of all relation entities, $E_R := \{e_{R_1}, e_{R_2}, \ldots, e_{R_m}\}$.*

Again, we extend the entity definition and value-function:

Definition 15 (Entities and value function (extended version 3)).

$$E = E_G \cup E_C \cup E_R \tag{5.12}$$

The set of all entities now includes all basic entities, all container entities, and all relation entities.

Consequently, the recursive value function needs to be extended. Let $b = (e, \tilde{d}) \in B, e \in E, \tilde{d} \in D, S \subseteq E_C$, initially $S = \{\}$:

$$val_r : B \times E_C \to \mathcal{P}(E)$$

$$val_r(b, S) = \begin{cases} \{e\}, & \text{\textit{case (1), if }} \tilde{d} = d, \\ \{\}, & \text{\textit{case (2), if }} \tilde{d} = \bar{d} \wedge e \in E_G, \\ \{\}, & \text{\textit{case (3), if }} b = \{\}, \\ \left\{ \begin{array}{l} R : \textit{for } c_{ij} \in C_i \textit{ do:} \\ \quad R = R \cup \\ \quad \quad val_r(e_{c_{ij}}, S \cup e_{C_i}) \\ \textit{end} \end{array} \right\} & \text{\textit{case (4), if }} \begin{cases} \tilde{d} = \bar{d} \wedge e \in E_C \\ \wedge e_{C_i} \notin S, \end{cases} \\ \{\}, & \text{\textit{case (5), if }} \begin{cases} \tilde{d} = \bar{d} \wedge e \in E_C \\ \wedge e_{C_i} \in S, \end{cases} \\ \{\}, & \text{\textit{case (6), if }} \tilde{d} = \bar{d} \wedge e \in E_R, \end{cases} \tag{5.13}$$

where C_i is the corresponding container to e, if $e \in E_C$. c_{ij} are the elements of C_i.

The above value-function (definition 15) equals to the previous version of the value-function (definition 11) but case (6). Case (6) deals with relation entities. The relation entities behave like basic entities. Direct entity structures of relations decompose through the val_r-function to the related relation entity. Indirect entity structures decompose to the empty set.

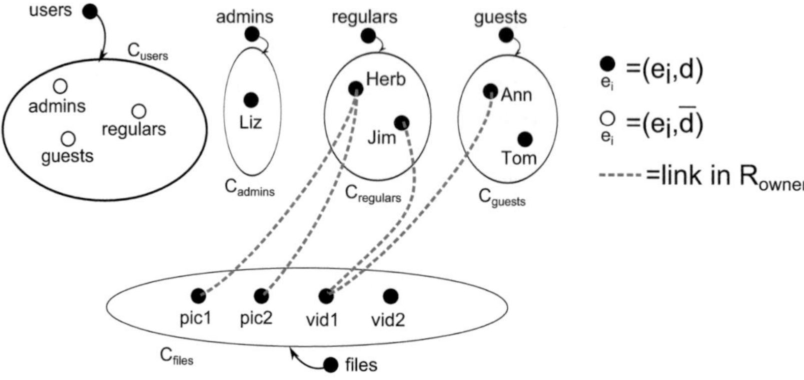

Figure 5.5.: Use case example of relations.

Example

We explain the usage of relations with the example illustrated in figure 5.5.

The example in figure 5.5 continues the container example (see figure 5.4). Besides the already introduced containers "users", "admins", "regulars" and "guests", a container "files" is defined with direct entity structures for the entities "pic1", "pic2", "vid1", and "vid2".

Let $C_{files} = \{(pic1, d), (pic2, d), (vid1, d), (vid2, d)\}$.
It follows for $Val(C_{files}) = \{pic1, pic2, vid1, vid2\}$.
Obviously, $Val(C_{users}) = \{Liz, Herb, Jim, Ann, Tom\}$.

We define relation R_{owner}:

$$R_{owner} \subseteq Val(C_{users}) \times Val(C_{files})$$
$$\text{with } \{(Herb, pic1), (Herb, pic2), (Jim, vid1), (Ann, vid1)\} \in R_{owner}$$

The files "pic1" and "pic2" are owned by the regular user "Herb", the file "vid1" has two owners, "Jim" being a "regular" user and "Ann" being a "guest". File "vid2" has no owner.

The definition of the above example makes use of an *explicit* relation definition. That is, all elements of the relation are explicitly enumerated. Another possibility of relation definitions are *implicit* definitions by boolean operators. Currently, the ADQL language definition does not support implicitly defined relations. Nevertheless, the ADQL concept itself has no constraints restricting relation definitions to explicit definitions.

Filtered 1-Projections

Filtered 1-projections are a composition of a filter operation and a projection. For the sake of shortness, we call "filtered 1-projections" "f1-projections", alternatively. Filtered 1-projections are used in ADQL to "decompose" relations. This is used mainly for queries. In the above example, the query "who is the owner of file pic1" can be asked.

We introduce the 1-filter operation:

Definition 16 (1-Filter). *Let R^n be a n-ary relation. $J = \{1, \ldots, n\}$ is the index set of the n-ary relation. Let $Dom_{R^n} = \times_{j \in J} Val(C_j) \cup \{\}$ be the domain of the relation including the empty set.*

We interpret the relation R^n as a table with n columns and m rows. Each row consists of a r_i with $r_i = (e_{i1}, e_{i2}, \ldots, e_{in}) \in R^n$. The n-tuples $r_1, r_2, \ldots, r_m$ are the m elements of the relation R^n.

Select the filter elements but leave one element unfiltered:
Choose an l with $1 \leq l \leq n$. Choose $n - 1$ entities satisfying the following conditions:
$e_{(1)} \in Val(C_1), \ldots e_{(l-1)} \in Val(C_{l-1}), e_{(l+1)} \in Val(C_{l+1}), \ldots e_{(n)} \in Val(C_n)$.
Let $r_{filter} = (e_{(1)}, \ldots, e_{(l-1)}, e_{(l+1)}, \ldots, e_{(n)})$ be the filter.
Let $Dom_{filter} = \times_{j \in J \setminus l} Val(C_i)$ be the domain of the filter.

We define a 1-filter function as:

$$
Dom_{R_i} \times Dom_{filter} \longrightarrow Dom_R
$$
$$
filter(R^n, r_{filter}) \mapsto \{r_m \mid \forall k : 1, \ldots, m : e_{k1} = e_{(1)} \wedge \cdots \wedge e_{k,l-1} = e_{(l-1)}
$$
$$
\wedge\, e_{k,l+1} = e_{(l+1)} \wedge \ldots \wedge e_{kn} = e_{(n)}\}
$$

$$(5.14)$$

We interpret a relation as a table, with each row representing a "link" of the relation and the columns representing the structure of the relation (a column is a tuple element of a relation element). An 1-filter on a n-ary relation requires $n-1$ bound and 1 unbound columns. When applied, the 1-filter returns those rows of the table which column entries match the filter. In SQL a filter corresponds to a (limited) WHERE-filter in SELECT statements.

Filters are not reflected in ADQL's syntax, as ADQL currently utilizes the combined function filtered 1-operation.

We continue with the introduction of a 1-projection:

Definition 17 (1-Projection)**.** *Let R^n be a n-ary relation. $J = \{1,\ldots,n\}$ is the index set of the n-ary relation. Let $Dom_{R^n} = \times_{j\in J} Val(C_j) \cup \{\}$ be the domain of the relation including the empty set.*

We interpret the relation R^n as a table with n columns and m rows. Each row consists of a r_i with $r_i = (e_{i1}, e_{i2}, \ldots, e_{in}) \in R^n$. The n-tuples $r_1, r_2, \ldots, r_m$ are the m elements of the relation R^n.

Select the projection dimension: Choose any but fixed $l \in J$.

We define an 1-projection:

$$Dom_{R^n} \times J \longrightarrow Val(C_{(l)})$$
$$proj(R^n, l) \mapsto \{e_{kl} \mid \forall k : 1, \ldots, m : \qquad (5.15)$$
$$r_k \in R^n \text{ with } e_{kl} \text{ is on } l\text{-th position of } r_k\}$$

When applied on a relation, an 1-projection cuts out $n - 1$ columns of the relation table and returns only one column called projection target. The result is a one-dimensional set.

Like filters, 1-projections are not represented in ADQL's syntax, as only the concatenation of filters and 1-projection is used.

We concatenate a 1-filter operation with a 1-projection operation:

Definition 18 (Filtered 1-projection (F1-projection))**.** *A filtered one projection, abbreviated as "F1-projection" is defined as:*

$$Dom_{R_i} \times Dom_{filter} \times J \longrightarrow Val(C_{(l)})$$
$$proj_{1F}(R_i^n, r_{filter}, l) \mapsto proj(filter(R_i^n, r_{filter}), l) = filter \circ proj \qquad (5.16)$$

For the syntactical representation of a filtered 1-projection we refer to 4.5.5.

An ADQL F1-projection transforms a relation to a set of entities.

The entities $e_{(1)}, e_{(2)}, \ldots, e_{(n-1)}$ are called the *bound entities* of the F1-projection. The corresponding containers $C_{(1)}, C_{(2)}, \ldots, C_{(n-1)}$ are called the *bound containers* of the F1-projection. The container $C_{(l)}$ is called the *unbound container* of the F1-projection. Another name for the unbound container is *target of the F1-projection.*

A F1-projection is a transformation from the space of the relation $Val(C_1) \times \cdots \times Val(C_n)$ to the space of the decomposed target container $Val(C_{(l)})$.

A F1-projection of a relation R_i^n requires $(n-1)$ bound entities and exactly one unbound entity on the l-th position of the n-tuples belonging to the relation.

The result of the F1-projection is a set of entities. These entities satisfy the condition that their related relation-tuples match all but the unbound entity in their tuples.

We provide an example continuing the above examples:

$$R_{owner} \mid (Herb, \bullet) = \{pic1, pic2\}$$
$$R_{owner} \mid (\bullet, vid1) = \{Jim, Ann\}$$
$$R_{owner} \mid (\bullet, vid2) = \{\}$$

The first example defines the entity *Herb* as bound entity. As the relation R_{owner} is defined on the decomposed containers $C_{users} \times C_{files}$, the container *users* is the bound container of the F1-projection. The second element of the tuple marks the position of the unbound container, which is C_{files}.

The first F1-projection evaluates all elements of the relation having *Herb* at the first tuple position. The resulting sets are stripped by all bound tuple positions, leaving only the component at the unbound position. As the entities *pic1* and *pic2* are both linked to *Herb* in the relation *owner*, the resulting set is $\{pic1, pic2\}$.

The second example is straight forward: The resulting container contains all those relation elements having the entity "vid1" at the second tuple position. These are "Jim" and "Ann". Here, the bound container is C_{files} with the bound entity "vid1". The unbound container is C_{users}.

The third example is similar to the second, but has a different bound entity "vid2". As the relation R_{owner} has no defined tuples with "vid2", the resulting set is empty.

ADQL uses the above F1-projections as a kind of query. "Show me the *owners* of the file *vid1*" is translated by the F1-projection $R_{owner} \mid (\bullet, vid1)$. In other words: Who is the *owner* of file *vid1*?

F1-Projections on Reflexive Relations

The definition of an ADQL relation allows reflexive F1-projections, thus a container can be part more than once in the F1-projection definition.

We provide as an example the definition of a proxy in an organization. In case, a user is not available due to vacation or illness, proxy users may be defined. For this, we introduce a relation "proxy": $R_{proxy} = Val(C_{users}) \times Val(C_{users})$.

We add two links to the relation, "Herb" has "Jim" as his proxy, "Jim" has "Ann" as his proxy. $(Herb, Jim), (Jim, Ann) \in R_{proxy}$.

To find out, who the proxies are, we utilize F1-projections:
$$R_{proxy} \mid (Jim, \bullet) = \{Ann\}$$
$$R_{proxy} \mid (\bullet, Jim) = \{Herb\}$$

The first F1-projection asks "who is the proxy of Jim". Consequently, the result is "Ann". In contrast, the second F1-projection asks "for whom is Jim the proxy". The answer for the latter question is "Herb".

The bullet • marks the position of the F1-projection target. This allows an unambiguous definition of F1-projections.

Summary of Relations

We summarize ADQL relations:

- Relations are defined on n decomposed containers.

- The n-ary elements of a relation are called links.

- F1-projections are a concatenation of 1-filters and 1-projections. They are used to transform a R_i^n relation to a set applying a filter and cutting out $n-1$ dimensions. A F1-projection has $(n-1)$ bound entities and exactly one unbound container. F1-projections are used for queries. The position of the bullet "•" marks the F1-projection target and allows unambiguous F1-projection definitions.

5.6. Variables, Bindings, Scopes

In order to be able to decide on access requests, a security system generally needs a set of rules (policies), a logical model and a description of the current system state. Variables are used in ADQL to represent the current system state. A set of variables representing a complete system state, is called a scope. Within a scope, decisions on access requests can be made by evaluating the rules. Therefore, we say, concerning the system state, a scope is sufficient to decide on access requests.

As ADQL is designed as a software service usable by third party products using ADQL as access management engine, several system states must be usable at the same time. This is why ADQL supports several parallel scopes.

Let us first introduce variables.

Definition 19 (Variable). *Let C be the set of all containers and V be the set of all variables.*

$$\exists C_i \in C \Rightarrow \exists \triangleright C_i \in V \tag{5.17}$$

$\triangleright C_i$ is called the associated variable to container C_i.

ADQL variables are closely related to containers. Each container automatically provides a variable whose symbol is derived from the container's name and whose possible values are a subset of the values of the container at execution time. For every container C_i a corresponding symbol $\triangleright C_i$ is defined.

A variable is used to express one part of a system state: While a container represents the possible values for a certain part, e.g. the "users", a variable describes the current system state of this part, e.g. the current user in state X is "Ann".

So far, we introduced the concept of variables. Next, we need to define the binding of a variable to a value and define some properties of such a binding.

Definition 20 (Binding of a variable). *Let $\triangleright C_i$ be a variable derived from container C_i. Let further $C_i' \in C$ be an arbitrary container, not necessarily related to container C_i.*

A variable $\triangleright C_i$ can be bound by the arbitrary container $C_i' \in C$.
We denote this binding by $X_{C_i} : \triangleright C_i = C_i'$.

A variable can be bound to a container. Generally, the binding of a variable can be arbitrarily chosen.

Definition 21 (Valid binding of a variable). *Let $\triangleright C_i$ be a variable derived from container C_i. Let further $C_i' \in C$ be an arbitrary container, not necessarily related to container C_i.*

A binding is said to be valid if $Val(C_i') \subseteq Val(C_i)$.

The binding of a variable is said to be "valid", if the assigned decomposed container consists only of entities also being part of the decomposed corresponding container of the variable. In other words, a binding is valid, if the variable is bount to a subset of the associated container.

Example   For example, let

$$Val(C_{users}) = \{Ann, Herb\}$$
$$Val(C_{permissions}) = \{read, write\}$$

With this definition, two variables have been defined implicitly, $\triangleright C_{users}$ and $\triangleright C_{permissions}$.

Let's have a look at some examples:

$$\triangleright C_{users} = \{(Ann, d)\} \qquad\qquad \Rightarrow Val(\triangleright C_{users}) = \{Ann\}$$
$$\triangleright C_{users} = \{(Ann, d), (Herb, d)\} \qquad \Rightarrow Val(\triangleright C_{users}) = \{Ann, Herb\}$$
$$\triangleright C_{users} = \{(read, d)\} \qquad\qquad \Rightarrow Val(\triangleright C_{users}) = \{read\}$$
$$\triangleright C_{users} = \{\}$$

The first binding is valid, as
$Val(C'_{users}) = \{Ann\} \subseteq Val(C_{users}) = \{Ann, Herb\}$.
The second binding is valid for the same reason. In contrast, the third binding is invalid: *read* does belong to the decomposed container $C_{permissions}$ and is not element of the decomposed container C_{users}. The last binding is valid, as the empty set is always included.

Universality of ADQL's variable concept   A counter argument against ADQL's way of defining variables is its universality: As there is exactly one variable defined for each container, a limitation in expressive power can be suspected concerning policy definitions. One may suspect that two or more variables are required with the type of one container.

We provide an example: Let us assume that for a certain policy the current user must be the proxy of another user. While modeling the proxy of a user with a relation and links, we need two variables for users. The user requesting access (*current user*) and the other user, who's proxy the current user is (*proxy user*). As both variables are derived from the container "users", there is only one variable $\triangleright C_{users}$.

On the one side, this argumentation is correct: ADQL does not support the possibility to introduce free variables in the sense, that variables can be explicitely defined and assigned a possible value domain, e.g. "users".

Nevertheless, on the other side, ADQL provides an easy concept to represent this scenario: Another container "proxy users" is introduced: $C_{proxyusers} = \{(e_{C_{users}}, \bar{d})\}$. The container "proxy users" is assigned to an indirect entity structure of the container entity C_{users}. With this trick, every entity being part of the container C_{users} becomes a member of the decomposed container $C_{proxyusers}$. As the decomposed containers are relevant for both, relation/link definitions and variable definitions, we now can represent the two variables from the value domain "users" needed for the proxy example.

Our argument for the relatively strict design of variables in ADQL is another: In case of free variables, the definition of a variable is of great importance. When used later in the context of policies and access checks, it is very important, that it is clear from which value domain a variable is from and how a variable can be identified. If there is confusion about a variable and its definition, unexpected access rights might be the result. ADQL avoids this source of errors by strictly linking the name of a variable to the name of a container.

For a further example we refer to 4.5.3.

5.6.1. Scopes

To represent system states it is necessary to be able to package several variable bindings together. We call these "packages" *scopes*. A scope is the representation of a certain system state in ADQL.

Definition 22 (Scope). *Let $X_1, X_2, \ldots, X_n$ be variable bindings with $X_j : \triangleright C_j = C'_j$.*

We define a scope S_i: $S_i = \{X_1, X_2, \ldots, X_n\}$

A scope S_i is a set of bindings. For each variable, a scope may contain one binding at most.

Definition 23 (Valid scopes). *A scope S_i is said to be* valid *if all of its bindings are valid.*

Definition 24 (Complete scope). *A scope S_i is said to be* complete, *if for all variables a binding is part of the scope.*

Examples:
We continue the above example. We have defined the containers C_{users}, C_{admins}, $C_{regulars}$, C_{guests}, and C_{files}.

$S_1 = \{\triangleright C_{users} = \{(Ann, d)\}, \triangleright C_{files} = \{(pic1, d), (pic2, d)\}\}$.

S_1 is not a complete scope, as there are no bindings for the variables C_{admins}, $C_{regulars}$, and C_{guests}.

To complete scopes, ADQL implicitly assigns empty sets to the missing variables. The complete scope will look like this:

$$S_1 = \{$$
$$\triangleright C_{users} = \{(Ann, d)\},$$
$$\triangleright C_{files} = \{(pic1, d), (pic2, d)\},$$
$$\triangleright C_{admins} = \{\},$$
$$\triangleright C_{regulars} = \{\},$$
$$\triangleright C_{guests} = \{\}$$
$$\}.$$

An interpretation of the above scope is, that *Ann* asks for access on two files, *pic1* and *pic2*.

In the above example, the scope definition is valid: "Ann" is an element of the decomposed container C_{users}, "pic1" and "pic2" are both elements of the decomposed container C_{files}, and the empty set is, of course, element of the decomposed containers C_{admins}, $C_{regulars}$, and C_{guests}.

5.6.2. Access Control on Variables and Scopes

Scopes are not defined to be part of the set of all entities E. This has one consequence: scopes cannot be used as entities in containers and relations. The result is that no access control can be established upon variables and scopes. In our understanding, this is not necessary: Access control is established upon facts, the model, and the policies. Access control is not required upon variables and their bindings, thus system states. Nevertheless, we know of some examples discussed in chapter 2, where the authors reasoned about access control on system states (e.g. the Model Z of McLean [McL90] applied on the original definition of the Bell-LaPadula-Model [BL73]). Therefore, if the binding of variables becomes relevant for access control, i.e. policies may be defined on bindings, variables and scopes have to be added to set E and the *value*-function has to be extended accordingly.

5.7. Tests

Next, we will introduce tests. Tests and policies build the "policy" layer of the ADQL architecture. Tests make yes-or-no decisions. If the test is fulfilled, the test is said to be passed. Its result is true. In the other case, a test is not passed, the result is false. ADQL defines its tests always boolean. Either it is passed or not.

An ADQL test is a three argument function. The first and second arguments (sometimes also referred to as "left" and "right" argument) are (a) a container, (b) a variable related to a container, or (c) an application of a term, which results in a container. The third argument is a boolean operator. It is operating on the two containers of the first two arguments. We will introduce operators in section 5.9. A test can only be evaluated within a scope. This is obvious, as variables have bindings only within a scope.

Definition 25 (Test). *Let $CV = C \cup V$ be the unified space of containers and variables. Let $CV_1, CV_2 \in CV$ be two elements from the unified container and variable space. op is a boolean operator of the operator space OP, $\mathcal{B}$ is the boolean space $\{true, false\}$. Then a test T_i is defined as follows:*

$$T_i : CV \times CV \times OP \longrightarrow \mathcal{B}$$
$$(CV_1, CV_2, op) \mapsto \mathcal{B} \tag{5.18}$$

A test is defined as a function on two containers or variables and a boolean operator. The result is boolean. As input, both arguments can either be a container or a variable. If the argument is a container, its value is scope-independent: Container definitions are global and not scope-dependent. Thus, containers work like constants in test definitions, although their value changes when the global container definition changes.

Please note: The return type of any application is of the type container. This means, that instead of a container, also any kind of application can be used for one of the first two arguments.

In case a variable is used in a test, its value is scope-dependent: a variable is assigned to different values in different scopes, so the values used for the test differs when changing the scope.

The operator op is an element of the set of ADQL's pre-defined operators OP. For the set of available operators we refer to section 5.9.

We call the first container the *test container* or the *left side* of the test. We refer by this term to the fact, that usually the first container is the container which gets compared. The second container is said to be the *comparative container* or the *right side* of a test. The latter term refers to the fact that often the second argument represents the benchmark or value against the test container is compared. Technically, there is no difference between the first and second test argument: E.g. it does not matter if the test container equals the comparative container or the comparative container equals the test container. The different terms are used to identify the position in the test expression.

Let us provide an example:
$$T_{userIsAnn} = (\triangleright C_{users}, \{(Ann, d)\}, \theta)$$

The test consists of three parameters. Parameter one is $\triangleright C_{users}$. It is the variable related to container C_{users}. The second parameter is a container. Its content is one association, (Ann, d). The third parameter is theta $"\theta"$. Although we did not introduce theta yet, it is a boolean operator. Its result is true, if the first and the second container share at least one element.

The test can then be evaluated. To become true, the test container and the comparative container need to have one common entity. The comparative container is defined to include "Ann" only. The logical conclusion is that the test is evaluated as true, if the test container includes at least "Ann" as well. This is the case, if "Ann" is bound to the variable $\triangleright C_{users}$. As variable bindings can only take place within scopes and tests can only be evaluated in the context of a scope, the scope needs to assign the variable $\triangleright C_{users}$ a container with at least the element (Ann, d). In other words: Within the current system state (represented by the scope), the current "users" needs to be "Ann". The test implements the question: "Is the current user Ann?".

Definition 26 (Set of tests). *The set of tests T is defined as set including all defined tests T_i. $T = \{T_1, T_2, \ldots, T_n\}$*

We introduce the set of all tests. It is simply the set of all defined tests in ADQL.

Next, we introduce entities for tests.

Definition 27 (Test entities). *For each test T_i we define a test entity e_{T_i}. The set E_T is the set of all test entities, $E_T := \{e_{T_1}, e_{T_2}, \ldots, e_{T_m}\}$.*

For each test defined in ADQL, a test-entity is defined, as well. The first refers to the test definition itself, while the latter is a symbol for the "test as an entity". Again, like with containers and relations, this definition allows us to include tests into access control policies. In other words, there can be tests about tests.

Again, we extend the definition of the entity definition and value-function:

Definition 28 (Entities and value function (extended version 4)).

$$E = E_G \cup E_C \cup E_R \cup E_T \tag{5.19}$$

The set of all entities now includes basic entities, container entities, relation entities, and test entities.

Consequently, the recursive value function needs to be extended. Let $b = (e, \tilde{d}) \in B, e \in E, \tilde{d} \in D, S \subseteq E_C$, initially $S = \{\}$:

$$val_r : B \times E_C \to \mathcal{P}(E)$$

$$val_r(b, S) = \begin{cases} \{e\}, & \text{\textit{case (1), if }} \tilde{d} = d, \\ \{\}, & \text{\textit{case (2), if }} \tilde{d} = \bar{d} \wedge e \in E_G, \\ \{\}, & \text{\textit{case (3), if }} b = \{\}, \\ \left.\begin{array}{l} R : \textit{for } c_{ij} \in C_i \textit{ do:} \\ \quad R = R\cup \\ \quad val_r(e_{c_{ij}}, S \cup e_{C_i}) \\ \textit{end} \end{array}\right\} & \textit{case (4), if } \begin{cases} \tilde{d} = \bar{d} \wedge e \in E_C \\ \wedge e_{C_i} \notin S, \end{cases} \\ \{\}, & \textit{case (5), if } \begin{cases} \tilde{d} = \bar{d} \wedge e \in E_C \\ \wedge e_{C_i} \in S, \end{cases} \\ \{\}, & \textit{case (6), if } \tilde{d} = \bar{d} \wedge e \in E_R, \\ \{\}, & \textit{case (7), if } \tilde{d} = \bar{d} \wedge e \in E_T, \end{cases} \tag{5.20}$$

where C_i is the corresponding container to e, if $e \in E_C$. c_{ij} are the elements of C_i.

The behavior of the *value*-function does not change much compared to the previous definition 15. Nothing changed but the addition of case (7). If assigned directly, the entities will decompose to their identity. If indirectly assigned, only container entities will be replaced by their content. Test entities evaluate to an empty set.

We have integrated tests to the ADQL entity definition. We have seen, that tests rely on boolean operators. Therefore, we will continue with operators in the next section.

Examples for tests can be found in section 3.2.

Summary of Tests

Let us wrap up on tests:

- Tests are used to decide upon access requests. They are part of the policy layer of ADQL.

- Tests are defined as boolean three-parameter functions: Two containers or variables (or applications, which return, when evaluated, containers) and a boolean operator.

- Tests are assigned to entities. The *value*-function has been adapted accordingly.

5.8. Policies

As the name suggests, a policy is part of the policy layer of ADQL, together with tests. Actually, policies are just sets of tests. A policy becomes true, if all tests of the policy are evaluated to true. Logically, policies are AND-concatenations of tests.

Definition 29 (Policy). *Let $T_{i1}, T_{i2}, \ldots, T_{in} \in T$ be tests.*
A policy P_i is defined as follows:

$$P_i = \{T_{i1}, T_{i2}, \ldots, T_{in}\} \tag{5.21}$$

As said, a policy is a set of tests. The logical interpretation of a policy is a logical AND-combination of its tests. To become true, all of its tests have to evaluate to true.

Definition 30 (Set of policies). *The set of policies P is defined as the set including all defined policies P_i. $P = \{P_1, P_2, \ldots, P_n\}$*

Like tests, we want to be able to refer to policies not only as policy but as entity. Again, we introduce special entities, the policy entities and integrate them to E and val.

Definition 31 (Test entities). *For each policy P_i we define a policy entity e_{P_i}. The set E_P is the set of all policy entities, $E_P := \{e_{P_1}, e_{P_2}, \ldots, e_{P_m}\}$.*

It is true, that: $\exists P_i \in P \Rightarrow \exists e_{P_i} \in E_P$

For each policy defined in ADQL, a policy entity is defined, as well. The first refers to the policy definition itself, while the latter is a symbol for the "policy as an entity". Again, like with containers and relations, this definition allows us to include policies into access control policies. In other words, there can be access checks on policies.

For the last time we extend the entity definition and the value-function:

Definition 32 (Entities and Value-Function (extended version 5)).

$$E = E_G \cup E_C \cup E_R \cup E_T \cup E_P \tag{5.22}$$

The set of all entities now includes basic entities, container entities, relation entities, test entities, and policy entities.

Consequently, the recursive value function needs to be extended for the last time. Let $b = (e, \tilde{d}) \in B, e \in E, \tilde{d} \in D, S \subseteq E_C,$ initially $S = \{\}$:

$$val_r : B \times E_C \to \mathcal{P}(E)$$

$$val_r(b, S) = \begin{cases} \{e\}, & \text{case (1), if } \tilde{d} = d, \\ \{\}, & \text{case (2), if } \tilde{d} = \bar{d} \wedge e \in E_G, \\ \{\}, & \text{case (3), if } b = \{\}, \\ \left. \begin{array}{l} R : \text{for } c_{ij} \in C_i \text{ do:} \\ \quad R = R \cup \\ \quad val_r(e_{c_{ij}}, S \cup e_{C_i}) \\ end \end{array} \right\} & \text{case (4), if } \begin{cases} \tilde{d} = \bar{d} \wedge e \in E_C \\ \wedge e_{C_i} \notin S, \end{cases} \\ \{\}, & \text{case (5), if } \begin{cases} \tilde{d} = \bar{d} \wedge e \in E_C \\ \wedge e_{C_i} \in S, \end{cases} \\ \{\}, & \text{case (6), if } \tilde{d} = \bar{d} \wedge e \in E_R, \\ \{\}, & \text{case (7), if } \tilde{d} = \bar{d} \wedge e \in E_T, \\ \{\}, & \text{case (8), if } \tilde{d} = \bar{d} \wedge e \in E_P, \end{cases} \quad (5.23)$$

where C_i is the corresponding container to e, if $e \in E_C$. c_{ij} are the elements of C_i.

Compared to the previous definition (definition 28) case (8) was added. Everything else is unchanged. If assigned directly, the entities will decompose to their identity. If indirectly assigned, only container entities will be replaced by their content. Policy entities evaluate to an empty set.

5.9. Operators

We will now introduce operators for ADQL. Operators are used with ADQL tests. An operator for ADQL tests has to fulfill the following requirements:

1. It must be a binary operator,

2. both operands have to be of the type container or variable $CV_i, CV_j \in CV$,

3. the result of the operation has to be either *true* or *false*.

Definition 33 (Operator). *Let $CV = C \cup V$ the union of all containers and variables. An ADQL operator is defined as a function:*

$$op : C \times C \longrightarrow \mathcal{B} \quad (5.24)$$

ADQL provides a set of built-in operators, discussed below. The operators can be divided into three classes:

1. First, so-called set operators θ and $\bar{\theta}$. They operate as the name suggests, on sets.

2. Second, the equal-operator class. They compare the content of containers.

3. Third, order operators like $\leq$. This operator class establishes an order on the elements of the sets which requires some data typing.

We will explain all three classes below.

Furthermore, ADQL provides a coding interface allowing the introduction of user-defined operators.

For examples explaining the operators below, we assume the following container definitions for the next sections:

$$\begin{aligned}
C_1 &= \{(Ann, d)\} \\
C_2 &= \{(Herb, d)\} \\
C_3 &= \{(C_1, \bar{d}), (C_2, \bar{d})\}
\end{aligned}$$

5.9.1. Set Operators

Operators in this class evaluate on sets: They interpret containers as sets. Predefined are the operators θ and its boolean inversion $\bar{\theta}$. Nevertheless, we already said, that ADQL supports user operators. User operators falling into this class are e.g. intersection or union.

θ (Theta) Operator

When applied, the θ-operator evaluates to the boolean function "intersection is not empty".

Side note: The symbol θ was chosen as it reminds us of the symbol generated when one draws a $\cap$-symbol over a $\oslash$-symbol.

Definition 34 (Theta Operator). *Let $CV_1, CV_2 \in CV$ be two containers or variables.*

$$\theta : CV \times CV \longrightarrow \mathcal{B}$$

$$\theta(CV_1, CV_2) \mapsto \begin{cases} \{true\}, & \text{if } Val(C_1) \cap Val(C_2) \neq \{\} \\ \{false\}, & \text{else} \end{cases} \tag{5.25}$$

The test becomes true if the values of CV_1 and CV_2 share at least one common entity

Example:

The symbol $\overset{?}{\neq}$ reads "is it not equal to?".

$$\theta : (C_1, C_3) = \{true\}$$

Proof:

$$Val(C_1) \cap Val(C_3) \overset{?}{\neq} \{\} \Leftrightarrow$$

$$\{Ann\} \cap Val(\{(Ann, d), (Herb, d)\}) \overset{?}{\neq} \{\} \Leftrightarrow$$

$$\{Ann\} \cap (\{Ann\} \cup \{Herb\})) \overset{?}{\neq} \{\} \Leftrightarrow$$

$$\{Ann\} \overset{?}{\neq} \{\}$$

This is $true$. As $\{Ann\}$ is a non-empty set, the test becomes $true$.

$\bar{\theta}$ (Not-Theta) Operator

The Not-Theta operator is defined to be the negation of the theta operator.

Definition 35 (Not-Theta). *Let $CV_1, CV_2 \in CV$ be two containers or variables.*

$$\bar{\theta} : CV \times CV \longrightarrow \mathcal{B}$$

$$\bar{\theta}(CV_1, CV_2) \mapsto \begin{cases} \{true\}, & if\ \theta(CV_1, CV_2) \mapsto \{false\} \\ \{false\}, & else \end{cases} \tag{5.26}$$

The not-theta operator is the logical NOT of the theta operator.

5.9.2. Equal Operators

The next class of operators are operators comparing the structure of containers and variables.

Equal-Operator "=="

The equal-operator, denoted by $==$, is defined by the following:

Definition 36 (Equal). *Let $CV_1, CV_2 \in CV$ be containers or variables. $A = Val(CV_1), B = Val(CV_2)$. A and B may be empty sets.*

$$== (CV_1, CV_2) \mapsto \begin{cases} \{true\}, & if \, \forall e \in A \cup B : \exists e \in A \iff \exists e \in B, \\ \{false\}, & else \end{cases} \tag{5.27}$$

To be equal in the sense of the operator $==$ the decomposed containers A and B have to have the same entities assigned to. Containers do not have an order, thus it is (and cannot) be relevant for the equal operator.

The "Equal"-operator requires no equality in the *structure* of the containers or variables. Only the decomposed containers have to be equal.

Not-Equal-Operator "$\neq$"

The Not-Equal-Operator is defined as the negation of the equal operator.

Definition 37 (Not-Equal). *Let $CV_1, CV_2 \in CV$.*

$$\neq (CV_1, CV_2) \mapsto \begin{cases} \{true\}, & if \, == (CV_1, CV_2) \mapsto \{false\} \\ \{false\}, & else \end{cases} \tag{5.28}$$

The not-equal-operator is the logical NOT of the equal operator.

5.9.3. Order Operators

In contrast to the above class of set operators, we discuss now order operators. We have seen that any container can be flattened to a set by the usage of the Val-function. However, establishing an order on the entities (elements) of the container (set) requires an order function.

So far, ADQL does this in a simple way and tries to interpret the entity symbol as a number. In terms of computer science it is a type cast from a string to an integer value. This cast may work, thus, the entity symbol can be interpreted as integer, or it may not work. In the latter case, the symbol is completely ignored.

Formally: When applying an operator from a class of order operators, ADQL typecasts the entity symbol in the following way:

Definition 38 (Type-Cast for entities). *Let e_i be an entity from E. Let $\mathcal{N}$ be the set of natural numbers. The function 'integertypecast' is a function type-casting Strings to numbers. We define the "order value" ov for e_i:*

$$ov : e_i \rightarrow \mathcal{N} \cup \{\}$$

$$ov : e_i \mapsto \begin{cases} integertypecast(e_i), & \text{if } e_i \text{ contains only digits,} \\ \{\}, & \text{else} \end{cases} \tag{5.29}$$

Next we introduce the set of type-casted entities.

Definition 39 (Type-Cast for containers). *Let $cv \in CV$ be an ADQL container or a variable. Let $e_1, \ldots, e_n$ be its decomposed entities. We define the "order value" OV for the container/variable cv:*

$$OV : CV \rightarrow \mathcal{P}(\mathcal{N} \cup \{\})$$

$$OV(cv) = ov(e_1) \cup \cdots \cup ov(e_n) \tag{5.30}$$

With the help of these definitions, we can assign a container or a variable to a set of integer numbers by type casting the entities to integer values, if possible.

Next, we define the maximum and the minimum value of a type-casted container.

Definition 40 (Definition of the max function). *Let $\mathcal{N}_\infty = \mathcal{N} \cup \{-\infty, +\infty\}$. Let $A \in \mathcal{P}(\mathcal{N} \cup \{\})$.*

$$max : \mathcal{P}(\mathcal{N} \cup \{\}) \rightarrow \mathcal{N}_\infty$$

$$max(A) = \begin{cases} -\infty, & \text{if } A = \{\}, \\ a_i, & \text{if } A \neq \{\} \text{ and } \forall j : a_i \geq a_j \text{ with } a_j \in A \end{cases} \tag{5.31}$$

The function max assigns a set of integers to its greatest value, $-\infty$ if the set is empty.

Definition 41 (Definition of the min function). *Let $\mathcal{N}_\infty = \mathcal{N} \cup \{-\infty, +\infty\}$. Let $A \in \mathcal{P}(\mathcal{N} \cup \{\})$.*

$$min : \mathcal{P}(\mathcal{N} \cup \{\}) \rightarrow \mathcal{N}_\infty$$

$$min(A) = \begin{cases} +\infty, & \text{if } A = \{\}, \\ a_i, & \text{if } A \neq \{\} \text{ and } \forall j : a_i \leq a_j \text{ with } a_j \in A \end{cases} \tag{5.32}$$

The function min assigns a set of integers to its smallest value, $+\infty$ if the set is empty.

With the help of the definitions of min and max we can now introduce the operators of the class "order operators".

$\prec$: Smaller-Than operator

Let $CV_1, CV_2 \in CV$ be two ADQL containers or variables.
The test $\prec (C_1, C_2)$ evaluates the following way:

$$\prec: CV \times CV \to \mathcal{B}$$

$$\prec (CV_1, CV_2) \mapsto \begin{cases} \{true\}, & \text{if } max(OV(CV_1)) < min(OV(CV_2)), \\ \{false\}, & \text{else} \end{cases} \tag{5.33}$$

The test becomes true if the largest type-cast-able element of CV_1 is still smaller than the smallest type-cast-able element of CV_2. If an element is not a member of the natural numbers $\mathcal{N}$, it is omitted. If either CV_1 or CV_2 are empty sets or contain no type-cast-able elements, min and max make use of their lower, respectively, upper boundary.

Examples:
$\prec (\{1\}, \{3\}) \mapsto \{true\}$
$\prec (\{3\}, \{1\}) \mapsto \{false\}$
$\prec (\{1, 2, 4\}, \{3\}) \mapsto \{false\}$
$\prec (\{1, 1000\}, \{\}) \mapsto \{true\}$

The first two examples are self-explanatory. The third example is $false$, as the largest value of $\{1, 2, 4\}$ is 4, and, therefore, not smaller than the smallest value of $\{3\}$, which is, of course, 3.

Another example:
$\prec (\{Alice, 1\}, \{Bob\}) \mapsto \{false\}$

Proof:
$max(OV(CV_1)) = max(\{1\}) = 1 < +\infty = min(\{\}) = min(OV(CV_2)).$

Please note, that in many cases instead of the correct operator $\prec$ the simpler symbol $<$ is used, although strictly seen, the latter symbol has not been introduced as a valid operator for tests.

$\preceq$: Smaller-Equal-Than operator

The Smaller-Equal-Than operator is defined the following way:

Definition 42 (Smaller-Equal). *Let $CV_1, CV_2 \in CV$:*

$$\preceq (CV_1, CV_2) \mapsto \begin{cases} \{true\}, & if\, max(OV(CV_1)) \leq min(OV(CV_2)), \\ \{false\}, & else \end{cases} \tag{5.34}$$

$\succ$: Greater-Than operator

The Greater-Than operator is defined accordingly to the smaller-than operator.

Definition 43 (Greater-Than). *Let $CV_1, CV_2 \in C$:*

$$\succ (CV_1, CV_2) \mapsto \begin{cases} \{true\}, & if\, max(OV(CV_1)) > min(OV(CV_2)), \\ \{false\}, & else \end{cases} \tag{5.35}$$

$\succeq$: Greater-Equal-Than operator

The Greater-Equal-Than operator is defined the following way:

Definition 44 (Greater-Equal). *Let $CV_1, CV_2 \in CV$:*

$$\succeq (CV_1, CV_2) \mapsto \begin{cases} \{true\}, & if\, max(OV(CV_1)) \geq min(OV(CV_2)), \\ \{false\}, & else \end{cases} \tag{5.36}$$

5.10. Summary of ADQL's Concepts

In this chapter we have defined and described the mathematical foundations of ADQL. Entities are the most basic concept in ADQL. Anything modeled in ADQL is an entity. E.g. users, files, permissions, etc.

Containers are used to collect entities. Entities can be assigned to containers by direct or indirect entity structures. Entities belong to the facts layer or sometimes to the model layer of ADQL. As containers can contain other containers, container hierarchies and networks can be established. The *val*-function is used, to decompose ("flatten") container hierarchies. Containers correspond to the model layer of ADQL.

Relations have been introduced as flexible connectors between n containers. They can be defined either explicitly by enumerating the links (elements of the relations) or implicitly through boolean functions. The latter is not yet integrated in ADQL. F1-projections can be defined on relations in order to transform relations into containers. This is used mainly for access queries. While relations belong to the model layer of ADQL, the link definitions belong to the facts layer.

Variables are used to represent certain aspects of a system state, e.g. used in access queries. E.g. the current *user* maybe *Ann*, i.e. the container variable $\triangleright user$ is bound to the value *Ann*. Such variable bindings can be packed to scopes. A scope represents a system state.

Containers and variables are used for tests. Two containers, the test container (or the left side of a test) and the comparative container (or the right side of a test) are compared by a boolean operator. The result is boolean, thus is either *true* or *false*. We introduced requirements for operators and suggested several default operators. The most important operator is theta θ. It compares two containers and resolves to true, if the intersection of both decomposed containers is not empty. If necessary, more operators can be introduced as long as they satisfy the defined requirements. Tests belong to the policy layer of ADQL.

The last concept to be introduced are policies. Policies are logical AND-concatenations of tests. In ADQL, policies are defined as sets of tests. To become true, all tests of a policy must evaluate to true for a certain scope. Like tests, policies belong to the policy layer of ADQL.

6. Use Cases for ADQL

In this chapter we present access control models and how they are expressed in ADQL. The aim of this chapter is to demonstrate the usage of ADQL as a meta access control language.

In this chapter we focus on our scientific targets (2) unification of theory and practice and (3) a step towards a meta model leaving the evaluation of the other goals for chapter 7. For the use case examples we chose the following access control models:

We start with the well-known Bell-LaPadula model as an example for a military use case. Its approach is quite different to the RBAC-like models. We aim to show that ADQL can not only model RBAC-like models or discretionary models, but also mandatory access control models. Additionally, several other access control models are based on the Bell-LaPadula model, e.g. the Chinese Wall model (see section 2.8).

The second use case example is a RBAC-like model used in a well-known software system, the SAP R/3 Enterprise Resource Planning software. This example shows the abilities of ADQL concerning the wide-spread RBAC-like world and how it can be used in ADQL.

As third example, we want to provide an extensive, complex and comprehensive access control model. Therefore, we took the use case of a software project at our institute with complex access control requirements. It is a kind of project management software which requires a 3-ary relationship between the core entities students, companies and university staff. This complex example aims to show more advanced features of ADQL which are not required in relatively simple RBAC-like models.

We undertook several more approaches to model access control models in ADQL together with some of our students. These results exist in the form of about a dozen seminar papers.

6.1. Bell-LaPadula Access Control Model

The Bell and LaPadula model [BL73, McL88] is described in detail in section 2.6.2. We repeat the fundamentals shortly: The model assigns subjects to so-called security levels, e.g. unclassified, classified, secret, top secret. The same happens to objects. Two access rights are defined, read and write. Write is defined here in the sense of "write but do not read", thus write-only.

Two policies decide on access:

- Simple Property: A subject may read objects only, if his clearance level (his security level) is not smaller than the security level of the accessed object. This is called the read-down principle or no-read-up principle.

- Star Property (*-property): On the other hand, a subject can write objects only, if the assigned clearance level of the subject is lower or equal to the object's security level.

The access control model   We analyze the model and see that we have the following concepts to model: "subjects", "objects", "permissions" and "security levels". We have at least two permissions, "read" and "write-only". Furthermore, we have two policies to model: (1) Subjects may read objects if their security level is higher or the same as the objects' security level. (2) Subjects may write objects, if their security level is lower or equal than the objects' security level.

The ADQL model definition reads as follows:

$$subjects = \triangle c();$$
$$objects = \triangle c();$$
$$permissions = \triangle c(read = \triangle e(), write = \triangle e());$$
$$securitylevels = \triangle c(1 = \triangle e(), 2 = \triangle e());$$

Obviously, we define containers for *subjects*, *objects*, *permissions*, and *securitylevels*. We define these concepts as containers, as we need variables to represent system states for these concepts: For an access control query, a specific subject will have to be defined, a specific object, and permissions. This simple example relies on two permissions, "read" and "write" (to be exact: "write-only"). However, if necessary, more permissions can be defined the same way. As security levels we introduce the levels "1" and "2". "2" can be interpreted as a higher security level, e.g. "secret", while "1" is a lower security level, e.g. "public".

Next, we introduce two relations:

$$plevel = \triangle r(subjects, securitylevels);$$
$$olevel = \triangle r(objects, securitylevels);$$

The *plevel* relation assigns a subject to a security level while the relation *olevel* assigns an object to a security level. We model these as relations, because a security level is a kind of property of a subject or an object, respectively.

With the above definitions, the model has been defined.

The policy definitions   We continue with policy definitions:

$$read\_down = \triangle p($$
$$\quad \triangle t(\triangleright permissions, \triangle c(read), \theta)$$
$$\quad \triangle t(\nabla \triangle pr(plevel)(\triangleright subjects, .), \nabla \triangle pr(olevel)(\triangleright objects, .), \geq),$$
$$);$$

The read-down (or no-read-up) policy is expressed by two tests:

1. The variable $\triangleright permissions$ must have a non-empty intersection with the anonymous container including the entity *read*. In other words, the requested permission must be read.

2. The filtered 1-projection of the subject's security level must be at least as high as the F1-projection of the object's security level.

Let us analyze the latter policy in detail:
$\nabla \triangle pr(plevel)(\triangleright subjects, .)$ is an ADQL application of a F1-projection definition. For details we refer to chapter 4. The F1-projection of a n-ary relation must have $(n - 1)$ bound and 1 unbound dimensions. The bound dimension in this F1-projection is $\triangleright subjects$, thus the variable related to the container "subject", in other words, the current subject. The unbound component is denoted by a dot ".". The definition of the relation *plevel* was $plevel = \triangle r(subjects, securitylevels)$. Therefore, the result of an application of this F1-projection is the container of all security levels of the current subject.

The second parameter of the test is $\nabla \triangle pr(olevel)(\triangleright objects, .)$: It evaluates to the security level of the current object.

The test operator is "$\geq$". As we've seen in chapter 5.9, the test becomes true, if the least numeric element of the first container is at least as high as the lowest numeric element of the second container. In our example, the security levels of the current subject must be at least as high as the security levels of the current object. If subject and object are assigned exactly one security level, it is equivalent to the simple security rule of Bell-LaPadula. If a subject is assigned several security levels, the smallest value is evaluated. If an object is assigned more than one security level, its highest assignment is taken into account. This

makes sense: If a document is classified the same time as "secret" and "top secret", it better gets treated as "top secret" – although one might argue, that such
multiple assignments have to be avoided entirely.

We go on with the star property:

$$write\_up = \triangle p($$
$$\triangle t(\triangleright permissions, \triangle c(write), \theta)$$
$$\triangle t(\nabla\triangle pr(plevel)(\triangleright subjects, .), \nabla\triangle pr(olevel)(\triangleright objects, .), \leq),$$
$$);$$

The rule is obviously clear as it follows the shape of the first policy. The requested permission has to be write(-only) and the subject's clearance level has
to be maximally as high as the security level of the request object.

The two policy definitions $read\_down$ and $write\_up$ are sufficient to represent
the policies of the Bell-LaPadula model.

Example facts for testing   To continue our use case, we provide some example facts for testing:

$$subjects = \triangle(Ann = \triangle e(), Herb = \triangle e());$$
$$objects = \triangle(fileL = \triangle e(), fileH = \triangle e());$$

$$plevel = \triangle r(subjects, securitylevels) : \{(Ann, 2), (Herb, 1)\};$$
$$olevel = \triangle r(objects, securitylevels) : \{(fileL, 1), (fileH, 2)\};$$

The example defines "Ann" and "Herb" as subject entities. Ann is the supervisor of Herb. Ann gets assigned the clearance level 2 while Herb is assigned
the clearance level 1. The file $fileL$ is assigned the security level 1, $fileH$ the
security level 2.

Scope definitions and example access checks   Let us do some scope definitions and access checks:

$$s_1 = \triangle s($$
$$\triangleright subjects = \triangle c(Ann),$$
$$\triangleright objects = \triangle c(fileH),$$
$$\triangleright permissions = \triangle c(read));$$
$$s_2 = \triangle s($$
$$\triangleright subjects = \triangle c(Ann),$$
$$\triangleright objects = \triangle c(fileH),$$
$$\triangleright permissions = \triangle c(write);$$

$$s_3 = \triangle s($$
$$\quad \triangleright subjects = \triangle c(Ann),$$
$$\quad \triangleright objects = \triangle c(fileL),$$
$$\quad \triangleright permissions = \triangle c(read));$$
$$s_4 = \triangle s($$
$$\quad \triangleright subjects = \triangle c(Ann),$$
$$\quad \triangleright objects = \triangle c(fileL),$$
$$\quad \triangleright permissions = \triangle c(write));$$

Four scopes are defined with the above commands. The first scope s_1 consists of three variable bindings. Variable $\triangleright subjects$ is bound to a newly defined container containing the entity "Ann" (we say, "subjects" is bound to "Ann"). Variable $\triangleright objects$ is bound to "fileH", "permissions" is bound to "read". This scope represents the query "Is 'Ann' allowed to 'read' object 'fileH?' ".

The other three scopes are defined accordingly.

The access checks will retrieve the following results. As in chapter 4, we use "==" as symbol to express equality. The symbol "=" is used to assign a value to a variable.

$$\nabla s_1 == \triangle c(true)$$
$$\nabla s_2 == \triangle c(true)$$
$$\nabla s_3 == \triangle c(true)$$
$$\nabla s_4 == \triangle c(false)$$

We provide a formal proof for s_4:
The application of a scope has been defined as repeated check of all policies until one policy returns true. Then the scope returns true. If no policy can be found returning true, the evaluation of the scope returns false. In other words, a scope application is an access check against all defined policies.

Formally:
$$\nabla s_4 == \nabla read\_down(s_4) \vee \nabla write\_up(s_4) == ?$$

We test the first policy $\nabla read\_down(s_4)$:
$$\nabla read\_down == \nabla \triangle p($$
$$\quad \triangle t(\triangleright permissions, \triangle c(read), \theta)$$
$$\quad \triangle t(\nabla \triangle pr(plevel)(\triangleright subjects, .), \nabla \triangle pr(olevel)(\triangleright objects, .), \geq),$$
$$)$$

We can rewrite the policy using the current scope definitions:

$$\nabla read\_down(s_4)$$
$$== \nabla \triangle p($$
$$\quad \triangle t(\triangle c(write), \triangle c(read), \theta)$$
$$\quad \triangle t(\nabla \triangle pr(plevel)(\triangle c(Ann), .), \nabla \triangle pr(olevel)(\triangle c(fileL), .), \geq),$$

$$
\begin{aligned}
&\quad)\\
&== \nabla\triangle p(\\
&\qquad \triangle t(\triangle c(write), \triangle c(read), \theta)\\
&\qquad \triangle t(\triangle c(2), \triangle c(1), \geq),\\
&\quad)\\
&== \nabla\triangle p(\\
&\qquad \triangle c(false),\\
&\qquad \triangle c(true),\\
&\quad)\\
&== \triangle c(false)
\end{aligned}
$$

The first policies evaluates to $false$ as the requested permission is $write$ while the policy requires $read$.

We continue with the second policy $\nabla write\_up(s_4)$:

$$
\begin{aligned}
\nabla write\_up &== \nabla\triangle p(\\
&\quad \triangle t(\triangleright permissions, \triangle c(write), \theta)\\
&\quad \triangle t(\nabla\triangle pr(plevel)(\triangleright subjects, .), \nabla\triangle pr(olevel)(\triangleright objects, .), \leq),\\
&\quad)
\end{aligned}
$$

Again, we evaluate accordingly to the current scope definition:

$$
\begin{aligned}
&\nabla write\_up(s_4)\\
&== \nabla\triangle p(\\
&\qquad \triangle t(\triangle c(write), \triangle c(write), \theta)\\
&\qquad \triangle t(\nabla\triangle pr(plevel)(\triangle c(Ann), .), \nabla\triangle pr(olevel)(\triangle c(fileL), .), \leq),\\
&\quad)\\
&== \nabla\triangle p(\\
&\qquad \triangle t(\triangle c(write), \triangle c(write), \theta)\\
&\qquad \triangle t(\triangle c(2), \triangle c(1), \leq),\\
&\quad)\\
&== \nabla\triangle p(\\
&\qquad \triangle c(true),\\
&\qquad \triangle c(false)),\\
&\quad)\\
&== \triangle c(false)
\end{aligned}
$$

The second policy evaluates to false as the security level of the requested document is lower than the clearance level of the subject.

We conclude:

$$
\nabla s_4 = \nabla read\_down(s_4) \vee \nabla read\_false(s_4)) = \triangle c(false) \vee \triangle c(false) = \triangle(false)
$$

$\square$

The proof of the other scopes is analogues.

We have seen in this subsection that the Bell-LaPadula model can be described easily in the ADQL formalism. It requires four containers, two relations and two policies. We demonstrated the formal definitions of the example of some example check accesses and proofed one access query in detail.

The complete ADQL expressions for this example can be found in listing 6.1. The figure makes use of alternative representation of the ADQL symbols. $\triangle$ is represented by 'DEF', ∇ by 'APP', and $\triangleright$ by 'ASSIGN'. Comments are prefixed by the hash sign (#). Containers, entities, and other concepts are also represented slightly different to be more readable.

The code shown in listing 6.1 can be copied in our ADQL Java implementation and will execute.

6.2. A Real-World Example: SAP R/3

We turn now to a RBAC-like model. SAP R/3 is a well-known and widely used Enterprise Resource Planning (ERP) software. The SAP R/3 system[1] is widely used by companies. The design of SAP R/3's access control architecture is depicted in figure 6.1. We refer to [AG08].

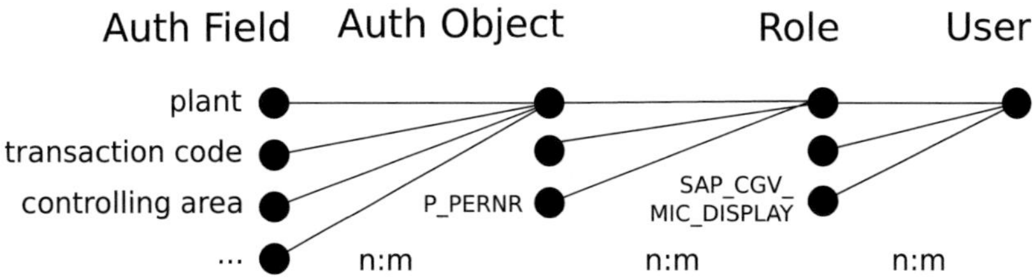

Figure 6.1.: Structure of the SAP R/3 access control model. We provide some examples for possible object names (e.g. P_PERNR)

Like in every RBAC-system, a subject (SAP calls subjects "users") can be assigned several (access control) roles. The relationship of roles to users is n:m as roles may be assigned to many users. Roles can be assigned names, descriptions and several more attributes as meta data describing it more closely. An example name for a role, as depicted in figure 6.1, is "SAP_CGV_MIC_DISPLAY".

---

[1]`http://www.sap.com/solutions/business-suite/erp/index.epx`, last accessed 2011-09-08

```
 1   # Bell−LaPadula Example
     # Tested: 18.3.2013 on cset 298:0c032e4d8aa6
 3
     # Define model (and some example facts)
 5   subjects = DEF CONTAINER(Ann = DEF ENTITY(), Herb = DEF ENTITY());
     objects = DEF CONTAINER(fileL = DEF ENTITY(), fileH = DEF ENTITY());
 7   permissions = DEF CONTAINER(read = DEF ENTITY(), write = DEF ENTITY());
     securitylevels = DEF CONTAINER(1 = DEF ENTITY(), 2 = DEF ENTITY());
 9
     # Relations with example facts
11   plevel = DEF RELATION(subjects, securitylevels):{(Ann,2),(Herb,1)};
     olevel = DEF RELATION(objects, securitylevels):{(fileL, 1),(fileH, 2)};
13
     # Define policies
15   'read_down' =
     DEF POLICY(
17       DEF TEST(ASSIGN permissions, DEF CONTAINER(read), theta),
         DEF TEST(
19         APP DEF PROJECTION(plevel)(ASSIGN subjects, .),
           APP DEF PROJECTION(olevel)(ASSIGN objects, .), >=));
21
     'write_up' =
23     DEF POLICY(
         DEF TEST(ASSIGN permissions, DEF CONTAINER(write), theta),
25       DEF TEST(
           APP DEF PROJECTION(plevel)(ASSIGN subjects, .),
27         APP DEF PROJECTION(olevel)(ASSIGN objects, .), <=));

29   # Define some example scopes
     s1 = DEF SCOPE(
31     ASSIGN subjects = DEF CONTAINER(Ann),
       ASSIGN objects = DEF CONTAINER(fileH),
33     ASSIGN permissions = DEF CONTAINER(read));
     s2 = DEF SCOPE(
35     ASSIGN subjects = DEF CONTAINER(Ann),
       ASSIGN objects = DEF CONTAINER(fileH),
37     ASSIGN permissions = DEF CONTAINER(write));
     s3 = DEF SCOPE(
39     ASSIGN subjects = DEF CONTAINER(Ann),
       ASSIGN objects = DEF CONTAINER(fileL),
41     ASSIGN permissions = DEF CONTAINER(read));
     s4 = DEF SCOPE(
43     ASSIGN subjects = DEF CONTAINER(Ann),
       ASSIGN objects = DEF CONTAINER(fileL),
45     ASSIGN permissions = DEF CONTAINER(write));

47   # Evaluate the scopes
     APP s1;   # access granted
49   APP s2;   # access granted
     APP s3;   # access granted
51   APP s4;   # access denied
```

Listing 6.1: Listing of the Bell-LaPadula use case example. The code can be executed in our ADQL implementation.

The naming conventions used by SAP say that this is a pre-configured role created by SAP (prefix SAP_), used in the module CGV in the sub-module MIC and allows display access.

Each role consists of so-called authorization objects ("auth objects"). The relationship between auth objects and roles are n:m. An auth object is a collection of several fields, called authorization fields or auth fields. Within an authorization object, each auth field is bound to a value. E.g. an auth field is named "plant" (see figure 6.1). It is assigned to the authorization object "P_PERSNR" and bound to the value 1000. Another auth field, "transaction code" is assigned to the same auth object with the value "HR03". The assigned values are not displayed in the figure.

SAP calls the execution of programs "transactions". These transactions must not be mistaken as database transactions as a SAP transaction is simply the execution of a certain program within SAP. It has nothing to do with the usual ACID rules. However, we perceive the naming of program execution as "transaction" as rather misleading but follow SAPs convention for this section.

We use the SAP-transaction HR03 as an example. The program HR03 displays information about staff. HR is the usual abbreviation for "human resources". To be able to execute this transaction, the user must own a role including the auth object "P_PERNR" with the auth field "transaction code" holding the value "HR03". When an SAP transaction (read: program) is executed, it checks all assigned roles of the current user. Dependent on the program, certain auth objects must be present in one (or several) roles. E.g. when executing the program HR03 the auth object "P_PERNR" must be present in at least one role of the user. The auth fields must match or contain the required values. E.g. a user wants to view staff data of plant 1000 "Karlsruhe Weststadt" then the auth object P_PERNR must contain the auth field plant with the value 1000. The auth fields, e.g. "plant", can, therefore, be used to limit the transaction to a certain plant.

An SAP transaction tc grants access if the following conditions are fulfilled:

For all $authobj$ in $authobjs$ required by SAP transaction tc:
For all $authfield$ in $authfields$ being part of $authobj$:
A role of the current user must contain $authobj$ with $authfield$ with $authfieldvalue$.

The ADQL model for SAP R/3   We model this access control model in ADQL. We start be defining the required concepts for the access control model.

The representation of the SAP access control model is depicted in figure 6.2. The model consists of containers for users, roles, authorization objects ("authobjs"),

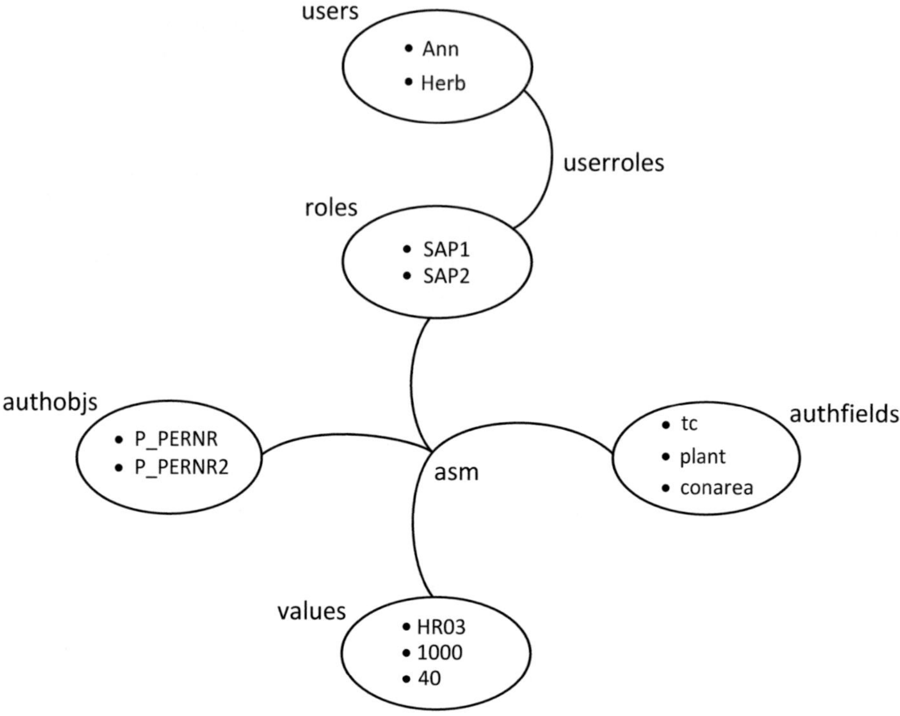

Figure 6.2.: SAP model represented in ADQL

authorization fields ("authfields"), and the values for the authorization fields ("values"). Two relations are defined: The relation "userroles" links users and their roles. The 4-ary relation role assignment ("asm") links roles, authorization objects, authorization fields, and values.

In ADQL this is formulated as:

$$users = \triangle c(),$$
$$roles = \triangle c(),$$
$$authfields = \triangle c(),$$
$$authobjs = \triangle c(),$$
$$values = \triangle c();$$

$$userroles = \triangle r(users, roles),$$
$$asm = \triangle r(roles, authobjs, authfields, values);$$

The ADQL policies for SAP SAP R/3 requires only one policy:

$$access = \triangle p($$
$$\quad \triangle t($$
$$\qquad \triangle pr(asm)(.,\triangleright authobjs, \triangleright authfields, \triangleright values),$$
$$\qquad \triangle pr(userroles)(\triangleright users,.)$$
$$\qquad \theta$$
$$\quad)$$
$$);$$

The policy consists of only one test. The first test part evaluates to all roles which include the currently requested authorization object, authorization field, and authorization field's value. The second test part evaluates all roles of the current user. Through this, the test and policy evaluate true, if the current user is assigned a role including the currently necessary authorization object, field, and value.

Example Facts We provide some example facts to demonstrate how the model works.

$$users = \triangle c(Ann = \triangle e(), Herb = \triangle e()),$$
$$roles = \triangle c(SAP1 = \triangle e(), SAP2 = \triangle e()),$$
$$authobjs = \triangle c(P\_PERNR = \triangle e(), P\_PERNR2 = \triangle e()),$$
$$authfields = \triangle c(tc = \triangle e(), plant = \triangle e(), conarea = \triangle e()),$$
$$values = \triangle c(HR03 = \triangle e(), 40 = \triangle e(), 1000 = \triangle e());$$

We define the users "Ann" and "Herb" and assign both to the container "users". Next, two roles are created, "SAP1" and "SAP2". As authorization objects we define "P_PERNR" and "P_PERNR2". Three authorization fields are introduced: "tc" for transaction code, "plant", and "conarea" for controlling area.

We populate the relations:

$$userroles = \triangle r(users, roles) : \{(Ann, SAP1), (Herb, SAP2)\};$$

Ann is assigned the role SAP1, Herb is assigned the role SAP2.

$$asm = \triangle r(roles, authobjs, authfields, values) :$$
$$\quad \{(SAP1, P\_PERNR, tc, HR03),$$
$$\quad (SAP1, P\_PERNR, plant, 1000),$$
$$\quad (SAP1, P\_PERNR, conarea, 40)\};$$

We introduce assignments for one example role SAP1. The role is assigned only one authorization object. The authorization fields are assigned the value $tc = HR03, plant = 1000$, and $conarea = 40$.

Example access queries We provided the model, the policy and example facts. Next, we continue with some example access queries.

We assume that the user "Ann" tries to execute the SAP transaction "HR03". Ann tries to access human resources data (HR03) related with plant 1000. The personnel belong to controlling area 40.

The SAP transaction HR03 creates related scopes:

$s_1 = \triangle s($
    $\triangleright users = \triangle c(Ann),$
    $\triangleright authobjs = \triangle c(P\_PERNR),$
    $\triangleright authfield = \triangle c(tc),$
    $\triangleright values = \triangle c(HR03));$
$s_2 = \triangle s($
    $\triangleright users = \triangle c(Ann),$
    $\triangleright authobjs = \triangle c(P\_PERNR),$
    $\triangleright authfield = \triangle c(plant),$
    $\triangleright values = \triangle c(1000));$
$s_3 = \triangle s($
    $\triangleright users = \triangle c(Ann),$
    $\triangleright authobjs = \triangle c(P\_PERNR),$
    $\triangleright authfield = \triangle c(conarea),$
    $\triangleright values = \triangle c(40));$

Please note, that three scopes are created, as SAP's logic requires checking not only one, but in this case three conditions. Generally, a separate scope is required for each authorization object a SAP transaction needs to check and for each authorization one scope for each authorization field has to be defined. This is not a characteristic of ADQL or ADQL's implementation of SAP's model. This requirement comes from the SAP model itself.

We evaluate the three scopes:

$\nabla s_1, \nabla s_2, \nabla s_3;$

In this case only one policy "access" has been defined.

$\nabla access(s_1) ==$
$== \nabla \triangle p(\triangle t($
    $\triangle pr(asm)(.,\triangleright authobjs, \triangleright authfields, \triangleright values),$
    $\triangle pr(userroles)(\triangleright users, .)))(s_1)$
$== \nabla \triangle p(\triangle t($
    $\triangle pr(asm)(., \triangle c(P\_PERNR), \triangle c(tc), \triangleright c(HR03)),$
    $\triangle pr(userroles)(\triangle(Ann), .)))$
$== \nabla \triangle p(\triangle t(\triangle c(SAP1), \triangle c(SAP1)))$
$== \triangle c(true)$

$$\nabla access(s_2) ==$$
$$== \nabla\triangle p(\triangle t($$
$$\triangle pr(asm)(., \triangleright authobjs, \triangleright authfields, \triangleright values),$$
$$\triangle pr(userroles)(\triangleright users, .)))(s_2)$$
$$== \nabla\triangle p(\triangle t($$
$$\triangle pr(asm)(., \triangle c(P\_PERNR), \triangle c(plant), \triangleright c(1000)),$$
$$\triangle pr(userroles)(\triangle(Ann), .)))$$
$$== \nabla\triangle p(\triangle t(\triangle c(SAP1), \triangle c(SAP1)))$$
$$== \triangle c(true)$$

$$\nabla access(s_3) ==$$
$$== \nabla\triangle p(\triangle t($$
$$\triangle pr(asm)(., \triangleright authobjs, \triangleright authfields, \triangleright values),$$
$$\triangle pr(userroles)(\triangleright users, .)))(s_3)$$
$$== \nabla\triangle p(\triangle t($$
$$\triangle pr(asm)(., \triangle c(P\_PERNR), \triangle c(conarea), \triangleright c(40)),$$
$$\triangle pr(userroles)(\triangle(Ann), .)))$$
$$== \nabla\triangle p(\triangle t(\triangle c(SAP1), \triangle c(SAP1)))$$
$$== \triangle c(true)$$

All three scopes evaluate true. Access can be granted. All three checks have to be issued by the SAP transaction and have to evaluate true. If one of the three checks returns *false*, access must be denied.

We demonstrated how SAP R/3's access control model can be modeled in ADQL. The model requires only one policy definition. However, due to the way how SAP R/3's access mechanism is designed, several access queries have to be issued for the execution of a single SAP program (transaction). To grant access, the SAP application program must issue these access queries and all have to evaluate to true.

The average numbers of required access requests is the product of all relevant authorization objects multiplied with the average number of authorization fields per authorization object.

The complete ADQL code is covered in listing 6.2.

6.3. Extended RBAC: E-Science Support for Students' Thesis in Cooperation with Companies

Our next example shows the access control model for an e-Science environment which supports students in writing their Bachelor or Master Thesis. Uni-

```
 1   # SAP R/3 Example
     # Tested 18.3.2013 on cset 298:0c032e4d8aa6
 3
     # Define model (and example data)
 5   users = DEF CONTAINER(Ann=DEF ENTITY(), Herb=DEF ENTITY());
     roles = DEF CONTAINER(SAP1=DEF ENTITY(), SAP2=DEF ENTITY());
 7   authobjs = DEF CONTAINER(
       'P_PERNR'=DEF ENTITY(),
 9     'P_PERNR2'=DEF ENTITY());
     authfields = DEF CONTAINER(
11     tc=DEF ENTITY(),
       plant=DEF ENTITY(),
13     conarea=DEF ENTITY());
     values = DEF CONTAINER(
15     HR03=DEF ENTITY(),
       40=DEF ENTITY(),
17     1000=DEF ENTITY());
 
19   userroles = DEF RELATION(users,roles):
       {(Ann,SAP1), (Herb,SAP2)};
21   asm = DEF RELATION(roles,authobjs,authfields,values):
       {(SAP1,'P_PERNR',tc,HR03),
23     (SAP1,'P_PERNR',plant,1000),
       (SAP1,'P_PERNR',conarea,40)};
25
     # Define policies
27   r3policy = DEF POLICY(DEF TEST(
      APP DEF PROJECTION(asm)(.,ASSIGN authobjs,ASSIGN authfields,ASSIGN values),
29    APP DEF PROJECTION(userroles)(ASSIGN users,.), theta));

31   # Define some example scopes
     s1 = DEF SCOPE(
33     ASSIGN users = DEF CONTAINER(Ann),
       ASSIGN authobjs = DEF CONTAINER('P_PERNR'),
35     ASSIGN authfields = DEF CONTAINER(tc),
       ASSIGN values = DEF CONTAINER(HR03));
37   s2 = DEF SCOPE(
       ASSIGN users = DEF CONTAINER(Ann),
39     ASSIGN authobjs = DEF CONTAINER('P_PERNR'),
       ASSIGN authfields = DEF CONTAINER(plant),
41     ASSIGN values = DEF CONTAINER(1000));
     s3 = DEF SCOPE(
43     ASSIGN users = DEF CONTAINER(Ann),
       ASSIGN authobjs = DEF CONTAINER('P_PERNR'),
45     ASSIGN authfields = DEF CONTAINER(conarea),
       ASSIGN values = DEF CONTAINER(40));
47
     # Evaluate the scopes
49   APP s1; # access granted
     APP s2; # access granted
51   APP s3; # access granted
```

Listing 6.2: Listing of the SAP R/3 use case example. The code can be executed in our ADQL implementation.

versities in their responsibility for the economic prosperity of their country have started to organize the writing of a Bachelor or Master Thesis as a joint university-company project in which a student investigates a company problem under the joint supervision of a professor, the professor's assistants and company employees interested in the problem investigated. A project usually lasts 3 months. After a project's official end the state of the project (and all related documents) should be frozen, so that all project members can only read the project-related material; except the academic supervisors, who still may upload new content. After a grace period of normally additional four weeks, non-university members loose access to all project resources. For competitive reasons, project related documents should only be accessible to project-related members, and only project members may upload project documents. On the other hand, some of the company documents are restricted to company members and the student. With regard to his own documents, the student initially keeps his documents private. However, as the project progresses, he makes documents accessible either to all project members or to university or company members. In any case, the owner of a document can always read it and change the document's visibility.

The Model Layer

Our access control model linked to these requirements is depicted in figure 6.3.

The basic model is a role-based access control model. Each user ($users$) can be assigned a specific role from $roles$. This is a typical RBAC model. As an extension, the assigned roles are linked to projects (from container pjs). Within each project, a user can be assigned to a project-specific role. Thus, roles are not assigned on a general, system-wide level, but the assignment is related to a specific project. E.g. the user $Ulrick$ may act as a university staff member in a project named $EM1$ while having no assigned role to project $EM2$. Consequently, $Ulrick$ has no access to project $EM2$. $Ulrick$ may even act as a company representative for a third project $KITspinoff$.

Each project has two time boundaries named project end ($pjend$) and a grace time period ($gracetime$). Access is granted, if the project has not ended. During the subsequent grace time, access is only possible for university staff members, who can upload files, and for file owners, who can change the document group of their files.

On the document side, each document is assigned to a project ($docpj$), to an owner (from $users$) and to a document group (from $roles$). The latter is re-

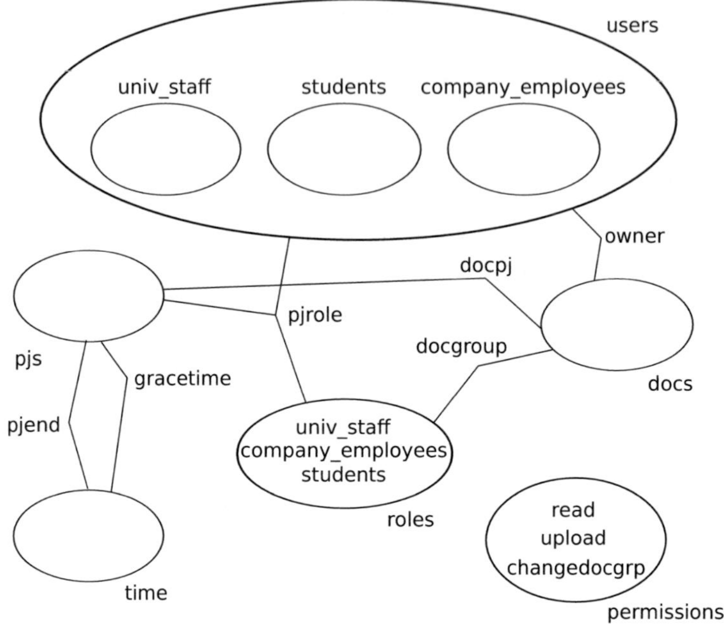

Figure 6.3.: Graphical representation of the model layer for the e-Science scenario. Containers are depicted as ellipses, relations as lines. "pj" is
an abbreviation for project.

quired to reason about access for documents: access is only permitted if the
document's group matches the project member's group.

To express the access control model in ADQL, we undertake the following
steps. We define several containers to group the users: university staff, students, and company employees. Further, we model a container for projects,
one for documents and one for permissions. To model the end date and the
grace period for a project we need a time container and two relations: one for
end date and one for the grace time. The grace time could also be expressed by
adding four weeks to the project end date. Nevertheless, we model it explicitly which allows grace times to vary (e.g. for later extensions or changes). As
every document has an owner, we define a relation between users and documents. We said that a user may have roles dependent on the project. Thus, we
model a project role as 3-tuple between users, roles, and projects. This allows
us to assign users in different roles for each project. Alternatively, one could
identify the role of a user in a project by the user's group membership, which
would then be fixed for all projects. However, this is not the model, we want to
build. Documents can be visible to students, university staff, the company or

the author only and are assigned to a project. For this requirement we model a document group and a document project assignment.

We provide the subsequent ADQL commands for the model:

$$users = \triangle c($$
$$\nabla(univ\_staff = \triangle c()),$$
$$\nabla(students = \triangle c()),$$
$$\nabla(company\_employees = \triangle c()));$$

The above command defines a container *users* and three more containers *univ_staff*, *students*, and *company_employees*. For each of the latter three containers, the application of each container is assigned to be a sub-element within *users*: If an entity, e.g. user *Herb* is assigned to be an element of the container *univ_staff*, he is also a member of *users*. If we avoided the application symbol ∇ here and assigned only one of the sub-containers itself to users (e.g. $users = \triangle c(univ\_staff = \triangle c())$), the container *univ_staff* itself would become a sub-element of *users* *but not* the elements of the container *univ_staff*, e.g. *Herb*. For further details, we refer to chapters 5 and 4.

We continue defining the model (remark: the abreviation "pjs" refers to projects):

$$pjs = \triangle c();$$
$$time = \triangle c();$$
$$docs = \triangle c();$$
$$permissions = \triangle c(read = \triangle e(), upload = \triangle e(), changedocgrp = \triangle e());$$
$$roles = \triangle c(univ\_staff, company\_employees, students);$$

The last command makes use of the previously defined symbols *univ_staff*, *company_employees*, and *students*. Here, we do not assign applications of the three containers like we did when defining *users*. Instead, we assign the symbols to be "direct" sub-elements of roles: If *Herb* is a sub-element of *univ_staff* he *does not automatically become* a sub-element of *roles*. Actually, this is what we want to model.

We go on:

$$pjend = \triangle r(pjs, time);$$
$$gracetime = \triangle r(pjs, time);$$
$$owner = \triangle r(docs, users);$$
$$docgroup = \triangle r(docs, roles);$$
$$docpj = \triangle r(docs, pjs);$$
$$pjrole = \triangle r(users, pjs, roles);$$

These are the access control model definitions.

The Policy Layer

The next step is to model the policies.

Policy 1: Read documents in the project First, we want to grant read access, if the grace period has not ended, the project document belongs to the project and the document has been assigned to be visible for the specific role within the project. E.g. a document A has been assigned to be visible for *company_employees*.

We define four tests and one policy:

$$perm\_read = \triangle t(\triangleright permissions, \triangle c(read), \theta);$$
$$ingrace = \triangle t(\triangleright time, \nabla \triangle pr(gracetime)(\triangleright pjs, .), <);$$
$$docgroup\_match = \triangle t($$
$$\nabla \triangle pr(pjrole)(\triangleright users, \triangleright pjs, .),$$
$$\nabla \triangle pr(docgroup)(\triangleright docs, .), \theta);$$
$$docpj\_match = \triangle t(\nabla \triangle pr(docpj)(\triangleright docs, .), \triangleright pjs, \theta) ;$$
$$pol\_read\_if\_pjrole : \triangle p(perm\_read, ingrace, docgroup\_match, docpj\_match);$$

The tests are:

1. *perm_read*: The binding of the variable associated with *permission* must have a non-empty intersection (this is, θ) with *read*. In other words, the requested permission is read.

2. *ingrace*: The test compares the current binding of the variable *time* with the result of a F1-projection. *time* has to be less than the value of the F1-projection. When evaluated, the F1-projection $\triangle pr(gracetime)(\triangleright pjs, .)$ returns the associated *time*s for the current binding of variable *pjs* in the relation *gracetime*. In other words, the F1-projection returns the grace-time(s) of the current project. Please note, that a project may have assigned more than one gracetime. For the definition of the operator $"<"$ we refer to section 5.9.

3. *docgroup_match*: Two F1-projections have to share at least one element. When evaluated, the first F1-projection $\triangle pr(pjrole)(\triangleright users, \triangleright pjs, .)$ returns the role(s) of the current user in the current project.
   The second F1-projection $\triangle pr(docgroup)(\triangleright docs, .)$ returns the assigned document group(s) (which are potentially the project-related user roles) of the current document. The test *docgroup_match* ensures that the current user has to be assigned the same project-specific role for the current project as the assignment of the current document.

4. *docpj_match*: The current document must be assigned to the current project.

The policy *pol_read_if_pjrole* is a logical AND-concatenation of all four tests. Shortly, read access is granted, if the project is in gracetime, the document is assigned to the project and the document is available for the user's project-related role.

Policy 2: Uploads before the end of the project   We continue with another policy: Uploads to a project are possible as long as the project has not ended and the user has at least one role in the project:

$$perm\_up = \triangle t(\triangleright permissions, \triangle c(upload), \theta);$$
$$intime = \triangle t(\triangleright time, \nabla \triangle pr(pjend)(\triangleright pjs, .), <);$$
$$anyrole = \triangle t(\nabla \triangle pr(pjrole)(\triangleright users, \triangleright pjs, .), roles, \theta);$$
$$pol\_upload = \triangle p(perm\_up, intime, anyrole);$$

Uploads are permitted, if

1. *perm_up*: The requested permission is "upload". The current binding of the variable associated with *permissions* has a non-empty intersection ("θ") with a container holding the element *upload*.

2. *intime*: The current time stamp is less than the project's end. Thus, the project has not been finished. The test is of the same shape as the test *ingrace* (see above).

3. *anyrole*: The current user is assigned at least to one role in the current project. If the F1-projection of the relation *pjrole* by the current project and user (which is resolved to all roles the users has in the project), matches any element in the container *roles*, the test evaluates to true.

Again, the policy *pol_upload* is a logical AND-concatenation of the three tests *perm_up*, *intime*, and *anyrole*. The policy *pol_upload* will allow access, if a user, who has got at least one project-specific role, wants to upload a file. The project must not be ended.

Policy 3: Uploads in gracetime   The third policy allows uploads within the grace period if the project role of the user is university staff:

$$upload\_in\_gracetime = \triangle p($$
$$\quad perm\_up,$$
$$\quad ingrace,$$
$$\quad \triangle t(\nabla \triangle pr(pjrole)(\triangleright users, \triangleright pjs, .), \triangle c(univ\_staff))$$
$$);$$

The policy *upload_in_gracetime* consists of three tests:

1. The test *perm_up*, which already has been defined. It evaluates true, if the currently requested permission is "upload".

2. The test *ingrace*, which, again, has already been defined earlier. The test evaluates true, if the current time is within the grace time period of the current project.

3. A new, third test. The first part of this third test is a F1-projection of the relation *pjrole*. The F1-projection evaluates the project-specific role of the current *user* in the current *project*, e.g. *univ_staff* or *company_employee*. The result of this F1-projection must match the container *univ_staff*. The third test is true, if the roles of the current user in the current project contain *univ_staff*.

We see that the third policy is true, if a university staff member tries to upload something and the project is in its grace period.

Policy 4: Owners can read and change the document group within the project's grace time period   The fourth policy we provide for our example allows the owner of a file to read it and change its document group as long as the project is in its grace period:

$$owner\_assign = \triangle p($$
$$\qquad \triangle t(\triangleright permissions, \triangle c(changedocgrp, read)),$$
$$\qquad ingrace,$$
$$\qquad \triangle t(\nabla \triangle pr(owner)(\triangleright docs, .), \triangleright users)$$
$$);$$

The policy *owner_assign* consists of three tests:

1. The requested permission must be either "read" or "changedocgrp". The latter means, that the document group of the current document can be changed.

2. The project must be within its grace time period.

3. The owner of the document must be the current user.

We have introduced four policies. Next, we continue with some example facts to demonstrate some access queries later.

Example Facts for The Facts Layer

We provide sample facts to be able to check access requests. We model one professor called "Herb" with his two assistants "Tom" and "Ulrick". The students "Mark" and "Ann" do their Bachelor thesis with "Tom", respectively "Ulrick", as their supervisor. "Mark" writes his thesis with the "CRM Ltd." company. At the company, the boss of "Mark" is "Ben". "Ann" cooperates with the "EM AG", where "Jim" is her boss.

"Mark" creates two documents A and B. The first one is a working document and, therefore, private. Document B is visible for the complete project. "Ann" has uploaded one document C which is visible to her and the company only.

$univ\_staff = \triangle c(Herb, Tom, Ulrick);$
$students = \triangle c(Mark, Ann);$
$company\_employees = \triangle c(Ben, Jim);$
$pjs = \triangle c(CRM1, EM1);$

The container $univ\_staff$ consists of the users "Herb", "Tom", and "Ulrick". The *students* are "Mark" and "Ann". The company employees *company_employees* are "Ben" and "Jim". Currently, two projects pjs exist, "CRM1" and "EM1".

$pjrole = \triangle r(users, pjs, roles) :$
$\quad \{(Mark, CRM1, students),$
$\quad (Ben, CRM1, company\_employees),$
$\quad (Tom, CRM1, univ\_staff),$
$\quad (Ann, EM1, students),$
$\quad (Ulrick, EM1, univ\_staff),$
$\quad (Jim, EM1, company\_employees)\};$

We define the project-specific roles of the users: Mark is a student in the project "CRM1". Ben is the company representative in the same project, while Tom is part of the university staff for this project.

For the project "EM1" Ann is a student member, Ulrick is part of the project's university staff and Jim is the company representative.

$docs = \triangle c(A, B, C);$

Three documents, A, B, and C, exist.

$owner = \triangle r(docs, users) :$
$\quad \{(A, Mark),$
$\quad (B, Mark),$
$\quad (C, Ann)\};$

The owner of documents A and B is "Mark", while the owner of document C is "Ann".

$docgroup = \triangle r(docs, roles) :$
  $\{(B, students),$
  $(B, univ\_staff),$
  $(B, company\_employees),$
  $(C, company\_employees)\};$

We define the roles for the documents: Document A is not assigned to any document role. Document B is assigned the document roles "students", "univ_staff", and "company_employees". Document C is assigned to "company_employees" only.

$docpj = \triangle r(docs, pjs) :$
  $\{(A, CRM1),$
  $(B, CRM1),$
  $(C, EM1)\};$

The documents are assigned to the projects. Document A and B belong to the project "CRM1", document C belongs to project $EM1$.

6.3.1. Check Access Requests

With the above model, policies, and facts access requests can be performed. Next, we will demonstrate one example access query.

$s = \triangle s($
  $\triangleright users = \triangle c(Tom),$
  $\triangleright pjs = \triangle c(CRM1),$
  $\triangleright docs = \triangle c(B),$
  $\triangleright permissions = \triangle c(read),$
  $\triangleright time = \triangle c(1300700213 = \triangle e())$
$);$

We define a scope s. Within this scope s the variable $users$ is bound to "Tom", thus, the current user is "Tom". Consequently, the current project is "CRM1", the current document is B, the current permission requested is "read", and the current time is "1300700213". We assume that this date is before the project's official end.

We execute the access query:
$\nabla s;$

To calculate the result for this query, we check all four defined policies until the first grants access.

The first policy of our use case reads (repeated from above):

$perm\_read = \triangle t(\triangleright permissions, \triangle c(read), \theta);$
$ingrace = \triangle t(\triangleright time, \nabla \triangle pr(gracetime)(\triangleright pjs, .), <);$
$docgroup\_match = \triangle t($
$\qquad \nabla \triangle pr(pjrole)(\triangleright users, \triangleright pjs, .),$
$\qquad \nabla \triangle pr(docgroup)(\triangleright docs, .), \theta);$
$docpj\_match = \triangle t(\nabla \triangle pr(docpj)(\triangleright docs, .), \triangleright pjs, \theta);$
$pol\_read\_if\_pjrole : \triangle p(perm\_read, ingrace, docgroup\_match, docpj\_match);$

We check the 4 tests of the policy *pol_read_if_pjrole* concerning the scope definition s:

1. $\nabla perm\_read(s)$
   $== \nabla \triangle t(\triangleright permissions, \triangle c(read), \theta)(s)$
   $== \nabla \triangle t(\triangle c(read), \triangle c(read), \theta)$
   $== \triangle c(true)$
   The first test of the policy is *true*.

2. $\nabla ingrace(s)$
   $== \nabla \triangle t(\triangleright time, \nabla \triangle pr(gracetime)(\triangleright pjs, .), <)(s)$
   $== \nabla \triangle t(\triangle c(1300700213), \nabla \triangle pr(gracetime)(\triangle c(CRM1), .), <)$
   $== \triangle c(true)$
   The second test of the policy is *true* as the project end date has not been reached.

3. $\nabla docgroup\_match(s)$
   $== \nabla \triangle t($
   $\qquad\qquad \nabla \triangle pr(pjrole)(\triangleright users, \triangleright pjs, .),$
   $\qquad\qquad \nabla \triangle pr(docgroup)(\triangleright docs, .), \theta)(s)$
   $== \nabla \triangle t($
   $\qquad\qquad \nabla \triangle pr(pjrole)(\triangle c(Tom), \triangle c(CRM1), .),$
   $\qquad\qquad \nabla \triangle pr(docgroup)(\triangle c(B), .), \theta)$
   $== \nabla \triangle t($
   $\qquad\qquad \triangle c(univ\_staff),$
   $\qquad\qquad \triangle c(students, univ\_staff, company\_employees), \theta)$
   $== \triangle c(true)$
   The third test evaluates *true*, as Tom is a member of the project-specific group *univ_staff* within project $CRM1$ and document B has been assigned to the groups *students*, *univ_staff*, and *company_employees*.

4. $\nabla docpj\_match(s)$
   $== \nabla \triangle t($
   $\qquad\qquad \nabla \triangle pr(docpj)(\triangleright docs, .),$

$$\begin{aligned}
&\qquad\qquad \rhd pjs, \theta)(s) \\
&== \nabla \triangle t(\\
&\qquad\qquad \nabla \triangle pr(docpj)(\triangle c(B), .), \\
&\qquad\qquad \triangle c(CRM1), \theta) \\
&== \nabla \triangle t(\triangle c(CRM1)), \triangle c(CRM1), \theta) \\
&== \triangle c(true)
\end{aligned}$$

The fourth test evaluates *true*: document B is assigned to project $CRM1$ which is the current project.

As all tests of the access condition are true, access is granted. Further access conditions need not to be checked.

The full listing, how it can be executed in our ADQL implementation can be found in listing 6.4.

6.4. Summary

In this chapter we demonstrated the usability and expressive power of ADQL with three examples. The first example showed how the Bell-LaPadula model can be expressed in ADQL. The second example covered a real-world RBAC-like model, specifically SAP's version of an RBAC-like model for the well-known SAP R/3 application. Our third example was an extended RBAC-like model making use of several relations, subject and object attributes and a 3-ary relation. For each example, we provided listings with the complete ADQL code and explained, how it can be used with our ADQL implementation.

```
1   # eScience Example
    # Tested 16.4.2013 on cset 310:067d012a5303
3
    # Define the model and some example facts
5   'univ_staff' = DEF CONTAINER(Herb=DEF ENTITY(),
      Tom=DEF ENTITY(), Ulrick=DEF ENTITY());
7   students = DEF CONTAINER(Mark=DEF ENTITY(), Ann=DEF ENTITY());
    'company_employees'=DEF CONTAINER(Ben=DEF ENTITY(), Jim=DEF ENTITY());
9   users = DEF CONTAINER(
      APP 'univ_staff', APP students, APP 'company_employees');
11
    pjs = DEF CONTAINER(CRM1=DEF ENTITY(), EM1=DEF ENTITY());
13  docs = DEF CONTAINER(A=DEF ENTITY(), B=DEF ENTITY(), C=DEF ENTITY());
    time = DEF CONTAINER(1300700214=DEF ENTITY());
15
    permissions=DEF CONTAINER(read=DEF ENTITY(), upload=DEF ENTITY(),
17    changedocgrp=DEF ENTITY());
    roles=DEF CONTAINER('univ_staff', 'company_employees', students);
19
    # Define relations for the model
21  pjend=DEF RELATION(pjs, time);
    gracetime=DEF RELATION(pjs, time):
23    {(CRM1,1300700214)};

25  pjrole = DEF RELATION(users, pjs, roles):
      {(Mark,CRM1,students), (Ben,CRM1,'company_employees'),
27    (Tom,CRM1,'univ_staff'), (Ann,EM1,students),
      (Ulrick,EM1,'univ_staff'), (Jim,EM1,'company_employees')};
29
    owner = DEF RELATION(docs, users):
31    {(A,Mark), (B,Mark), (C,Ann)};

33  docgroup = DEF RELATION(docs, roles):
      {(B,students), (B,'univ_staff'),
35    (B,'company_employees'), (C,'company_employees')};

37  docpj = DEF RELATION(docs, pjs):
      {(A,CRM1), (B,CRM1), (C,EM1)};
```

Listing 6.3: Listing of the extended RBAC e-Science use case example (first part). The code an be executed in our ADQL implementation.

```
40    # Now define the policies
      # Policy 1
42    'perm_read' = DEF TEST(
        ASSIGN permissions,
44      DEF CONTAINER(read));
      ingrace = DEF TEST(
46      ASSIGN time,
        APP DEF PROJECTION(gracetime)(ASSIGN pjs,.), <);
48    'docgroup_match' = DEF TEST(
        APP DEF PROJECTION(pjrole)(ASSIGN users, ASSIGN pjs, .),
50      APP DEF PROJECTION(docgroup)(ASSIGN docs, .));
      'docpj_match' = DEF TEST(
52      APP DEF PROJECTION(docpj)(ASSIGN docs,.),
        ASSIGN pjs);
54    'pol_read_if_pjrole' = DEF POLICY(
              'perm_read',ingrace,'docgroup_match','docpj_match');
56
      # Policy 2
58    'perm_up' = DEF TEST(
        ASSIGN permissions,
60      DEF CONTAINER(upload));
      intime = DEF TEST(
62      ASSIGN time,
        APP DEF PROJECTION(pjend)(ASSIGN pjs,.), <);
64    anyrole = DEF TEST(
        APP DEF PROJECTION(pjrole)(ASSIGN users, ASSIGN pjs, .),
66      roles);
      'pol_upload' = DEF POLICY('perm_up', intime, anyrole);
68
      # Policy 3
70    'upload_in_gracetime' = DEF POLICY(
        'perm_up',
72      ingrace,
        DEF TEST(
74        APP DEF PROJECTION(pjrole)(ASSIGN users, ASSIGN pjs, .),
          DEF CONTAINER('univ_staff')));
76
      # Policy 4
78    'owner_assign' = DEF POLICY(
        DEF TEST(ASSIGN permissions, DEF CONTAINER(changedocgrp,read)),
80      ingrace,
        DEF TEST(APP DEF PROJECTION(owner)(ASSIGN docs, .), ASSIGN users));
82

84
      # Scope definition
86    s1 = DEF SCOPE(
        ASSIGN users = DEF CONTAINER(Tom),
88      ASSIGN pjs = DEF CONTAINER(CRM1),
        ASSIGN docs = DEF CONTAINER(B),
90      ASSIGN permissions = DEF CONTAINER(read),
        ASSIGN time = DEF CONTAINER(1300700213 = DEF ENTITY())
92    );

94    # Evaluate the scope
      APP s1;  # access granted
```

Listing 6.4: Listing of the extended RBAC e-Science use case example (second part). The code an be executed in our ADQL implementation.

7. Implementing ADQL as Software Service

In this chapter we will describe our academic prototype implementing ADQL.

We aim for our scientific goals (1) "access component as a service" and (4) "scalable and fast service". We want to achieve goal (1) by describing the service implementation of our prototype. We show that ADQL can and has been implemented as a software service with the usual components, a back end and a front end. Goal (4) is approached by providing runtime profiles and execution times. We provide examples and show how fast these examples execute using our implementation.

ADQL binaries and online documentation are available at `http://iism.kit.edu/em/ref/adql`.

7.1. ADQL's Implementation: General Architecture

The general architecture of our ADQL implementation is depicted in figure 7.1.

As usual for an IT-service, ADQL's architecture is split in a front-end and a back-end. The back-end consists of the code executed on the service's server. The back-end is described in section 7.2. The front-end consists of the libraries imported and used by applications which want to use the ADQL service (ADQL's API) or are applications which use the ADQL service. The front-end is described in section 7.3. The intermediate object is the "Result Object" encapsuling service requests and answers. It is described in section 7.4.

Project History The initial steps of ADQL have been undertaken using the name "Community Administration Platform (CAP)" in the mentioned project "WeKnowIt". We have found, the former names have been partially misleading. For this reason, and because since the end of the project significant efforts have been put into the design and code, we changed the name to ADQL. First

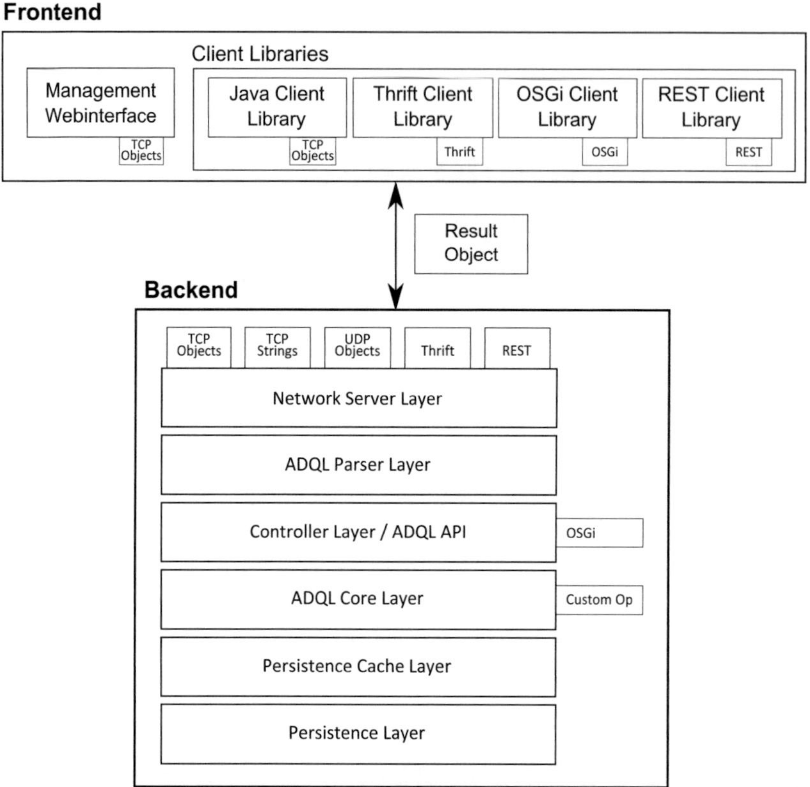

Figure 7.1.: General architecture of our Access Definition and Query Language implementation.

work about ADQL has been published in a regular deliverable for the project [SS09]. This deliverable is based on version 1.2 of our ADQL prototype.

This work is based on ADQL version 3.0, exactly, Mercurial revision "7120faa6b7c6" from 2012-09-10.

7.2. Back End Design and Architecture

Our back end implementation of ADQL has been written in Java, currently compiling under Java v1.7 (but backward compatible to Java v1.5). As platform we chose the Intel/AMD i386/i586/i686 platform, compatible with 32-bit and 64-bit operating systems. Due to the platform-specific JavaVM implementations, we tested our code in Linux and Windows 7 and 8 systems. Other platforms with JavaVM support are probable usable, but were not tested by us.

As parser and compiler generator for parsing ADQL as a language we use the Java Compiler Compiler (JavaCC)[1].

The current implementation has about 35,000 lines of code.

7.2.1. Back End Architecture and Modules

When we tried to find a definition for the phrase "software architecture" interestingly enough, we were not able to find a commonly accepted wording. Instead a huge set of definitions has been suggested:

Garlan and Perry suggest "the structure of the components of a program/system, their interrelationships, and principles and guidelines governing their design and evolution over time" [GP95, p.269].

Booch, Rumbaugh, and Jacobson define: "An architecture is the set of significant decisions about the organization of a software system, the selection of the structural elements and their interfaces by which the system is composed, [together] with their behavior, as specified in the collaborations among those elements, [and] the composition of these structural and behavioral elements into progressively larger subsystems, [and] the architecture style that guides this organization: the static and dynamic elements and their interfaces, their collaborations, and their composition" [BRJ05, p.31f].

IEEE 1471 defines "the fundamental organization of a system embodied in its components, their relations to each other, and to the environment, and the principles guiding its design and evolution" [IEE].

Further definitions and a discussion can be found in [CBB+10, p.3ff].

We will follow the definition of Garlan and Perry.

ADQL back end module's architecture stack is depicted in figure 7.2. We will iteratively explain all layers and interfaces.

---

[1]`http://javacc.java.net`, last accessed 2013-04-02

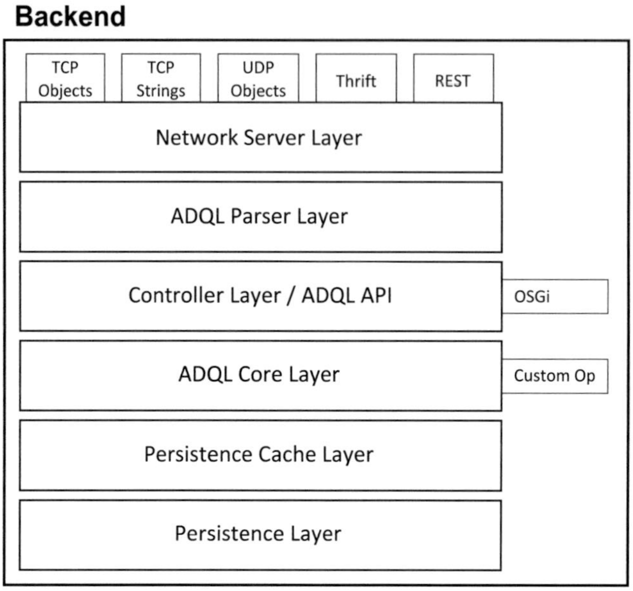

Backend

TCP Objects | TCP Strings | UDP Objects | Thrift | REST

Network Server Layer

ADQL Parser Layer

Controller Layer / ADQL API — OSGi

ADQL Core Layer — Custom Op

Persistence Cache Layer

Persistence Layer

Figure 7.2.: Back end architecture of our Access Definition and Query Language implementation

7.2.2. Persistence Layer

A persistence layer is used to permanently save ADQL's model, facts, and policies. It persists even if the ADQL code execution is stopped or re-started. As persistence storage system we use a relational database system.

The ADQL persistence module was developed to access the persistence storage (the database management engine). The targets for this layer are:

- make database access transparent for the above layers,

- automatically manage database access,

- support the usage of several, distributed databases by vertical division,

- support access via different database user,

- support SSL and non-SSL connections.

For our current implementation we chose PostgreSQL [Gro10] as database management system. PostgreSQL supports transactions since quite a long time, is open-source and scalable. However, there is no technical, mandatory reason for PostgreSQL. ADQL's persistence layer also supports other relational database management systems, like MySQL [Cor11], Oracle, or other relational DBMS supported by Hibernate.

Our ADQL prototype switched from a self-developed cache and persistence module in version 1.2 to Hibernate in version 1.3. Major concerns existed concerning runtime efficiency of the code and scalability. Without providing details in this work, our findings can be summarized in the following:

- The code complexity and readability became much better after switching to Hibernate. The code size was reduced by about 30%.

- The efficiency for direct database access was almost the same as with handwritten SQL-code. There was a tiny increase in answering times with Hibernate.

- The cache performance was almost completely lost. While the handwritten cache and persistence layer increased the performance of repeated access queries by approx. 200%, Hibernate's automatic caching mechanisms did not show any significant improvements.

Although losing the runtime gain by the manual caching mechanism, we decided to continue the development using Hibernate. The idea was, to re-implement a manual caching layer based on Hibernate and regain cache effects – which was not undertaken so far.

The usage of Hibernate and the add-on Hibernate Annotations allowed us to integrate persistence functionality into ADQL code in a simple and efficient way. We provide an example for the Java entity definition of an ADQL entity in listing 7.1.

The Java annotation `@Entity` defines the Java class to be persistent. The annotation `@DiscriminatorColumn` describes how child class instances are handled concerning database storage. With the selected strategy, one table is used for `ADQLEntity` and all child class instances: if a class inherits from `ADQLEntity`, its instances are stored in the same table as `ADQLEntity` itself. The discriminator column "discriminator" is used to distinguish the actual class types. The annotation `@Cache` defines the Hibernate cache query and database strategy for this entity.

The simple fact of the existence of the getter- and setter methods for the attributes `id` and `externalId` is enough to define the related database tables and property types. The additional annotations of `id` define the property to be the table key generated by a (Postgres) sequencer. The attribute `externalId` is associated with a unique constraint.

```
1   @Entity
    @DiscriminatorColumn(name = "discriminator",
3     discriminatorType = DiscriminatorType.STRING)
    @Cache(usage = CacheConcurrencyStrategy.NONSTRICT_READ_WRITE)
5   public class ADQLEntity implements Serializable, ADQLProperties {

7     private static final long serialVersionUID = 39601073033505345510L;

9     private Long id;
      private String externalId;
11

      public ADQLEntity() {
13      super();
      }
15

      public ADQLEntity(String externalId) {
17      this.externalId = externalId;
      }
19

      @SequenceGenerator(name="entity_seq",sequenceName="entity_seq")
21    @Id
      @GeneratedValue(strategy=GenerationType.SEQUENCE, generator="entity_seq")
23    public Long getId() {
        return id;
25    }

27    public void setId(Long id) {
        this.id = id;
29    }

31    @Column(unique = true)
      public String getExternalId() {
33      return externalId;
      }
35

      public void setExternalId(String externalId) {
37      this.externalId = externalId;
      }
39

      (...)
41  }
```

Listing 7.1: Listing of an excerpt of the ADQLEntity Java class

ADQL's database schema   We continue by explaining the database schema used by ADQL.

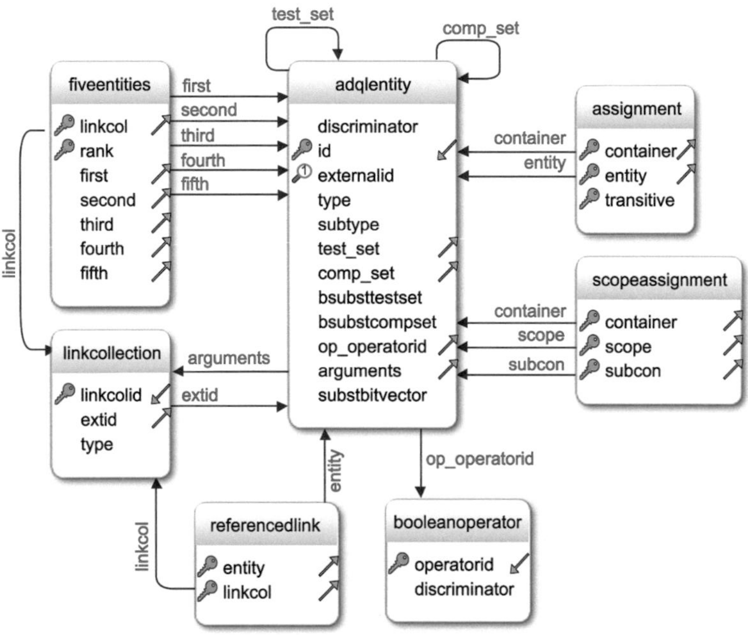

Figure 7.3.: Database schema of ADQL's persistence layer

Figure 7.3 depicts the schema. The central table is "adqlentity" holding the basic information about all ADQL objects. This includes not only entities, but also containers, relations, F1-projections, tests, policies, scopes and applications. The assignments of entities to a container are stored in the table "assignment". Scope definitions are stored in the table "scopeassignment". Available ADQL operators can be found in the table "booleanoperator". Links (elements) of relations are stored in the tables "linkcollection" and "fiveentities". We continue explaining the tables below.

We provide some example database entries. The minimal example code creating database entries for all basic ADQL concepts is depicted in figure 7.4. By this code, an entity "Ann" is defined. Ann is assigned to a container "users". On this container, a relation "relproxy" is defined, linking the container "users" with itself. A F1-projection "projproxy" is created on the relation. This F1-

projection is used in a test "testproxy" comparing the application of this F1-projection with an anonymous container holding the entity Ann. Finally, a policy named "testproxy", utilizing the test, is created.

The resulting database entries from this code are depicted in table 7.1. We explain them in the following.

```
1   Ann = DEF ENTITY();
    users = DEF CONTAINER(Ann);
3   relproxy = DEF RELATION(users, users):{(Ann,Ann)};
    projproxy = DEF PROJECTION(relproxy)(ASSIGN users,.);
5   testproxy = DEF TEST(APP projproxy, DEF CONTAINER(Ann), theta);
    policyproxy = DEF POLICY(testproxy);
```

Figure 7.4.: Listing of an example code creating database entries of all ADQL concepts

discriminator	id (PK)	externalid	type	sub- type	test _set	comp _set	bsub stte stset	bsub stco mpset	op_ opera torid	argu ments	subst btvec tor
ADQLEntity	302	Ann	E								
ADQLContainer	303	users	S	CONT							
ADQLRelation	304	relproxy	R							50	
ADQLProjection	305	projproxy	J		304					52	1
ADQLApplication	350		A		305						
ADQLContainer	351		S	CONT							
ADQLTest	352	testproxy	R		350	351	FALSE	FALSE	theta		
ADQLPolicy	400	policyproxy	P								

Table 7.1.: Example of the table "adqlentity" resulting from the listing in figure 7.4

The central table is "adqlentity". ADQL entities, containers, relations, F1-projections, tests, and policies are stored in this table. The primary key is "id", a big integer. The primary key is an internal identifier and auto-incremented for each new table entry. Technically, it is an auto-generated sequence. The "externalid" holds the externally given symbol name for an entity. To ensure uniqueness of external identifiers, the field is defined unique. E.g. the ADQL command $Ann = \triangle e()$ defines an entity and assigns it to the symbol "Ann". Ann will be stored in the "externalid" field, while the identifier "id" is auto-chosen by the DBMS. In the depicted example, Ann received the internal id 302.

The "type" field is a single character indicating the type of the database entry.

You can see that the entity "Ann" is of type "E" for "entity". The abbreviation "S" is used for containers, "R" for relations, "J" for F1-projections, "A" for applications, "T" for tests, and "P" for policies. The "discriminator" field is de-facto a duplicate of the field "type". However, the discriminator field is automatically introduced by the persistence framework Hibernate which we cannot influence. This comes from Hibernate's default behavior to store all entities of not only a class but a whole class hierarchy in one database table. As super and child classes may differ in their persistent attributes, the table includes the hull of all persistent attributes, thus all attributes of all classes of the hierarchy. To be able to distinguish the type of an entry, the class name is stored in the discriminator field. Consequently you can see, that "Ann" is an instance of the Java class `ADQLEntity`, while "users" is an instance of the Java class `ADQLContainer`, and so on.

The field "subtype" is only present for backward compatibility and not used anymore. In previous ADQL versions, different types of containers have been supported. This behavior became obsolete by introducing unified, generalized containers.

The fields "test_set" and "comp_set" stem from test entries. For tests, they contain a reference to the two containers of the test. However, the field "test_set" is overloaded with several other meanings. We explain the different interpretations with the following examples:

- Test: In the example shown in table 7.1, the first test set of the test 352 is entry 350. The object with the id 350 is an application of a F1-projection with the id 305.

- Application: You see that the field "test_set" for an applications is used in a different context, namely a reference of the object the application is defined upon.

- F1-projections: The object with the id 305 is a F1-projection. For F1-projections, the field "test_set" contains a reference to the relation it is defined on. This relation is entry 304.

Let's go back to the test definition 352 and the field "comp_set". The field "comp_set" holds a reference to the second test container, in this case container 351. The fields "bsubsttest" and "bsubstcomp" are boolean. They are used exclusively for tests. If true, the "test" or "comp" reference is marked to be a variable or, if false, a fixed value. The field "op_operation" is also exclusively used by tests. The field holds a reference to the operator, the tests makes use of. In the given example this is "theta".

The field "arguments" is used for relations referencing the primary key of table "linkcollection". In the table "linkcollection" parts of relation definitions are stored. It shows on which containers the relation is defined (we refer to the description of the table "linkcollection"). As with relations, for F1-projections the field "arguments" is used in the same way.

The field "substbtvector" is a binary vector. A bit of the vector is set 1 (true), if in the corresponding F1-projection the argument is a variable, and 0 (false) if the argument is a container or an application (we refer to section 5.5).

The table "assignment" (see figure 7.3) is used to store the assignments of entities to containers. As the database relation is n:m the table has two primary keys, "container" referencing the container id from the table "adqlentity" and "entity" referencing the assigned entity id from the table "adqlentity". Thus, each assignment is described by one table entry. The field "transitive" is obsolete and only there for backward-compatibility.

The table "scopeassignment" (see figure 7.3) is used to store scope assignments. For a specific scope "scope", a container "container" is assigned a certain value "subcon". All fields (scope, container, subcon) are referencing an entry in "adqlentity" as foreign key.

The tables 7.2 and 7.3 continue the example resulting from the listing in figure 7.4 concerning the database table "linkcollection" and "fiveentities", respectively.

linkcol (PK)	extid	type
50	304	Relation
51	304	Link
52	304	Projection

Table 7.2.: Example of the table "linkcollection" resulting from the listing in figure 7.4

linkcol (PK)	rank (PK)	first	second	third	fourth	fifth
50	0	303	303			
51	0	302	302			
52	0	303				

Table 7.3.: Example of the table "fiveentities" resulting from the listing in figure 7.4

You can see that the table "linkcollection" has three entries. The primary key is generated from an independent sequence generator and is not related to any other key, thus, it is not a foreign key. The field "extid" is a foreign key of the central table "adqlentity" referencing the relation 304 "relproxy".

The "type" field tells, what kind of type the entry is:

- "Relation" is used as descriptor for a relation, thus, which containers the relation is defined on. Which containers these are can be seen from table "fiveentities". The "linkcol" field references as primary key the corresponding field from the table "linkcollection" as foreign key. The fields "first" to "fifth" hold references to the central table "adqlentity". We explain the example of $linkcol = 50$. It is of the type "relation", thus, a definition for the relation 304 which collections it is defined on. The involved containers are 303 (users) and 303 (user). We see, that relation 304 (relproxy) is defined on $users \times users$.

- "Link" is used to describe a link of a relation. A link is an element of a relation. The link with the id $linkcol = 51$ is part of relation 304 (relproxy). In table "fiveentities" you can see that this link is defined from entity 302 (Ann) to entity 302 (Ann).

- "Projection" describes the definition of a F1-projection. In the given example, the id $linkcol = 52$ describes a F1-projection on relation 304 (relproxy). Its projection elements are stored in the field first to fifth by omitting an entry for the F1-projection target.

The above database schema was chosen to combine relatively quick access by omitting too many field accesses for the DBMS with flexibility: Theoretically, a relation can be n-ary, thus link n relations. To map a n-ary relation to a database, generally a table in the form (relation, rank, entity) would be necessary. However, for a n-ary relation this would lead to n read/write accesses to the table for one link. With m links, the access count sumarizes to $n \times m$, thus be of $O(n^2)$.

In our chosen database schema we decided to model up to 5-ary relations with only one database entry for each link. Therefore, if a relation is of the type $1 - ary$ to $5 - ary$ only one database access is required to read a link. In such cases with up to m links, only m accesses are required, thus, linear instead of quadratic.

However, in case of a relation with an order higher than 5, a second (third, ...) entry with a rank 1 (or higher) is established. Consequently, a 10-ary relation requires 2 entries in the table "fiveentities", a 13-ary relation requires 3 entries, and so on. We based this design on the assumption, that, practically, most relations will be of the order 5 or below leading to only linear access times for relation links.

The table "booleanoperator" holds an index of all defined and available ADQL operators. The table is automatically populated by Hibernate: If a class (e.g. theta) inheriting the `ADQLOperator` class exists, Hibernate auto-generates a corresponding entry in the "boleanoperator" table, allowing to be referenced by the "op_operatorfield" of the table "adqlentity".

The table "referencedlink" is used for link caching to support faster link retrieval.

7.2.3. Persistence Module and Database Cache

The next layer of ADQL's back end is the persistence module and database cache. The purpose of this layer is two-fold: it serves as database cache and is used for the pre-calculation of access queries.

Database Cache   First, this layer is used to cache database queries and answers in memory. If the same request to the persistence layer is issued several times during the cache period of this request, a (costly) database query can be avoided by utilizing the previous answer to this query.

As we have said in the previous section, since version 1.3 of ADQL we switched to Hibernate [JBo10] as persistence layer. Hibernate's development was started by open source developers lead by Galvin King in 2001. His target was to create an easy-to-use persistence framework for Java. Later JBoss Inc. supported the Hibernate community, hired leading developers and integrated it into the JBoss Application Server (which is not used for ADQL). Today, Hibernate is available for Java and .NET. Its functionality has grown far beyond a persistence layer framework. The result was that as caching mechanisms we could only rely on the standard features of Hibernate.

We did some minor testing with the standard caching capabilities of the Hibernate framework. Hibernate offers a "second-level cache"[2] allowing to define several cache strategies like hash-tables, EHCache, OSCache, and so on. We did some not too extensive checks enabling and disabling the Hibernate cache features but found no measurable improvements in access or query times. With these disappointing results we decided not to focus on Hibernate's caching mechanisms for now. However, for future work we aim to do a more intensive research about the caching capabilities of Hibernate as we confess that our investigations about these features have been shallow. In the current version of ADQL, caching is not available.

---

[2]`http://docs.jboss.org/hibernate/orm/3.3/reference/en/html/performance.html`, last accessed 2013-03-20

Access Pre-Calculation   We started working on the idea of pre-calculating "atomic" access rights derived from the model and facts layer. "Atomic" is defined here in the sense, that no calculation has to be done to find out, if access can be granted, instead the current variable bindings can be matched against pre-calculated database tables in $O(1)$ to decide upon an access request.

Example: We say that Alice and Bob are users (fact). There exists a file "file1" (fact). All users may read "file1" (policy). As long as no changes in model, facts, and policies occur, the policies can be pre-calculated to "atomic" access rights. In this case, "Alice can read file1" and "Bob can read file1". If calculated and stored properly in a database schema, a request "can Bob read file1?" can be answered by simply finding the related database entry.

First tests and results promise that most policies can be pre-calculated and that the answering times can be improved by at least one order of magnitude.

However, there are policies which are not or quite hard to pre-calculate: Policies making use of orders or total orders: It is easy to pre-calculate policies like $user = Alice, permission = read, file = file1$. It becomes more complex if a policy uses orders like "Alice may read file1 *from now on*". To pre-claculate the test "from now on" is very expensive (or impossible). It is not an exact value which can be looked up in a database table ("from now on" is true for any date from now into the future), but has either to be calculated ("is '2100' greater equal 'now'?") or pre-calculated for any possible value (thus any date in the future). We immediately see that some tests can be pre-calculated and others are very expensive (in terms of storage) to pre-calculate.

This extension is future work.

7.2.4. ADQL's Core Layer, Controller, and Parser

The ADQL implementation follows the model-viewer-controller (MVC) paradigm ([GHJ94, KP88]). The MVC paradigm separates data (model) from data representation (view) and data processing (controller). It was suggested by Krasner and Pope for the language Smalltalk and adopted as a coding paradigma. However, MVC is not seen as a classic software pattern but described as a software paradigm.

ADQL's model is defined in the "core layer". The controller is represented by the "controller layer". As the ADQL server part does not include "view" in its usual meaning, this part is omitted. However, defining "view" in a broader sense, the visual representation of ADQL can be interpreted as the ADQL language, thus represented in the ADQL parser layer.

Core Layer   The ADQL core layer contains the data model of ADQL. Besides the model, the ADQL functions "define" and "apply" are implemented on this level, together with several internal, auxiliary functions.

Custom operators have to be defined on this layer (see section 5.9).

The core is implemented in Java. It consists of 33 classes and about 3500 lines of code. Each class represents a concept of ADQL, like ADQL Entity, ADQL Container, and so on. The classes are supplemented by auxiliary classes which represent e.g. combined database keys, intermediate data types and helper methods.

Controller   The ADQL controller consists of one major and some auxiliary classes. The major class is "the" controller, thus, organizing the program flow. Its methods are invoked by the parser layer. For example, the controller has methods (functions) for creating new entities, calculating applications, evaluating access requests and so on. The controller fetches persistent entities from the database storage, changes its properties and saves new or changed entities back to the database. Anything related to program control and program flow is represented in the controller.

The controller consists of about 2000 lines of code.

Parser   To be able to handle the formal ADQL language, a parser and the definition of the syntax is required. As parser generator we decided to use JavaCC[3]. The "Java Compiler Compiler" is a parser generator for use with Java applications. As the website says, "a parser generator is a tool that reads a grammar specification and converts it to a Java program that can recognize matches to the grammar"[4]. We utilized JavaCC in version 5.0.

Technically, JavaCC is a parser generator. This means, JavaCC is used to define a language (expressed by a BNF-like syntax). JavaCC is a LL(k) parser. It can parse a subset of context-free grammars. LL is the abbreviation for left-left: the parser parses from left to right and builds a left-most derivation of the input. k refers to the the parser characteristic to handle k "lookaheads" when parsing a sentence ([ASU86]).

The syntax definition file for JavaCC, called the "language file", is compiled to Java sources (`.java`-files) which can be compiled, again, to bytecode using the usual Java compiler. Note, that JavaCC language files are compiled twice: The first compilation creates Java sources from the JavaCC sources. The second

---

[3]`http://javacc.java.net`, last accessed 2013-04-02
[4]`http://javacc.java.net`, last accessed 2013-04-02

compilation creates bytecode from the Java sources which can be executed, as usual, with a Java Virtual Machine. The first compilation also creates methods and classes necessary to read expressions of the defined language.

```
   public ADQLContainer container() :
2  {
     ID id = null;
4    ADQLContainer container = null;
   }
6  {
     (
8      LOOKAHEAD({ getToken(2).kind != Equals && getToken(1).kind != Def })
       id = identifier()
10   | LOOKAHEAD({ getToken(2).kind == Equals || getToken(1).kind == Def })
       [ id = identifier() < Equals > ] < Def > container = containerDefAnonym()
12   )
     {
14     if (container == null) container = controller.getContainer(id);
       else if (id != null) controller.renameEntity(container, id);
16     return container;
     }
18 }
```

Figure 7.5.: Example listing of the JavaCC code. The example shows the language definition and reference of an ADQL container.

Figure 7.5 shows a short example of JavaCC code. The snippet depicts one part of the ADQL container definition (or reference). The header defines a `public` method (which correlates with a non-terminal symbol) `container()` with no arguments, return type `ADQLContainer`. It is followed by a block "{}" containing variable definitions. The second block consists of the syntax definition of the language interpreted by the parser. The JavaCC syntax itself follows a BNF-like syntax.

The complete block reads:

```
      (
2       LOOKAHEAD({ getToken(2).kind != Equals && getToken(1).kind != Def })
        id = identifier()
4     | LOOKAHEAD({ getToken(2).kind == Equals || getToken(1).kind == Def })
        [ id = identifier() < Equals > ] <Def> container = containerDefAnonym()
6     )
```

We see, that the outer construct of this block reads " (. . . | . . .) ". Following
BNF, the parser accepts two alternatives:

- The first alternative is `id = identifier()`. The statement invokes a
  method `identifier()`, which parses further input. This method is related to a non-terminal symbol, here "identifier". We do not show the
  composition of the non-terminal symbol "identifier" in our example here,
  however, in the real implementation, this symbol is, of course, defined.
  The result of this non-terminal/method is assigned the variable `id`, which
  is of the type `ID` following the definition of the first definition block of the
  `container`.

- The second alternative reads
  `[id=identifier() <Equals>]`
  `<Def> container=containerDefAnonym()`.
  It starts with an optional part `[]` including an `identifier()` non-
  terminal assigned to the variable `id` and a terminal-symbol `Equals`. The
  definition of the terminal symbol `Equals` is not shown in our example
  but is simply defined as the fixed literal "=". This first optional part is
  followed by a terminal symbol `Def`, the definition symbol of ADQL ($\triangle$
  or `DEF`). Next, a non-terminal symbol `containerDefAnonym()` follows
  which invokes in JavaCC a method with the same name. The result value
  is assigned the variable `container` of the type `ADQLContainer`.

We continue explaining the `LOOKAHEAD` lines: To distinguish both alternatives,
it is not enough to parse only the next, following token, as both expressions may
start with the non-terminal symbol `identifier`. Therefore, a "look-ahead"
has to be used, meaning, that not only the next token decides on the alternative,
but in this case the next two tokens. The expression

```
LOOKAHEAD({ getToken(2).kind != Equals && getToken(1).kind
!= Def })
```

is interpreted in the following way:
"Use this alternative, if the next but one token (`getToken(2).kind`) is not the terminal symbol `Equals` and (`&&`) the next token (`getToken(1).kind`) is not the terminal symbol `Def`. The second look-ahead definition can be interpreted correspondingly.

The last block reads:

```
   {
2    if (container == null) container = controller.getContainer(id);
     else if (id != null) controller.renameEntity(container, id);
4    return container;
   }
```

It contains Java code which is executed after interpreting the previous block. We see, that in the given example, a method `getContainer(id)` is called utilizing a `controller` instance, if the container is null (did not previously exist). If the id of the container is not null, the method renames the container.

The implementation of the parser generator consists of about 900 lines of code for the v3 (Lamdba-style) syntax, and about 1500 lines of code for the v2 (SQL-style) syntax.

7.2.5. Network Server Layer

The network server layer is responsible for starting several listening threads on server side network sockets and for waiting for connecting clients. The current ADQL implementation supports the following connection types:

- *TCP Strings*: The TCP string service supports plain text input and returns String representations of the resulting objects and queries. Its standard port is 1228. To test a running ADQL service, the command "`telnet <server> 1228`" can be used. An example is shown in figure 7.6 sending the command "`Ann = DEF ENTITY();`".

- *TCP Objects*: To support structured, machine-readable connections, the TCP object port can be used. It is running on TCP port 1227 by default. For communication it makes use of the intermediate object "Result Object" described in section 7.4. This type of connection is used by the ADQL web management interface (see section 7.3).

```
1   $ telnet localhost 1228
    Trying 127.0.0.1...
3   Connected to localhost.
    Escape character is '^]'.
5   Ann = DEF ENTITY();

7   FLAGS: CmdSuccess: + | AccessGrant: - | Quit: -
    RESULT OBJECTS:
9   ADQLEntity (extId=Ann, id=1650)
    LOG:
11  Created entity (anonymous) [$1650]
    Renamed $1650 to Ann.
```

Figure 7.6.: Example connection to the network layer using the TCP string port.

- *UDP Objects*: Like "TCP objects", the interface "UDP objects" is implemented. Basically, it uses the same connectivity like TCP objects but uses UDP instead of TCP as transport layer protocol.

- *Thrift*: Thrift is an interface definition language. It was initially developed by Facebook (see [Sle07]) as a core part of Facebook's internal web service communication structure. After being made Open Source, it became an Apache project[5]. Basically, Thrift supports language independent, reliable object transmission through network communication. To use it, the object(s) to be transmitted are defined using the "interface definition language", actually a language to define complex data types. Thrift binaries are then generating the code libraries necessary to transmit these objects between clients and servers in many of today's computer languages like Java, C++, Python, PHP, Ruby, Erlang, and others. These created code binaries are usable by the client and server code abstracting from transmission and communication layers.

  ADQL implements a Thrift interface for Java on the server side and by this supports any client communication utilizing Thrift.

- *REST*: The "Representational State Transfer" was suggested by Roy Fielding [Fie00]. REST is an architectural style which forces the program to represent all objects and methods of a service as an URL. In most cases these objects and methods are represented in a structured hierarchy. We do not want to go into further details here, as REST is only one of many interfaces for ADQL and not in the focus of this work. Together with one of our students, Matthias Eckstein [Eck12] we implemented an early release of a REST interface for ADQL.

---

[5] `http://thrift.apache.org`, last accessed 2013-04-02

7.3. Front End Design and Architecture

We continue with the design and architecture of the front end of our ADQL implementation. The architecture of the front end is depicted in figure 7.7. We provide four libraries which can be imported by business software: a Java client library, a Thrift client library, an OSGi client library, and an REST client library. Besides, we provide a web management interface. All components are described below.

Frontend

Client Libraries				
Management Webinterface	Java Client Library	Thrift Client Library	OSGi Client Library	REST Client Library
TCP Objects	TCP Objects	Thrift	OSGi	REST

Figure 7.7.: Front end architecture of our Access Definition and Query Language implementation.

Java Client Library   The Java client library is basically a Java library which can be imported by clients which want to use ADQL as access control service. The client library consists of three classes:

- *ADQLConnection*: The class establishes a connection to the ADQL back end server. The server details, like IP/URL and port, are stored in the config file `server.properties`.
  It is sufficient to call the constructor of the class `ADQLConnection` to establish a server communication. Alternatively, an overloaded constructor can be used to override the values stored in the config file.

  Communication with the server takes place by calling the method `ResultObject executeADQLCommand(String command)`.
  The ADQL command to be issued is sent to the server. The result of the command is returned by the server through the intermediate object `ResultObject` (see section 7.4).

- *ADQLScope*: Instead of sending native ADQL commands to the server using the above class, for access queries a simplified alternative is provided by the class `ADQLScope`. The class allows to define ADQL states by assigning values to ADQL variables through the methods `public void set(String variable, String value, TTL ttl)`. The variable `variable` is assigned the value `value`. The flag time-to-live (`TTL`) is used to express if the variable binding is deleted after the next access query or remain constant until manually erased. This can be used to keep certain variable bindings for several subsequent access queries.

  The method `public ResultObject checkAccess()` is then used to send an access query to the server using the previously provided variable bindings. The result value is the intermediate `ResultObject`.

- *ADQLScopeCallbackInterface*: To support inversion of control, a callback interface is provided. It can be implemented by third-party code to define classes or methods which are called back when access queries take place.

Management Web Interface   ADQL's Management Web Interface is a web application using the Google Web Toolkit (GWT)[6] as web framework.

The goal of the web interface is to provide a web based graphical user interface (GUI) to communicate with the ADQL back end. It can be used to define and change access models, facts, and policies in a graphical way instead of using "dry" ADQL commands.

A screenshot showing the web interface is depicted in figure 7.8.

- *Session Control*: The web interface allows connections to many ADQL back ends. The back end, to connect to, can be defined within the session control tab.

- *Entities*: The tab "entities" is depicted in the screenshot. All available entities are listed in the left screen part. When selected, the right part of the screen shows information about this entity: Its properties (id, externalid, type, and subtype), and to which containers (here called "sets") the entity is assigned to. The up- and down buttons can be used to assign the selected entity to containers. The button "Create a new one" can be used to create a new entity. By marking an entity and pressing the button "Delete selected" the marked entities are deleted.

---

[6]`https://developers.google.com/web-toolkit`, last accessed 2013-04-02

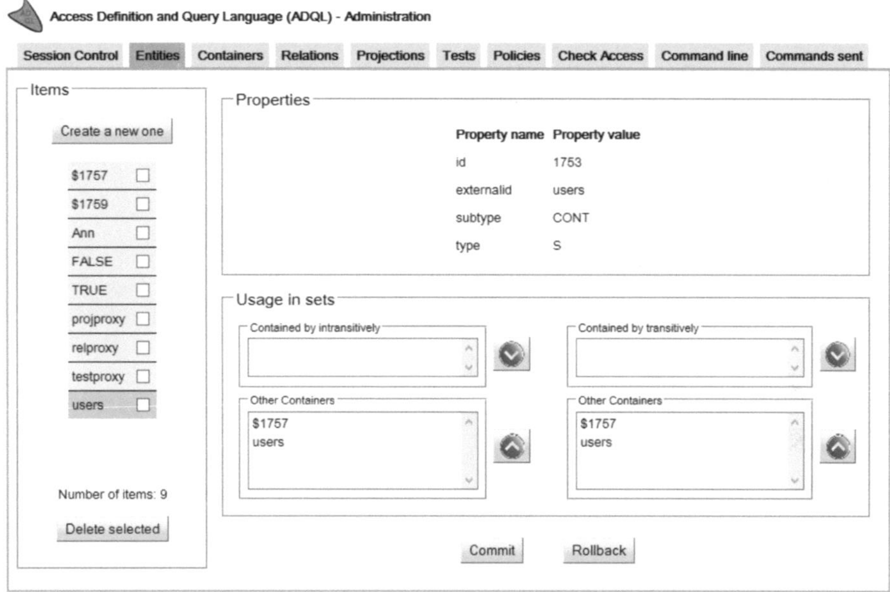

Figure 7.8.: Screenshot of the ADQL Management Web Interface

- *Containers, Relations, F1-projections, Tests, Policies*: These tabs are used to manage the ADQL concepts of the respective name. For the sake of short-ness we do not depict and describe all of these tabs one by one. Summarizing the tabs, they show properties and usage of defined concepts and allow creating new ones, deleting existing, and changing their properties and assignments.

- *Check Access*: The "check access" tab allows issuing access queries and receiving the results.

- *Command Line*: The tab "command line" offers a command line in the browser which can be used to issue native ADQL commands to the server.

- *Commands sent*: The tab "commands sent" shows a history of previously sent commands and their results. This features allows to see what commands have been generated by the GUI and check for errors.

Thrift, OSGi, and REST client   As described in the back end (see section 7.2), ADQL supports Thrift, OSGi, and REST interfaces. Consequently, for all three interfaces client libraries are available.

7.4. Intermediate Layer: Design and Architecture

The object `ResultObject` represents the intermediate object between ADQL clients and ADQL servers. Whenever an ADQL command is sent to the ADQL back end, the back end answers with an instance of the class `ResultObject`.

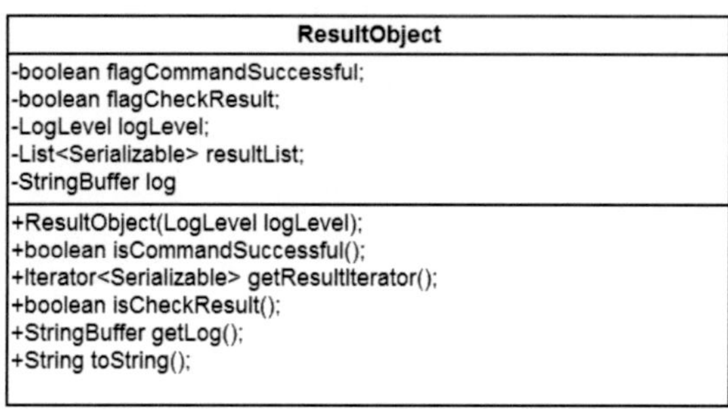

Figure 7.9.: UML class diagram of the class ResultObject

Figure 7.9 depicts the UML class diagram. The `ResultObject` consists of two private flags. `flagCommandSuccessful` is set `true` by the back end if the last command or command sequence could be executed successfully and without any error. The flag `flagCheckResult` becomes `true`, if the last command or command sequence included an access query and access was granted. Otherwise, the flag is `false`, also, if the last command or command sequence did not contain an access check query. If the last command sequence contained several access queries, the flag contains the result for the last access query in the sequence. Both flags can be retrieved using the getter methods `isCommandSuccessful()` and `isCheckResult()`.

In case, a command or command sequence returns an ADQL concept (e.g. an entity, container, ...), this ADQL object is contained in the `resultList` and can be retrieved through the iterator getter method `getResultIterator`. All ADQL concepts implement the interface `Serializable` and can thus be included in the list.

The `StringBuffer log` contains logging information from the back end containing relevant logging information related to last command or command sequence. The preferred `logLevel` (TRACE, DEBUG, INFO, WARN, ERROR, MANDATORY) can be set by using client parameters.

Finally, `String toString()` creates a recursive textual representation of the object `ResultObject` including objects in the `resultList` and logging information. This method is used by the "TCP String" interface (see section 7.6).

7.5. Using ADQL as Software Service

In this section we want to show, which steps have to be taken to use ADQL as access control service for third party software. We refer to the third party software as "business software". The business software can be of any kind (e.g. web service, application, app, ...). To be able to use ADQL, an ADQL instance must either run on the same physical node or the ADQL instance must be reachable through a network connection.

ADQL takes the role of a policy decision point (PDP).

To be able to decide on access requests, ADQL has to know the following concepts:

- Model: What are the conditions that can be used to make decisions on? E.g.: we have users.

- Facts: What are the facts that we have to decide on? E.g.: There is a user called Ann.

- Scope: What is the current situation to decide on? E.g.: the current user is Ann.

- Policy: What are the rationals / the rules we base our decision on? E.g.: Ann as superuser can do anything.

Below we will describe all steps that have to be followed to include ADQL's access control in the business software.

7.5.1. Decide on the Model

Before even anything concerning access control can be implemented in the business software, it has to be defined what the concepts are that access control makes its decisions on. We provide an example: The business software implementing ADQL's access control wants to make use of users, objects, permission and time. It becomes immediately clear that then the concepts of user, object, permission and time must be introduced. If ADQL's access control does not know about time, no decision can be made upon it. We see that it has to be defined what the *model* is on which the access control is based on.

Apart from the above concepts the (access control relevant) attributes of the concepts have to be defined. Again, we provide examples: An object might have an owner (which is a user), a user might have a proxy (being another user) and so on. So we have two things that have to be defined: the concepts and their attributes. Of course, attributes are also a concept.

- The access control containers have to be defined. An access control container is a set of entities which can be bound to a variable at runtime. Containers are what we called a concept above. A container is a collection of possible runtime conditions. Containers may be organized in hierarchies or networks. E.g. user, object, permission, time.

- The access control relations have to be defined. An access control relation inter-relates two or more access control containers. E.g. the owner of an object (object - user relation) or the proxy of a user (user - user relation).

This task has to be done by the software designers of the business software considering the requirements of their customers. It requires analysis and abstract thinking. Anything that has been defined in the access control model can be used later to model policies on, which means can be used to make decisions on, if access is granted or denied. Of course, anything not being part of the access control model can later not be used to make decisions on.

Please note, that it is not necessary to make decisions on possible values of the containers yet: We do not need to know if there is a user named "Ann" or "Herb", how many users exist and so on. This will be specified later.

7.5.2. Implement Access Checks in the Software

The next step is to write the business software. When writing the code a developer may come to a point when an access check is required to decide whether to continue as wished or deny access. The developer simply calls ADQL's access control software service and wait for it to make a simple yes or no decision. RFC2904 [FHdL$^+$00] calls these software service the policy decision point (PDP).

We do not want the developer to deal with details about any access control mechanism or policy. In the simplest case such a line of code looks like

```
  if adqlscope.checkAccess()
2    continue;
  else
4    break;
```

The method `adqlscope.checkAccess()` is a called by the business software. `adqlscope` is an instance of the class `ADQLScope` included in the ADQL client library (see section 7.3).

In the literature, RFC2904 [FHdL+00] outsources these kind of calls to the so-called policy enforcement point (PEP). A PEP requires an inversion-of-control, that is, the business code is called by the access control component: Not the business logic calls the access control component, but the access control calls the business logic. We argue that this approach is uncommon, as access control is a part of the business logic and not business logic a part of access control.

7.5.3. Provide the Facts

To be able to make a decision, the policy decision point PDP needs to know the facts. For example, if the concept (access control container) "user" has been defined, the PDP needs to know, which users exist (e.g. Ann, Herb, Jim, Liz).

Therefore, the PDP needs a mechanism to learn about the entities. RFC 2904 assigns this task to the policy information point (PIP).

Anyhow, when writing code as a software developer, two ways are possible: (1) The PIP asks the business software to retrieve this information (inversion-of-control approach) when the PIP needs to know (e.g. during an access check) or (2) the PIP is told through a function call, when such an entity is created in the business software (direct approach).

- Example code for the first approach could look like below.

```
adqlscope.getExternalContainer("users", BusinessCode.getUsers());
```

The access control component is told, that all `users` can be retrieved by calling the method `BusinessCode.getUsers()`. This functionality is not yet implemented in our current prototype.

- A direct function call informing the PIP about a fact at its creation time could look like this:

```
1   adqlconnection.executeADQLCommand
       ("users = DEF CONTAINER(Ann = DEF ENTITY());");
```

Here, the access control service is informed about the existence of a user "Ann".

Both approaches have advantages and disadvantages: In the case of a direct approach, all changes (i.e. creations and deletions) in access control relevant facts have to be propagated to the external access control service. The facts are stored twice, in the business application and the access control service. This includes the risk of data inconsistency.

The direct approach can evaluate access checks faster: The definition of a container with all its entities is known to the PIP. No (remote) function calls have to be issued, which can take quite a time to be answered. Furthermore, it allows the possibility of pre-calculation access check queries.

The above advantages of a direct approach are the disadvantages of the indirect approach, and vice versa.

7.5.4. Learn the Current System State

To make an access control decision, it is necessary to know about the current system state (current situation), e.g. who wants to do what. Let us assume the access control containers "users" and "objects" exist. The decision to grant or deny access can only be made, if ADQL knows which user wants to gain access on which object. Obviously, without this knowledge, a decision cannot be made.

There are two possible ways, to find out about the current binding of an access control container. First, ADQL can ask another service (the policy information point, PIP [FHdL$^+$00]). Second, ADQL has been told about the current binding before the decision has to be made.

Actually, both situations have to be dealt with by another piece of code in the business software. The first case can be handled by a call-back function (precisely, the address of code in memory or the network to be called when the current binding needs to be evaluated).

```
adqlscope.set("time", System.currentTimeMillisADQL(), TTL.nonpermanent);
```

This example tells ADQL it can retrieve the current time by calling the function `System.currentTimeMillisADQL()`. Please note, that this function must implement the interface `ADQLScopeCallbackInterface` from the client library.

The second case can be handled by the simple code lines below telling ADQL the current user is "Ann":

```
1   adqlscope.set("user", "Ann", TTL.nonpermanent);
```

It is only a question of syntax how to handle web service calls like REST, SOAP and others. Therefore, we will not discuss this further.

7.5.5. Defining Policies

The policies, which define the conditions for access, are created when the business software is installed for the customer. This is usually a task for the system administrators. For convenience, a graphical user interface like the ADQL WebGui can be used. Alternatively, native ADQL commands can be issued to the ADQL service.

7.6. ADQL Back End Performance

In this section we describe the result of several performance tests we did for the ADQL back end. All tests are based on ADQL version 2.6pre1.

As test system we used an 8-core Intel system (Intel Xeon CPU X5355 @ 2.66GHz). The memory used by the Java Virtual machine was 71 MB. The test system was using Linux with a 2.6 kernel. As persistence storage we used PostgreSQL in version 8.4. The Postgres server was running on the same node as the JVM.

All tests were done using a test software written in C. The C program simply reads test commands from a file and repeats sending the commands to the ADQL back end. The results sent back by the ADQL back end are analyzed for errors but not handled any further. The log files for these tests are available from the author.

We tested several variations:

- *Normal Core*: The normal core was the standard ADQL back end, using no specializations and compiled straight from the sources. As connection interface, the TCP String interface was used. The connection was made over the local loopback interface, thus testing software and ADQL back end were running on the same machine.

- *Parser with and without logging*: We wanted to know the influence of network overhead. Using communication through a network, in our case TCP, may result in lower performance as the whole network software stack has to be processed to receive commands and answers. To circumvent this effect and measure how large this effect is, we tested a variant where the test software was connected directly to the parser without using a network connection.

  The variant was split into two sub-variants: As we wanted to evaluate the influence of creating and including logging information on the side of the back end, we disabled all logging functionality in one sub-variant ("without logging or w/o logging"). The other sub-variant made use of standard logging features ("with logging").

- *Controller with and without logging*: To find out the influence of the parser on the run time performance, we created two test alternatives avoiding the parser code completely. The parser is used to interpret ADQL commands (delivered as a text sequence) and call corresponding methods from ADQL's core.

  To find out, how time consuming the parsing is, we connected the test software directly to the ADQL core by direct Java function calls avoiding any parsing. As ADQL's back end is a software stack, consequently, also the network stack was avoided. Therefore, the "controller" variant is expected to be the fasted variant, as it omits network and parser overhead.

  Again, we split this variant into two sub-variants, one with and the other without logging in the back end.

As test case we used the "traveler scenario". The complete ADQL listing is depicted in the appendix. The traveler scenario defines containers for "users", "pictures", "trips", "roles", "permissions", and "stages". Each "user" can be assigned "roles". A "user" can be part of a "trip", as well as "pictures" can be assigned to "trips". A "trip" can be assigned a stage, either "duringtrip", or "published". The scenario uses 4 policies consisting of 9 tests.

For the tests the persistence store was initiated with the traveler scenario. Then, one access request was sent to the back end repeatedly. The access request results in a "deny" so that all policies and tests have to be tested.

The core was restarted and re-initialized after each sequence. No other requests or connections were sent to the core during the tests. All versions were tested sending the command 100, 200, 400, 800, 1600, 3200, 6400, 12800, 25600, 51200, and 102400 times. By this sequence we wanted to measure the start-up costs for the core. All variants were tested three times with every sequence length. The average was calculated for all three runs of every variant and sequence length.

Times	1st test	2nd test	3rd test	Average (ms)	Cmds p.s.	Cmd duration (μs)
100	648	705	548	634	158	6337
200	1100	1104	1031	1078	185	5392
400	1948	1864	1710	1841	217	4602
800	3664	3164	3015	3281	244	4101
1600	5622	6036	4730	5463	293	3414
3200	12103	10632	9832	10856	295	3392
6400	21282	24104	25248	23545	272	3679
12800	49384	47014	47540	47979	267	3748
25600	96325	95025	95147	95499	268	3730
51200	194689	191593	192531	192938	265	3768
102400	394533	377621	378652	383602	267	3746

Table 7.4.: Results table for the "normal variant" of the check access performance test of the traveler scenario

Times	1st test	2nd test	3rd test	Average (ms)	Cmds p.s.	Cmd duration (μs)
100	247	237	246	243	411	2433
200	367	340	371	359	557	1797
400	780	673	735	729	548	1823
800	1459	1341	1494	1431	559	1789
1600	2686	2683	2800	2723	588	1702
3200	5425	5416	5429	5423	590	1695
6400	10839	10820	10849	10836	591	1693
12800	21661	21629	23821	22370	572	1748
25600	43256	43210	45283	43916	583	1715
51200	86540	88350	90333	88408	579	1727
102400	173213	191172	177721	180702	567	1765

Table 7.5.: Results table for the "controller variant with logging" of the check access performance test of the traveler scenario

Tables 7.4, 7.5, 7.6, 7.7, and 7.8 show the test results. Figure 7.10 depicts the

Times	1st test	2nd test	3rd test	Average (ms)	Cmds p.s.	Cmd duration (μs)
100	282	245	237	255	393	2547
200	433	359	352	381	524	1907
400	864	698	872	811	493	2028
800	1414	1273	1396	1361	588	1701
1600	2551	2540	2607	2566	624	1604
3200	5325	5314	5167	5269	607	1646
6400	10461	10474	10493	10476	611	1637
12800	20716	20637	20555	20636	620	1612
25600	42925	41148	41167	41747	613	1631
51200	85409	82132	82313	83285	615	1627
102400	164945	163992	164872	164603	622	1607

Table 7.6.: Results table for the "controller variant without logging" of the check access performance test of the traveler scenario

Times	1st test	2nd test	3rd test	Average (ms)	Cmds p.s.	Cmd duration (μs)
100	534	540	449	508	197	5077
200	912	920	778	870	230	4350
400	1730	1797	1552	1693	236	4233
800	3128	3193	3024	3115	257	3894
1600	6630	6092	5991	6238	257	3899
3200	11847	12692	11748	12096	265	3780
6400	22764	24120	22814	23233	275	3630
12800	45628	50412	45713	47251	271	3691
25600	94666	92578	92203	93149	275	3639
51200	191288	185218	184247	186918	274	3651
102400	372788	368869	369042	370233	277	3616

Table 7.7.: Results table for the "parser variant with logging" of the check access performance test of the traveler scenario

Times	1st test	2nd test	3rd test	Average (ms)	Cmds p.s.	Cmd duration (μs)
100	678	712	479	623	161	6230
200	1109	1062	833	1001	200	5007
400	1944	1817	1636	1799	222	4498
800	3607	3267	3216	3363	238	4204
1600	5728	5614	5627	5656	283	3535
3200	11953	11060	11077	11363	282	3551
6400	22396	22113	23012	22507	284	3517
12800	45105	44125	46590	45273	283	3537
25600	92487	88407	90252	90382	283	3531
51200	177023	177041	178698	177587	288	3469
102400	356901	355522	357484	356636	287	3483

Table 7.8.: Results table for the "parser variant without logging" of the check access performance test of the traveler scenario

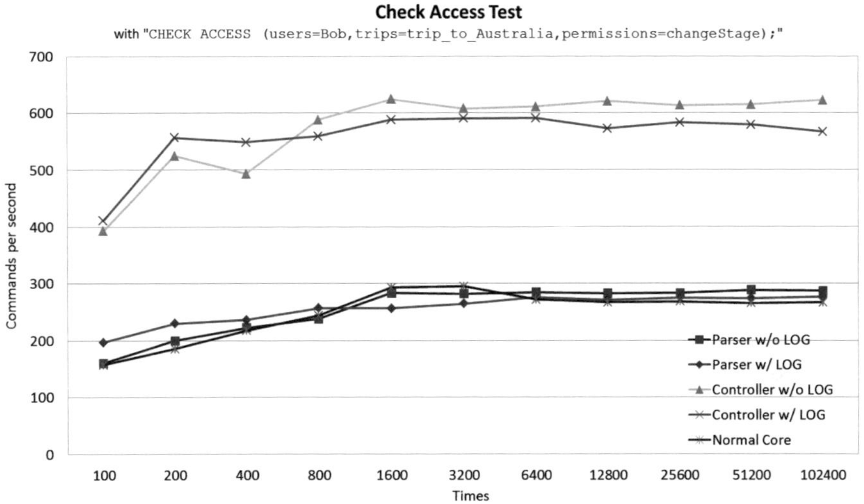

Figure 7.10.: Check access performance test of the traveler scenario

commands per seconds processed by the ADQL back end for all tested variations and sequence lengths.

As expected, the performance tests with full functionality and all back end layers enabled ("normal core"), are the slowest variant. Anything else would be counter-intuitive. The "normal core" starts up with 158 commands per second for the first 100 commands, improving with every command sequence processed (see table 7.4). Please note, that this is not caused by caching mechanisms used in the back end, as no caching has been enabled for all tests. When the startup phase has been overcome, the performance levels out at about 270 commands per second (see table 7.4). The test results of 1600 and 3200 command repetitions are higher, 293 and 295, respectively. This result is surprising, as we would have expected the results to be monotonically increasing. It might be the effect of the Java garbage collector, who starts up just after 3200 repeats and slows down the system. However, we did not explicitly test for this effect.

From figure 7.10 we can see that the "parser" variants do influence the back end performance only marginally (see also tables 7.7 and 7.8). The tests "controller with and without logs" and "normal core" share almost the same performance. The "normal control" includes the complete network stack, while the variant "controller with and without logging" omits the network stack. This finding leads to the conclusion that the network stack requires only a very small, probably fixed, percentage of the performance and does not significantly change the overall performance.

Furthermore, we see that logging does not have a heavy influence on the performance (see tables 7.8). This observation is repeated with the "controller" variant (see and 7.6), although, logging has a bigger influence on the latter variant than on the "parser" variant.

Concerning the variants "controller", which omit the parser (and the network stack), doubles the performance relative to the "normal" variant (see table 7.5). The commands operated per second stabilize at about 580 commands per second with logging and 610 commands per second without logging. We conclude that the parser requires about 50% of the total performance of the back end.

In this section we have shown that for the use case "traveler scenario" the average number of access checks processed per second is roughly about 300. About 50% of the processing time is required by the parser, the other 50% by ADQL's internal logic and the persistence storage. Logging does have a minor influence on the performance only.

7.7. Performance of Other Access Control Implementation

In this section we provide examples of the performance of other access control implementations.

Performance of a RBAC Access Control at CERN Gysin et al. [GPC[+]07b] describe their implementation of a standard RBAC access control model for the accelerator control system at CERN. The implementation was done by a cooperation of CERN and Fermilab. Their implementation pre-calculates atomic access rights from facts and policies and stores them in a structure Gysin et al. call "access map". For their performance test they used 20 rules and 2000 rule access maps. Their findings were:

- The size of the access map has little influence on the answering times.

- Logging has little effect on the answering times.

- Gysin et al. used RSA verification for access requests. The verification algorithm alone took between 0.15 ms and 5 ms per request, dependent on the RSA key length.

- Dependent on the architecture (2-tier, 3-tier) the answering time was about 0.7 ms per request (2-tier, 512-bit RSA key length) for a 2000 rule environment in the best case.

It is difficult to compare the findings of Gysin et al. with our own results. Gysin et al. use pre-calculation in their approach which operates as a cache for access result calculations. Consequently, their finding that the amount of rules stored in the model did not influence the answering times significantly, is conclusive. How could it? Using pre-calculation, the number of policies can only influence the time necessary to pre-calculate the access results and not the lookup time of the latter.

Second, Gysin et al. use RSA-based verification which we do not. Gysin et al. report execution times for RSA verification of 0.15 ms (512-bit RSA key length) but we cannot say for sure if we can simply subtract these values from the answering times to calculate RSA-free processing times. If we do so, a typical answering time of Gysin et al. would be $0.7ms - 0.15ms = 0.55ms$. Our ADQL implementation currently offers around $\frac{1000}{287} = 3.48ms$ per request.

The finding that logging influences answering times only marginally is consistent with our own findings.

The approach of Gysin et al. and our own approach differ too much to be able to compare both in detail and infer better or worse performance.

However, both approaches deliver answering times in the same order of magnitude. If we assume, that access control mechanisms for the accelerator control at CERN are time-critical, we can conclude that our current ADQL implementation is also fast enough for this kind of scenario.

Performance of XACML implementations Another performance test has been reported by Turkmen and Crispo [TC08]. They compare three open-source implementations of XACML on specific policy and request settings. They tested implementations from Sun, "Sun XACML", XACMLight (offering only parts of the functionality of XACML), and XACML Enterprise. Turkmen and Crispo verified their test cases concerning the amount of policies (1,100,1k,10k) and rules (10,50,100,500,1k).

We describe some of their results:

- XACML Enterprise evaluated 10 policies with 1000 rules in 125 ms.

- XACML Light evaluated 10 policies with 1000 rules in 6 s.

- Suns XACML's performance lies between the other two test candidates.

It is difficult to compare the results of Turkmen and Crispo with the results for ADQL. Dependent how "rules" are counted, our own performance test scenario can be seen to have around 200 "rules" (counting symbols and symbol references in our test scenario). However, both approaches do not match so they can be hardly compared.

We can conclude that an answering for an access request towards an XACML implementation consisting of 10 policies and 1000 rules is about 125 ms (XACML Enterprise) or 6 s (XACML light). ADQLs answering time with about 200 symbols and 4 policies is around 3.48 ms.

If we assume that the XACML implementations can be used in production environments, ADQL can as well, as ADQL's answering times are 2 (XACML Enterprise) or 3 (XACML light) orders of magnitude faster than XACML implementations.

However, we are aware that this first comparison between quite different access control implementations cannot be seen as a real benchmark as the test setups differ in many points. We leave this for future work.

7.8. Summary

In this chapter we aimed for three objectives:

- First, we described the architecture of ADQL's back end, front end, and intermediate layer. Our ADQL implementation is a software service following the MVC paradigm. It can be accessed by several interfaces, like TCP string, TCP objects, REST, and Thrift. This finding is related to target (1) of this work, "by describing the service implementation of our prototype" and proof, that a generalized access control model, like ADQL, can be implemented as a concrete and operative software service.

- Second, we described the steps necessary to use ADQL's implementation for a business software as PDP/PEP/PIP providing access control functionality. We aimed to show that the operative ADQL prototype can be applied to productive scenarios.

- Third, we showed the performance of ADQL. We aimed to demonstrate that ADQL is fast enough to answer access requests in a proper time appropriate for production environments. We think, that about 300 access requests per second is indeed fast enough for this goal and could verify this by comparing ADQL answering times with a RBAC implementation for CERNs accelerator control system and XACML implementations.

8. Conclusion

In this work we suggest an access control model, the Access Definition and Query Language (ADQL), and its implementation as a software service used by business applications to factor access control out of the business application itself.

ADQL is a context-free formal computer language. It is implemented as a usable software service. ADQL is a meta language in the sense that it can be used to work like existing access control models. More specifically, ADQL is used to define the concepts which can then be used to formulate the conditions which decide if access is granted or denied. As example, ADQL allows to introduce the concepts "users", "objects", and "time". Policies can be formulated to grant access for specific users to specific objects on certain time slots.

ADQL consists of two parts: the formal language and the software service. While the formal language describes the concepts and basics of ADQL as a meta access control model, the software is an implementation interpreting ADQL language expressions and inferencing on facts, if for specific conditions access may be granted or must be denied.

ADQL has four aims:

- It wants to close the gap between the constantly reused Role Based Access Control (RBAC) models in industry / practice on the one side, and the large number of access control models suggested by the academic world.

- Second, our suggested model is a configurable meta model. This means, that the model can be configured to mimic existing access control models, e.g. discretionary access control models (i.e., the HRU model), mandatory access control models (i.e., Bell-LaPadula, ChineseWall, ...), RBAC-like models ($RBAC_{0-3}$, TRBAC, ...), and others.

- Third, the access control model is implemented as an existing, usable software service. The software service can be used by business applications to decide if operations are allowed or denied.

- Fourth, the access control model and its implemented service support features like flexibility, delegation, and (user) empowerment. Flexibility is meant in a sense, that the service can be configured to work like standard access control models. Delegation means, that access control is based on delegation and must support features like proxies and delegation of access rights from one user to another. This results in empowerment of the user allowing the user to decide upon the access control model being used for his data.

Our work introduces the motivation for such an approach in chapter 1. We show that privacy will be an important matter in the future, especially related to social networks, like Facebook, Google plus and other personal data. After this motivational part, we show that for software designers, developers, and administrators access control is mostly a recurring task. We analyze existing software libraries and frameworks and find, that to our knowledge, no configurable software exists which could handle the access control part for business software. Consequently, access control code in software is rewritten for each application again, mostly utilizing application specialized adaptations of standard RBAC-models. This approach misses the chance of code re-usage. The chapter closes by laying out of the aims of our work.

Chapter 2 provides an overview of some major points in the history of access control. The chapter starts by providing the major design principles for access control models of Saltzer and Schroeder [SS75]. Although perhaps not all of their principles formulated back in 1975 are still valid, we still see major learning points for present access control services. As for any scientific discipline, it is important to define the important terms to avoid misunderstandings. So we provide definitions of important terms related to access control model like "account" and "user", next. We continue with a history of access control. We introduce the background and models of the discretionary access control models, mandatory access control models, role based access control and models derived from role based access control models. Another part of this chapter are important standards, especially relevant RFCs and the "eXtensible Access Control Markup Language" (XACML) standardized by OASIS. Interesting ideas come from the world of the "semantic web" which we describe as well as logic-based authorization models.

The chapters 3, 4, and 5 describe the foundations of our own approach, the Access Definition and Query Language (ADQL). Chapter 3 is an informal introduction to ADQL. It utilizes a motivational example for access control requirements and shows, how these requirements are implemented in ADQL. The chapter aims to provide an example to make it easier for the reader to understand the language syntax and its underlying concepts.

The complete syntax of ADQL is presented in chapter 4. Concerning its syntactical structure, ADQL leans towards the famous Lambda calculus, although purpose, syntax, and semantic differ from the latter. However, like the Lambda calculus, ADQL knows definitions and applications. Definitions change the internal state of the access control system, applications are operations executed on the internal state, which do not change the internal state itself. Symbol definitions referencing applications are exempted here. Strictly seen, symbol definitions change the internal state of our access control system.

The underlying concepts of ADQL are described in chapter 5. ADQL makes use of set theory also utilizing relations, filters, projections, boolean tests, and logical AND- and OR-concatenations. ADQL calls its concepts entities, containers, relations, filtered 1-projections, tests, policies, variables, and scopes. Containers can be organized in hierarchies allowing hierarchically organized entities, e.g. user group hierarchies, object hierarchies, organizational hierarchies.

Chapter 6 demonstrates with three use cases how ADQL can be used to model access control. The first example shows how ADQL can be used to work like the Ball-LaPadula model. We show that ADQL requires two policies and few model definitions to mimic Bell-LaPadula. The second example provided is SAP R/3 ERP's access control model. SAP is a large German software company offering a widely-spread enterprise resource planning software. We show how the access control model of SAP R/3 can be modeled in ADQL. ADQL requires only one policy and a few definitions to emulate the model. Our last use case example is an extended RBAC model which stems from an e-science project supporting students' thesis in cooperation with companies. We demonstrate how ADQL can be used to handle project-related roles, hierarchical organizations and model time-dependent access rights.

The implementation of ADQL as a software service is described in section 7. We picture the design of the software service allowing ADQL to work as a policy decision point (PDP), policy enforcement point (PEP), and as policy information point (PIP). In addition to the architecture, we show how business software can utilize ADQL as external service to take responsibility for access decisions. We describe the steps software developers have to follow, to include ADQL as service in their business software. ADQL offers several state-of-the-art interfaces for client requests, e.g. TCP, UDP, REST, OSGi, and Thrift. A basic web management graphical user interface allows to avoid pure textual communication with the service. The chapter closes by an analysis of the performance of ADQL indicating that ADQL is fast enough to be used in production environments although it is an academic prototype.

Future Work To further improve the performance of AQDL's service implementation, we want to work on intelligent caching and caching update mechanisms. Related to further improving execution times, especially the relatively costly parser layer, we want to re-implement ADQL in C.

8. Conclusion

To avoid duplicated facts storage, we think of implementing interfaces to external data storages, like LDAP, external databases, and fast and reliable mechanisms to retrieve such data.

On the conceptional side we want to implement the possibility of free, explicit variable definitions avoiding situations where "artificial" containers have to be utilized representing two variables. Further, supporting implicitly defined relations can gain ADQL more flexibility. Another extension is a more flexible and not so strictly interrelated definition of filters and projections. For practical purposes, we also plan adding the support for incremental updates of existing definitions. E.g., adding an entity to an existing container without having to re-define the container as a whole.

Appendix

A. Backus-Naur-Form of ADQL v3.0

$$
\begin{aligned}
\langle\text{Expression}\rangle \;&\models\; \langle\text{Term}\rangle \;"\,;"\; \mid\; \langle\text{Term}\rangle \;"\,;"\; \langle\text{Expression}\rangle \\
\langle\text{Term}\rangle \;&\models\; \epsilon \;\mid\; \langle\text{Definition}\rangle \;\mid\; \langle\text{Application}\rangle \\[6pt]
\langle\text{Definition}\rangle \;&\models\; \langle\text{Entity}\rangle \;\mid\; \langle\text{Container}\rangle \;\mid\; \langle\text{Relation}\rangle \\
 &\qquad \mid\; \langle\text{Projection}\rangle \;\mid\; \langle\text{Test}\rangle \;\mid\; \langle\text{Policy}\rangle \;\mid\; \langle\text{Scope}\rangle \\
\langle\text{Application}\rangle \;&\models\; \langle\text{NamedApplication}\rangle \;\mid\; \langle\text{AnonApplication}\rangle \\
\langle\text{NamedApplication}\rangle \;&\models\; \langle\text{ExtSymbol}\rangle"="\langle\text{AnonApplication}\rangle \\
\langle\text{AnonApplication}\rangle \;&\models\; \nabla \;"("\; \langle\text{Term}\rangle \;")"\; "("\; \langle\text{Scope}\rangle \;")" \\[6pt]
\langle\text{Entity}\rangle \;&\models\; \langle\text{ExtSymbol}\rangle \;\mid\; \langle\text{EntityDef}\rangle \\
 &\qquad \mid\; \langle\text{ExtSymbol}\rangle"="\langle\text{EntityDef}\rangle \\
\langle\text{EntityDef}\rangle \;&\models\; \triangle e \;"("\; ")" \\[6pt]
\langle\text{Container}\rangle \;&\models\; \langle\text{Symbol}\rangle \;\mid\; \langle\text{ContainerDef}\rangle \\
 &\qquad \mid\; \langle\text{ExtSymbol}\rangle"="\langle\text{ContainerDef}\rangle \\
\langle\text{ContainerDef}\rangle \;&\models\; \triangle c \;"("\; \langle\text{Terms}\rangle \;")" \\
\langle\text{Terms}\rangle \;&\models\; \langle\text{Term}\rangle \;\mid\; \langle\text{Term}\rangle \;","\; \langle\text{Terms}\rangle \\[6pt]
\langle\text{Variable}\rangle \;&\models\; \triangleright\langle\text{Symbol}\rangle \\[6pt]
\langle\text{Relation}\rangle \;&\models\; \langle\text{Symbol}\rangle \;\mid\; \langle\text{RelationDef}\rangle \\
 &\qquad \mid\; \langle\text{ExtSymbol}\rangle"="\langle\text{RelationDef}\rangle \\
\langle\text{RelationDef}\rangle \;&\models\; \langle\text{RelationHead}\rangle \\
 &\qquad \mid\; \langle\text{RelationHead}\rangle \;":"\; \langle\text{RelationBody}\rangle \\
\langle\text{RelationHead}\rangle \;&\models\; \triangle r \;"("\; \langle\text{Containers}\rangle \;")" \\
\langle\text{Containers}\rangle \;&\models\; \langle\text{Container}\rangle \;\mid\; \langle\text{Container}\rangle \;","\; \langle\text{Containers}\rangle
\end{aligned}
$$

A. *Backus-Naur-Form of ADQL v3.0*

$$
\begin{aligned}
\langle\text{RelationBody}\rangle &\models \text{''\{'' }\langle\text{Tuples}\rangle\text{ ''\}''} \\
\langle\text{Tuples}\rangle &\models \langle\text{Tuple}\rangle \mid \langle\text{Tuples}\rangle\text{ '',''}\langle\text{Tuple}\rangle \\
\langle\text{Tuple}\rangle &\models \text{''('' }\langle\text{SymbolList}\rangle\text{ '')''} \\
\langle\text{SymbolList}\rangle &\models \langle\text{Symbol}\rangle \mid \langle\text{Symbol}\rangle\text{ '',''}\langle\text{SymbolList}\rangle \\[6pt]
\langle\text{Projection}\rangle &\models \langle\text{Symbol}\rangle \mid \langle\text{ProjDef}\rangle \mid \langle\text{ExtSymbol}\rangle\text{''=''}\langle\text{ProjDef}\rangle \\
\langle\text{ProjDef}\rangle &\models \triangle\text{pr ''('' }\langle\text{Relation}\rangle\text{ '')'' ''('' }\langle\text{ProjTuple}\rangle\text{ '')''} \\
\langle\text{ProjTuple}\rangle &\models \text{''.'' '',''}\langle\text{VarContApps}\rangle \mid \langle\text{VarContApps}\rangle\text{ '','' ''.''} \mid \\
&\quad\ \langle\text{VarContApps}\rangle\text{ '','' ''.'' '',''}\langle\text{VarContApps}\rangle \\
\langle\text{VarContApps}\rangle &\models \langle\text{VarContApp}\rangle \mid \langle\text{VarContApp}\rangle\text{ '',''}\langle\text{VarContApps}\rangle \\
\langle\text{VarContApp}\rangle &\models \langle\text{Variable}\rangle \mid \langle\text{Container}\rangle \mid \langle\text{Application}\rangle \\[6pt]
\langle\text{Test}\rangle &\models \langle\text{Symbol}\rangle \mid \langle\text{TestDef}\rangle \mid \langle\text{ExtSymbol}\rangle\text{''=''}\langle\text{TestDef}\rangle \\
\langle\text{TestDef}\rangle &\models \triangle\text{t ''('' }\langle\text{TestBody}\rangle\text{ '')''} \\
\langle\text{TestBody}\rangle &\models \langle\text{VarContApp}\rangle\text{ '',''}\langle\text{VarContApp}\rangle\text{ '',''}\langle\text{Operator}\rangle \\[6pt]
\langle\text{Policy}\rangle &\models \langle\text{Symbol}\rangle \mid \langle\text{PolicyDef}\rangle \\
&\quad\ \mid \langle\text{ExtSymbol}\rangle\text{''=''}\langle\text{PolicyDef}\rangle \\
\langle\text{PolicyDef}\rangle &\models \triangle\text{p ''('' }\langle\text{Tests}\rangle\text{ '')''} \\
\langle\text{Tests}\rangle &\models \langle\text{Test}\rangle \mid \langle\text{Test}\rangle\text{ '',''}\langle\text{Tests}\rangle \\[6pt]
\langle\text{Scope}\rangle &\models \langle\text{Symbol}\rangle \mid \langle\text{ScopeDef}\rangle \\
&\quad\ \mid \langle\text{ExtSymbol}\rangle\text{''=''}\langle\text{ScopeDef}\rangle \\
\langle\text{ScopeDef}\rangle &\models \triangle\text{s ''('' }\langle\text{VarAssignments}\rangle\text{ '')''} \\
\langle\text{VarAssignments}\rangle &\models \langle\text{VarAssignment}\rangle \\
&\quad\ \mid \langle\text{VarAssignment}\rangle\text{ '',''}\langle\text{VarAssignments}\rangle \\
\langle\text{VarAssignment}\rangle &\models \langle\text{Variable}\rangle\text{ ''=''}\langle\text{Container}\rangle \\[6pt]
\langle\text{Operator}\rangle &\models \text{theta} \mid < \mid <= \mid > \mid >= \mid == \mid \,!= \\[6pt]
\langle\text{Symbol}\rangle &\models \langle\text{ExtSymbol}\rangle \mid \langle\text{IntSymbol}\rangle \\
\langle\text{ExtSymbol}\rangle &\models \langle\text{ExtIdentifier}\rangle \\
\langle\text{IntSymbol}\rangle &\models \langle\text{IntIdentifier}\rangle
\end{aligned}
$$

$$\langle\text{SpecialContainers}\rangle \models \triangle c(\mathit{true}) \mid \triangle c(\mathit{false})$$

$$\langle\text{ExtIdentifier}\rangle \models \langle\text{RegularId}\rangle \mid \langle\text{EscapedId}\rangle$$
$$\langle\text{IntIdentifier}\rangle \models \langle\text{InternalId}\rangle$$
$$\langle\text{RegularId}\rangle \models \langle\text{letter}\rangle \mid \langle\text{digit}\rangle$$
$$\mid \langle\text{RegularId}\rangle\langle\text{letter}\rangle \mid \langle\text{RegularId}\rangle\langle\text{digit}\rangle$$
$$\langle\text{EscapedId}\rangle \models ''''' \langle\text{anychar}\rangle '''''$$
$$\langle\text{InternalId}\rangle \models ''\$'' \langle\text{digit}\rangle$$
$$\langle\text{letter}\rangle \models A \dots Z a \dots z$$
$$\langle\text{digit}\rangle \models 0 \dots 9$$
$$\langle\text{anychar}\rangle \models \mathit{any\ UTF\text{-}8\ symbol\ but}\ '$$
$$\mid \mathit{any\ UTF\text{-}8\ symbol\ but}\ ' \langle\text{anychar}\rangle$$

ϵ is the null terminal.

$\nabla, \triangle, \triangleright, \triangle e, \triangle c, \triangle r, \triangle pr, \triangle t, \triangle p, \triangle s, \mathit{true}, \mathit{false}$ are fixed strings.

B. Traveler Scenario

```
1
   ###########################
3  # Definition of the model #
   ###########################
5
   START TRANSACTION;
7
   CREATE CONTAINERS users, pics, trips;
9  CREATE CONTAINERS roles, permissions, stages;
   CREATE ENTITIES roles: {organizer, traveler, visitor};
11 CREATE ENTITIES permissions: {read, upload, changeStage};
   CREATE ENTITIES stages: {duringtrip, published};
13
   CREATE RELATIONS
15 user_role(users, roles),
   user_trip(users, trips),
17 pic_trip(pics, trips),
   in_stage(trips, stages);
19
   CREATE CONTAINER permSet_read: {read};
21 CREATE CONTAINER permSet_upload: {upload};
   CREATE CONTAINER permSet_change_stage: {changeStage};
23
   CREATE CONTAINER stageSet_published: {published};
25 CREATE CONTAINER stageSet_duringtrip: {duringtrip};
27 CREATE CONTAINER roleSet_organizerOrTraveler: {organizer, traveler};
   CREATE CONTAINER roleSet_organizer: {organizer};
29
   CREATE TEST currentPerm_eq_read:
31   ([permissions], permSet_read);
   CREATE TEST currentPerm_eq_upload:
33   ([permissions], permSet_upload);
   CREATE TEST currentPerm_eq_changestage:
35   ([permissions],  permSet_change_stage);
   CREATE TEST tripOfCurrentUser_eq_currentTrip:
37   (user_trip([users], .), [trips]);
   CREATE TEST tripOfCurrentUser_eq_tripOfCurrentPic:
39   (user_trip([users], .), pic_trip([pics], .));
   CREATE TEST stageOfCurrentTrip_eq_duringtrip:
41   (in_stage([trips], .), stageSet_duringtrip);
   CREATE TEST stageOfTripOfCurrentPic_eq_published:
43   (in_stage(pic_trip([pics], .), .), stageSet_published);
   CREATE TEST roleOfCurrentUser_eq_organizerOrTraveler:
45   (user_role([users], .), roleSet_organizerOrTraveler);
   CREATE TEST roleOfCurrentUser_eq_organizer:
47   (user_role([users], .), roleSet_organizer);

49 CREATE POLICY tripmembers_can_read:
```

```
       {
51          currentPerm_eq_read,
            tripOfCurrentUser_eq_tripOfCurrentPic
53     };
       # This POLICY does not depend on current stage.
55

57     CREATE POLICY all_can_read_if_published:
       {
59          currentPerm_eq_read,
            stageOfTripOfCurrentPic_eq_published
61     };
       # This POLICY does not depend on trip membership.
63
       CREATE POLICY upload_rule:
65     {
            currentPerm_eq_upload,
67          tripOfCurrentUser_eq_currentTrip,
            roleOfCurrentUser_eq_organizerOrTraveler,
69          stageOfCurrentTrip_eq_duringtrip
       };
71
       CREATE POLICY change_stage_rule:
73     {
            currentPerm_eq_changestage,
75          roleOfCurrentUser_eq_organizer,
            tripOfCurrentUser_eq_currentTrip,
77          stageOfCurrentTrip_eq_duringtrip
       };
79
       COMMIT;
81
       #########
83     # Facts #
       #########
85
       START TRANSACTION;
87
       CREATE ENTITIES users: {Alice, Bob, Cindy, Daniel};
89     CREATE ENTITIES trips: {trip_to_Australia, trip_to_Brasil};
       CREATE ENTITIES pics: {picOfRio_jpg};
91
       CREATE LINKS in_stage:
93       {(trip_to_Australia, duringtrip), (trip_to_Brasil, duringtrip)};
       CREATE LINKS user_role:
95       {(Alice, visitor), (Bob, traveler), (Cindy, organizer), (Daniel, visitor)};
       CREATE LINKS user_trip:
97       {(Alice, trip_to_Australia), (Bob, trip_to_Australia),
         (Cindy, trip_to_Australia), (Daniel, trip_to_Brasil)};
99     CREATE LINKS pic_trip:
         {(picOfRio_jpg,trip_to_Brasil)};
101
       # additional facts, which are part of request-flow below:
103    # CREATE ENTITIES pics: {nicePic_jpg};
       # CREATE LINKS pic_trip: {(nicePic_jpg,trip_to_Australia)};
105
       COMMIT;
107
       ####################
109    # Example requests #
       ####################
111
       START TRANSACTION;
113    # all changes in the context of the example requests will be
```

```
      # reverted in the end
115
      CHECK ACCESS
117     ([users] := {Bob},
         [trips] := {trip_to_Australia},
119      [permissions] := {changeStage});
      # denied
121
      CHECK ACCESS
123     ([users] := {Bob},
         [trips] := {trip_to_Brasil},
125      [permissions] := {upload});
      # denied
127
      CHECK ACCESS
129     ([users] := {Bob},
         [trips] := {trip_to_Australia},
131      [permissions] := {upload});
      # granted
133

135   CREATE ENTITIES pics: {newNicePic_jpg};
      CREATE LINKS pic_trip: {(newNicePic_jpg, trip_to_Australia)};
137
      CHECK ACCESS
139     ([users] := {Alice},
         [pics] := {newNicePic_jpg},
141      [permissions] := {read});
      # granted
143
      CHECK ACCESS
145     ([users] := {Alice},
         [pics] := {picOfRio_jpg},
147      [permissions] := {read});
      # denied
149
      CHECK ACCESS
151     ([permissions] := {read},
         [pics] := {newNicePic_jpg},
153      [users] := {Daniel});
      # denied
155
      CHECK ACCESS
157     ([users] := {Alice},
         [trips] := {trip_to_Australia},
159      [permissions] := {upload});
      # denied
161
      CHECK ACCESS
163     ([users] := {Cindy},
         [trips] := {trip_to_Brasil},
165      [permissions] := {changeStage});
      # denied
167
      CHECK ACCESS
169     ([users] := {Cindy},
         [trips] := {trip_to_Australia},
171      [permissions] := {changeStage});
      # granted
173
      DELETE LINKS in_stage: {(trip_to_Australia, duringtrip)};
175   CREATE LINKS in_stage: {(trip_to_Australia, published)};

177   CHECK ACCESS
```

```
            ([users]      := {Alice},
179         [pics]        := {newNicePic_jpg},
            [permissions] := {read});
181     # granted

183     CHECK ACCESS
            ([permissions] := {read},
185         [pics]        := {newNicePic_jpg},
            [users]       := {Daniel});
187     # granted

189     CHECK ACCESS
            ([permissions] := {upload},
191         [trips]       := {trip_to_Australia},
            [users]       := {Bob});
193     #denied

195     CHECK ACCESS
            ([permissions] := {changeStage},
197         [trips]       := {trip_to_Australia},
            [users]       := {Cindy});
199     #denied    --> maybe further ac desirable, to get positive result here

201     CHECK ACCESS
            ([permissions] := {upload},
203         [trips]       := {trip_to_Australia},
            [users]       := {Cindy});
205     #denied    --> maybe further ac desirable, to get positive result here

207     # rollback to get rid of example data
        ROLLBACK;
```

Listing B.1: Listing of the Traveler Scenario

List of Figures

2.1. Timeline of a selection of historically important contributions in access control 11
2.2. Overview of the terms user, session, principal, and subject and their relationships following [Ben06, p.10]. 18
2.3. Representation of the example protection state as access control list 24
2.4. Representation of the example protection state as capability list . 25
2.5. Composition of objects in the Chinese Wall policy following [BN89, p.208] 30
2.6. Elements of the Core RBAC model [FKC07, p.64] 31
2.7. Architecture and data flow of XACML. Taken from [Mos05, p.17]. 41
2.8. Authorization model of Woo and Lam [WL92, p.38]. 46

3.1. Graphical illustration of the simple RBAC example. 52

4.1. Illustration of the container example 2 68
4.2. Access control model defined by Mironov [Mir12, p.10] demonstrating a use case scenario for the requirement of two variables for a container. 69
4.3. Example of a container hierarchy built through indirect entity structures 81

5.1. Structure of the logical layers of ADQL 93
5.2. Example showing the mapping of facts in an information system to the ADQL environment. 95
5.3. Example of a recursive container definition. Full circles represent a tuple in the form $b_i = (e_i, d)$, empty circles $b_i = (e_i, \bar{d})$. 101
5.4. Use case of a recursive container definition for user groups. . . . 103
5.5. Use case example of relations. 106

6.1. Structure of the SAP R/3 access control model. We provide some examples for possible object names (e.g. P_PERNR) 133
6.2. SAP model represented in ADQL 136

6.3. Graphical representation of the model layer for the e-Science scenario. Containers are depicted as ellipses, relations as lines. "pj" is an abbreviation for project. 142

7.1. General architecture of our Access Definition and Query Language implementation. 154
7.2. Back end architecture of our Access Definition and Query Language implementation 156
7.3. Database schema of ADQL's persistence layer 159
7.4. Listing of an example code creating database entries of all ADQL concepts 160
7.5. Example listing of the JavaCC code. The example shows the language definition and reference of an ADQL container. 167
7.6. Example connection to the network layer using the TCP string port. 170
7.7. Front end architecture of our Access Definition and Query Language implementation. 171
7.8. Screenshot of the ADQL Management Web Interface 173
7.9. UML class diagram of the class ResultObject 174
7.10. Check access performance test of the traveler scenario 183

List of Tables

1.1. Overview of existing software frameworks / libraries and their authentication and authorization features. 4

2.1. Example of a protection state as access matrix 22
2.2. Representation of the example protection state as authorization table 23

7.1. Example of the table "adqlentity" resulting from the listing in figure 7.4 160
7.2. Example of the table "linkcollection" resulting from the listing in figure 7.4 162
7.3. Example of the table "fiveentities" resulting from the listing in figure 7.4 162
7.4. Results table for the "normal variant" of the check access performance test of the traveler scenario 181
7.5. Results table for the "controller variant with logging" of the check access performance test of the traveler scenario 181
7.6. Results table for the "controller variant without logging" of the check access performance test of the traveler scenario 182
7.7. Results table for the "parser variant with logging" of the check access performance test of the traveler scenario 182
7.8. Results table for the "parser variant without logging" of the check access performance test of the traveler scenario 182

Bibliography

[AG08] SAP AG. *ADM940 - Berechtigungskonzept AS ABAP Schulungshandbuch*. SAP, Walldorf, Germany, 2008.

[Alg86] Suad Algic. *Relational Database Technology*. Texts and Monographs in Computer Science. Springer, New York, 1986.

[All11] OSGI Alliance. Open Services Gateway Initiative (OSGi). `http://www.osgi.org/Main/HomePage`, 2011. last accessed 2011-03-15.

[And72] James P. Anderson. Computer Security Technology Planning Study. Volume 2. Technical report, Electronic Systems Division (AFSC), Airforce Systems Command, Hanscom Field, Bedford, MA, October 1972.

[ASU86] Alfred V. Aho, Ravi Sethi, and Jeffrey D. Ullman. *Compilers: Principles, Techniques, and Tools*. Addison Wesley, 1st edition, January 1986.

[Bar64] Paul Baran. *IX. Security, Secrecy, and Tamper-Free Considerations*, volume 9 of *On Distributed Communications*. The RAND Corporation, Santa Monica, CA, August 1964.

[Bar85] H.P. Barendregt. *The Lambda Calculus, Its Syntax and Semantics (Studies in Logic and the Foundations of Mathematics, Volume 103). Revised Edition*. North Holland, Amsterdam, revised edition, November 1985.

[Bar09] Steve Barker. The next 700 access control models or a unifying meta-model? In *Proceedings of the 14th ACM symposium on access control models and technologies*, SACMAT '09, pages 187–196, New York, NY, USA, 2009. ACM.

[BBF01] Elisa Bertino, Piero Andrea Bonatti, and Elena Ferrari. TRBAC: a temporal role-based access control model. *ACM Transactions on Information and System Security (TISSEC)*, 4(3):191–233, 2001.

[Ben06] Messaoud Benantar. *Access Control Systems*. Springer, New York, 2006.

[BFIM98] T. Berners-Lee, R. Fielding, U.C. Irvine, and L. Masinter. Uniform resource identifiers (URI): generic syntax. http://www.ietf.org/rfc/rfc2396.txt, August 1998. last accessed: 2011-02-26.

[BFS67] G. Bender, D. N. Freeman, and J. D. Smith. Function and design of DOS/360 and TOS/360. *IBM Systems Journal*, 6(1):2–21, 1967.

[BHJV08] J. Bock, P. Haase, Q. Ji, and R. Volz. Benchmarking OWL reasoners. In *ARea08: Workshop on Advancing Reasoning on the Web: Scalability and Commonsense*, pages 119–132, Vienna, Austria, 2008.

[Bib77] K. J. Biba. Integrity considerations for secure computer systems. Technical report, The Mitre Corporation, Bedford, MA, USA, April 1977.

[BL73] D. E. Bell and Leonard J. LaPadula. Secure computer systems: Mathematical foundations and model. Technical Report MTR-2547, Vol I, MITRE Corp., Bedford, MA, USA, November 1973.

[BLHL$^+$01] T. Berners-Lee, J. Hendler, O. Lassila, et al. The semantic web. *Scientific American*, 284(5):34–43, 2001.

[BLS10] Petter Bae Brandtzaeg, Marika Lueders, and Jan Havard Skjetne. Too many facebook Friends? Content sharing and sociability versus the need for privacy in social network sites. *International Journal of Human-Computer Interaction*, 26(11-12):1006–1030, 2010.

[BN89] David F.C. Brewer and Micheal J. Nash. The chinese wall security policy. In *Proceedings of the IEEE Symposium on Security and Privacy*, pages 206–228, Los Alamitos, CA, USA, 1989. IEEE Computer Society.

[BPS$^+$11] Tim Bray, Jean Paoli, C. M. Sperberg-McQueen, Eve Maler, and Francois Yergeau. Extensible markup language (XML) 1.0 (Fifth edition). `http://www.w3.org/TR/2008/REC-xml-20081126/`, May 2011. last accessed: 2011-05-30.

[BRJ05] Grady Booch, James Rumbaugh, and Ivar Jacobson. *The Unified Modeling Language User Guide*. Addison-Wesley Professional, 2 edition, May 2005.

[Bur11]   Leon Burkard. *Entwurf und Bewertung einer Resource Oriented Architecture (ROA) auf Basis von REST als Referenzarchitektur fuer die Anbindung von Mobile Devices an ein Backendsystem fuer Smart-Metering.* Bachelor Thesis. Karlsruhe Institute of Technology, Karlsruhe, Germany, October 2011.

[CBB$^+$10]   Paul Clements, Felix Bachmann, Len Bass, David Garlan, James Ivers, Reed Little, Paulo Merson, Robert Nord, and Judith Stafford. *Documenting Software Architectures: Views and Beyond.* Addison-Wesley Professional, 2 edition, October 2010.

[CH10]   Jason Crampton and Michael Huth. An authorization framework resilient to policy evaluation failures. In Dimitris Gritzalis, Bart Preneel, and Marianthi Theoharidou, editors, *Computer Security – ESORICS 2010*, volume 6345 of *Lecture Notes in Computer Science*, pages 472–487. Springer Berlin / Heidelberg, 2010. 10.1007/978-3-642-15497-3_29.

[Cir03]   M. Cirspin. RFC 3501 - Internet Message Access Protocol - Version 4rev1. `http://www.faqs.org/rfcs/rfc3501.html`, March 2003. accessed 2011-02-22.

[CMA00]   Michael J. Covington, Matthew James Moyer, and Mustaque Ahamad. Generalized role-based access control for securing future applications. Technical Report GIT-CC-00-02, Georgia Tech College of Computing, Georgia, 2000. accessed 2013-03-12.

[Coh09]   Noam Cohen. Wikipedia to limit changes to articles on people. `http://www.nytimes.com/2009/08/25/technology/internet/25wikipedia.html`, August 2009. accessed 2012-10-19.

[Con07]   The World Wide Web Consortium. XML path language (XPATH). `http://www.w3.org/TR/xpath20/`, January 2007. accessed at 2010-01-31.

[Cor11]   Oracle Corporation. MySQL Database Management System. `http://www.mysql.com`, May 2011. accessed at 2011-05-15.

[Cro06]   Douglas Crockford. The application/json media type for JavaScript object notation (JSON). `http://tools.ietf.org/html/rfc4627`, July 2006. last accessed 2011-05-30.

[CSC72]   F. J. Corbat, J. H. Saltzer, and C. T. Clingen. MULTICS: the first seven years. In *Proceedings of the Joint Computer Conference*, AFIPS '72 (Spring), pages 571–583, New York, NY, USA, 1972. ACM. ACM ID: 1478950.

[CW87]   David D. Clark and David R. Wilson. A comparison of commercial and military computer security policies. In *IEEE Symposium on Security and Privacy*, pages 184–194, Los Alamitos, CA, USA, 1987. IEEE Computer Society.

[DdVPS02] Ernesto Damiani, Sabrina De Capitani di Vimercati, Stefano Paraboschi, and Pierangela Samarati. A fine-grained access control system for XML documents. *ACM Transactions on Information and System Security (TISSEC)*, 5:169–202, May 2002. ACM ID: 505590.

[Dec10]   Michael Decker. Location-aware access control: An overview. *International Journal on Computer Science and Information System (IJCSIS)*, 5(1):26–44, 2010.

[DLHH09]   Bernhard Debatin, Jennette P. Lovejoy, Ann-Kathrin Horn, and Brittany N. Hughes. Facebook and online privacy: Attitudes, behaviors, and unintended consequences. *Journal of Computer-Mediated Communication*, 15(1):83–108, 2009.

[DM89]   John E. Dobson and John McDermid. Security models and enterprise models. In C.E. Landwehr, editor, *Database Security, II: Status and Prospects*, pages 1–39. North-Holland Publishing Co, New York, January 1989.

[Eck12]   Matthias Eckstein. *Bachelorarbeit: Design und Implementierung einer REST Schnittstelle fuer einen Policy Decision and Enforcement Point Bachelorarbeit*. Karlsruhe Institute of Technology, Karlsruhe, Germany, September 2012.

[ESMW01]   Ed Ellesson, John Strassner, Bob Moore, and Andrea Westerinen. RFC 3060: Policy core information model – version 1 specification. `http://tools.ietf.org/html/rfc3060`, February 2001. last accessed: 2011-10-7.

[FHdL+00] Stephen Farrell, Matt Holdrege, Cees T.A.M. de Laat, Pat R. Calhoun, Leon Gommans, John R. Vollbrecht, Betty de Bruijn, and George M. Gross. RFC 2904: AAA authorization framework. `http://tools.ietf.org/html/rfc2904`, August 2000. last accessed: 2011-10-7.

[Fie00]   Roy Thomas Fielding. *Architectural styles and the design of network-based software architectures*. PhD thesis, University of California, Irvine, CA, 2000.

[Fis05]   Ken Fischer. Ars technica: Wikipedia embraces wider vandal lockout scheme. `http://arstechnica.com/old/content/2005/12/5790.ars`, December 2005. accessed 2011-02-22.

[FJK+08] T. Finin, A. Joshi, L. Kagal, J. Niu, R. Sandhu, W. Winsborough, and B. Thuraisingham. ROWLBAC: representing role based access control in OWL. In *Proceedings of the 13th ACM Symposium on Access Control Models and Technologies - SACMAT '08*, pages 73–82, Estes Park, CO, USA, 2008.

[FK92] David F. Ferraiolo and D. Richard Kuhn. Role-based access controls. pages 554 – 563, Baltimore MD, 1992.

[FKC07] David Ferraiolo, D. Richard Kuhn, and Ramaswamy Chandramouli. *Role-based access control, 2.ed.* Artech House, Boston/London, 2007.

[FLG00] Stephen Farrell, de Cees T.A.M. Laat, and George M. Gross. RFC 2906: AAA authorization requirements. http://tools.ietf.org/html/rfc2906, August 2000. last accessed: 2011-10-7.

[Fou06] OpenLDAP Foundation. RFC 4512: Lightweight directory access protocol (LDAP): directory information models. http://tools.ietf.org/html/rfc4512, June 2006. accessed 2011-02-22.

[GB05] Rajeev Gupta and Manish Bhide. A Generic XACML Based Declarative Authorization Scheme for Java. In Sabrina de Capitani di Vimercati, Paul Syverson, and Dieter Gollmann, editors, *Computer Security – ESORICS 2005*, volume 3679 of *Lecture Notes in Computer Science*, pages 44–63. Springer Berlin / Heidelberg, 2005.

[GD71] G. Scott Graham and Peter J. Denning. Protection. pages 417–429. ACM Press, 1971.

[GHJ94] Erich Gamma, Richard Helm, and Ralph E. Johnson. *Design Patterns. Elements of Reusable Object-Oriented Software.* Addison-Wesley Longman, Amsterdam, 1st ed., reprint. edition, October 1994.

[GM03] Simon Godik and Tim Moses. eXtensible access control markup language (XACML), version 1.0. Technical report, February 2003.

[GP95] David Garlan and Dewayne E. Perry. Introduction to the special issue on software architecture. *IEEE Transactions on Software Engineering*, 21:269–274, April 1995. ACM ID: 205314.

[GPC+07a] S. Geysin, A.D. Petrov, P. Charrue, W. Gajewski, V. Kain, K. Kostro, G. Kruk, S. Page, and M. Peryt. Role-Based access control for the accelerator control system at CERN. In *International Conference on Accelerator and Large Experimental Physics Control Systems*, pages 90–92, Knoxville, Tennessee, USA, 2007.

[GPC⁺07b] S. Gysin, A. D. Petrov, P. Charrue, W. Gajewski, V. Kain, K. Kostro, G. Kruk, S. Page, and M. Peryt. Role-based access control for the accelerator control system at CERN. In *Proceedings of International Conference on Accelerator and Large Experimental Physics Control Systems 2007*, pages 90–92, Knoxville, Tennessee, USA, 2007.

[Gro10] PostgreSQL Global Development Group. PostgreSQL Database Management System. `http://www.postgresql.org/`, February 2010. accessed at 2011-02-27.

[Haf06] Katie Hafner. Growing wikipedia refines its 'Anyone can edit' policy. *The New York Times*, June 2006. accessed 2011-02-22.

[Har12] Dick Hardt. The OAuth 2.0 authorization framework. `http://tools.ietf.org/html/draft-ietf-oauth-v2-3`, July 2012. accessed at 2012-10-21.

[HdBG⁺00] M. Holdrege, B. de Bruijn, L. Gommans, D. Spence, J. Vollbrecht, G. Gross, C. de Laat, S. Farrell, and P. Calhoun. RFC 2905: AAA authorization application examples. `http://tools.ietf.org/html/rfc2905`, August 2000. last accessed: 2011-10-7.

[Her00] Shai Herzog. RFC 2748: The COPS (Common open policy service) protocol. `http://tools.ietf.org/html/rfc2748`, January 2000. last accessed: 2011-10-7.

[HKY95] T. Howes, S. Kille, and W. Yeong. RFC 1777: Lightweight directory access protocol. `http://tools.ietf.org/html/rfc1777`, March 1995. accessed 2011-02-22.

[HMPR04] A. R. Hevner, S. T. March, J. Park, and S. Ram. Design science in information systems research. *MIS quarterly*, 28(1):75–105, 2004.

[HR78] M.H. Harrison and W.L. Ruzzo. Monotonic protection systems. In R. Demilo, editor, *Foundations of Secure Computations*. Academic Press, 1978.

[HRU76] Michael A. Harrison, Walter L. Ruzzo, and Jeffrey D. Ullman. Protection in operating systems. *Communications of the ACM*, 19(8):461–471, 1976.

[HS10] Jerome Howard Saltzer. Jerome Howard Saltzer: Curriculum vitae. `http://web.mit.edu/afs/athena.mit.edu/user/other/a/Saltzer/www/vita.html`, May 2010. accessed 2011-02-22.

[IEE] IEEE 1471. IEEE standard 1471 - ISO/IEC 42010. `http://www.iso-architecture.org/ieee-1471/`. accessed at 2011-05-19.

[Int97] Lucas D. Introna. Privacy and the computer: Why we need privacy in the information society. *Metaphilosophy*, 28(3):259–275, 1997.

[JBo10] JBoss Community Team. Hibernate. `http://www.hibernate.org/`, February 2010. accessed at 2011-03-15.

[JSSS01] Sushil Jajodia, Pierangela Samarati, Maria Luisa Sapino, and V. S. Subrahmanian. Flexible support for multiple access control policies. *ACM Trans. Database Syst.*, 26(2):214–260, June 2001.

[KBCW06] L. Kagal, T. Berners-Lee, D. Connolly, and D. Weitzner. Using semantic web technologies for policy management on the web. In *Proceedings of the National Conference on Artificial Intelligence*, volume 21, pages 1337–1344, 2006.

[Knu64] Donald E. Knuth. Backus normal form vs. backus naur form. *Commun. ACM*, 7(12):735–736, December 1964.

[KP88] Glenn E. Krasner and Stephen T. Pope. A cookbook for using the model-view controller user interface paradigm in smalltalk-80. *Jornal of Object-Oriented Programming*, 1(3):26–49, August 1988.

[Lam71] Butler W. Lampson. Protection. In *Proceedings of the Fifth Princeton Symposium on Information Sciences and Systems*, pages 437–443. Princeton University, January 1971.

[Lam74] Butler W. Lampson. Protection (Reprint). *ACM SIGOPS Operating Systems Review*, 8:18–24, January 1974.

[LWQ+09] Ninghui Li, Qihua Wang, Wahbeh Qardaji, Elisa Bertino, Prathima Rao, Jorge Lobo, and Dan Lin. Access control policy combining: theory meets practice. In *Proceedings of the 14th ACM symposium on Access control models and technologies*, pages 135–144, Stresa, Italy, 2009. ACM.

[McL88] J. McLean. The algebra of security. In *IEEE Symposium on Security and Privacy*, Oakland, CA, 1988.

[McL90] John McLean. The specification and modeling of computer security. *IEEE COMPUTER*, 23(1):9—16, 1990.

[Mel05] A. Melnikov. RFC 4314 - IMAP4 access control list (ACL) extension. `http://www.faqs.org/rfcs/rfc4314.html`, December 2005. Accessed 2011-02-22.

[Mir12] Antim Mironov. *Seminararbeit: Access Control for Health Care Systems*. Number WS2011/2012 in Masterseminare. Karlsruhe Institute of Technology, Karlsruhe, Germany, June 2012.

[Mos05] Tim Moses, editor. *eXtensible Access Control Markup Language (XACML) Version 2.0*. OASIS Standard. OASIS Open, February 2005.

[MS70] R. A. Meyer and L. H. Seawright. A virtual machine time-sharing system. *IBM Systems Journal*, 9(3):199–218, 1970.

[NBL09] Qun Ni, Elisa Bertino, and Jorge Lobo. D-algebra for composing access control policy decisions. In *Proceedings of the 4th International Symposium on Information, Computer, and Communications Security*, ASIACCS '09, pages 298–309, New York, NY, USA, 2009. ACM. ACM ID: 1533097.

[Net03] Microsoft Tech Net. What are security principals? `http://technet.microsoft.com/en-us/library/cc780957(WS.10).aspx`, March 2003. last accessed: 2011-08-08.

[Not96] LouAnna Notargiacomo. Role-based access control in ORACLE7 and trusted ORACLE7. In *Proceedings of the first ACM Workshop on Role-based access control*, RBAC '95, New York, NY, USA, 1996. ACM.

[oD83] U.S. Department of Defense. Trusted computer system evaluation criteria. Technical Report DoD 5200.28-STD, U.S. Department of Defense, December 1983.

[Oh10] Sejong Oh. New role-based access control in ubiquitous e-business environment. *Journal of Intelligent Manufacturing*, 21(5):607–612, October 2010.

[Org72] Elliott I. Organick. *The multics system: an examination of its structure*. MIT Press, Cambridge, MA, 1972.

[PYG00] Dimitrios Pendarakis, Raj Yavatkar, and Roch Guerin. RFC 2753: A framework for policy-based admission control. `http://tools.ietf.org/html/rfc2753`, January 2000. last accessed: 2011-10-7.

[Rei80] R. Reiter. A logic for default reasoning. *Artificial Intelligence*, 13(12):81–132, April 1980.

[Rig00] Carl Rigney. RFC2866: RADIUS accounting. `http://tools.ietf.org/html/rfc2866`, June 2000. last accessed: 2012-09-18.

[Ris10] Erik Rissanen. eXtensible access control markup language (XACML) version 3.0 committee draft 03. Technical report, March 2010.

[RKY06] Indrakshi Ray, Mahendra Kumar, and Lijun Yu. LRBAC: a location-aware role-based access control model. In Aditya Bagchi and Vijayalakshmi Atluri, editors, *Information Systems Security*, number 4332 in Lecture Notes in Computer Science, pages 147–161. Springer Berlin Heidelberg, January 2006.

[RR06] D. Recordon and D. Reed. OpenID 2.0: a platform for user-centric identity management. In *Proceedings of the second ACM workshop on Digital identity management*, pages 11–16, Alexandria, Virginia, USA, 2006. ACM.

[Sal74] Jerome H. Saltzer. Protection and the control of information sharing in multics. *Communications of the ACM*, 17:388–402, July 1974. ACM ID: 361067.

[Sam96] Vipin Samar. Unified login with pluggable authentication modules (PAM). In *Proceedings of the 3rd ACM conference on Computer and communications security*, CCS '96, pages 1–10, New York, NY, USA, 1996. ACM. ACM ID: 238177.

[SCFY96] Ravi S. Sandhu, Edward J. Coyne, Hal L. Feinstein, and Charles E. Youman. Role-based access control models. *Computer*, 29(2):38–47, 1996.

[Ser06] Jim Sermersheim. RFC 4511: Lightweight directory access protocol (LDAP): the protocol. `http://tools.ietf.org/html/rfc4511`, June 2006. accessed 2011-02-22.

[SFK00] Ravi Sandhu, David Ferraiolo, and Richard Kuhn. The NIST model for role-based access control: towards a unified standard. In *Symposium on Access Control Models and Technologies: Proceedings of the fifth ACM workshop on Role-based access control*, volume 26, pages 47–63, Berlin, 2000.

[SGS12] Andreas C. Sonnenbichler and Andreas Geyer-Schulz. ADQL: a flexible access definition and query language to define access control models. In Pierangela Samarati, editor, *Proceedings of the International Conference on Security and Cryptography 2012*, Rome, July 2012. The Institute for Systems and Technologies of Information, Control and Communication (INSTICC).

[SHC$^+$01] Mark Scherling, An-Ni Huynh, Mark Carlson, Andrea Westerinen, Bob Quinn, Shai Herzog, John Strassner, and John Schnizlein. RFC 3198: Terminology for Policy-Based management. `http://tools.ietf.org/html/rfc3198`, November 2001. last accessed: 2011-10-7.

[Sil01a] Len Silverston. *The Data Model Resource Book, Vol. 1: A Library of Universal Data Models for All Enterprises*. Wiley, revised edition, volume 1 edition, March 2001.

[Sil01b] Len Silverston. *The Data Model Resource Book, Vol. 2: A Library of Data Models for Specific Industries*. Wiley, revised edition, volume 2 edition, March 2001.

[Sla09] Brennon Slattery. Wikipedia changes editing policy. `http://www.networkworld.com/news/2009/082609-wikipedia-changes-editing.html`, August 2009. accessed 2011-02-22.

[Sle07] Mark Slee. Thrift: We're giving away code. `http://blog.facebook.com/blog.php?post=2261927130`, April 2007. last accessed: 2012-10-18.

[SLH06] Nigel Shadbolt, Tim Lee, and Wendy Hall. The semantic web revisited. *Intelligent Systems, IEEE*, 21(3):96–101, 2006.

[Son13] Andreas C. Sonnenbichler. Social access control. In *Proceedings of the 2nd Workshop on Customer Empowerment*, Karlsruhe, Germany, January 2013. Karlsruhe Institute of Technology. to appear.

[SS75] J.H. Saltzer and M.D. Schroeder. The protection of information in computer systems. *Proceedings of the IEEE*, 63(9):1278–1308, 1975.

[SS94] R.S. Sandhu and P. Samarati. Access control: principle and practice. *Communications Magazine, IEEE*, 32(9):40–48, 1994.

[SS09] Andreas C. Sonnenbichler and Felix Schwagereit. Prototype Of A Community Management Platform. Deliverable D4.2, Karlsruhe Institute of Technology, Karlsruhe, Germany, June 2009.

[ST83] Ray Switzer and Ralph B. Taylor. Sociability versus privacy of residential choice: Impacts of personality and local social ties. *Basic and Applied Social Psychology*, 4(2):123–136, 1983.

[SV01] Pierangela Samarati and Sabrina De Capitani di Vimercati. Access control: Policies, models, and mechanisms. In *Revised versions of lectures given during the IFIP WG 1.7 International School on Foundations of Security Analysis and Design on Foundations of Security Analysis and Design: Tutorial Lectures*, pages 137–196. Springer-Verlag, 2001.

[TC08] Fatih Turkmen and Bruno Crispo. Performance evaluation of XACML PDP implementations. In *Proceedings of the 2008 ACM Workshop on Secure Web Services*, SWS '08, pages 37–44, New York, NY, USA, 2008. ACM.

[Ter05a] Daniel Terdmian. Growing pains for wikipedia - CNET news. `http://news.cnet.com/Growing-pains-for-Wikipedia/2100-1025_3-5981119.html`, December 2005. accessed at 2012-10-19.

[Ter05b] Daniel Terdmian. In search of the wikipedia prankster - CNET news. `http://news.cnet.com/In-search-of-the-Wikipedia-prankster/2008-1029_3-5995977.html?tag=st.num`, December 2005. acessed at 2012-10-19.

[Tur38] A. M. Turing. On computable numbers, with an application to the entscheidungsproblem. *Proceedings of the London Mathematical Society*, 2(42):230–265, 1938.

[Vol06] John Vollbrecht. *The Beginnings and History of RADIUS*. Interlink Networks, LLC., Michigan, USA, 2006.

[W3C11] W3C. RDF tech standards. `http://www.w3.org/standards/techs/rdf`, May 2011. last accessed 2011-05-30.

[War70] Willis Ware, editor. *Security Control Systems for Computer Systems (U): Report of Defense Science Board Task Force on Computer Security*. The RAND Corporation, Santa Monica, CA, February 1970.

[wik12a] History of wikipedia. `http://en.wikipedia.org/w/index.php?title=History_of_Wikipedia&oldid=518638766`, October 2012. Page Version ID: 518638766, access at 2012-10-19.

[wik12b] Wikipedia biography controversy. `http://en.wikipedia.`
`org/w/index.php?title=Wikipedia_biography_`
`controversy&oldid=516537849,` October 2012. Page Version
ID: 516537849, accessed 2012-10-19.

[WJL09] Qihua Wang, Hongxia Jin, and Ninghui Li. Usable access control in collaborative environments: authorization based on people-tagging. In *Proceedings of the 14th European conference on Research in computer security*, ESORICS'09, pages 268–284, Berlin, Heidelberg, 2009. Springer-Verlag.

[WL92] Thomas Y. C. Woo and S.S. Lam. Authorization in distributed systems: a formal approach. In *Proceedings of the 1992 IEEE Computer Society Symposium on Research in Security and Privacy*, Austin, TX, USA, May 1992.

[WRRS00] Steve Willens, Allan C. Rubens, Carl Rigney, and William Allen Simpson. RFC 2865: Remote authentication dial in user service (RADIUS). `http://tools.ietf.org/html/rfc2865,` June 2000. last accessed: 2012-09-18.

[YT05] E. Yuan and J. Tong. Attributed based access control (ABAC) for web services. In *Proceedings of the International Conference on Web Services (ICWS)*, pages 569–578, 2005.

[ZCH+00] Glen Zorn, Pat R. Calhoun, Tom Hiller, Peter J. McCann, Gopal Dommety, Bernard Aboba, Steven M. Glass, and Hajime Shiino. RFC2989: criteria for evaluating AAA protocols for network access. `http://tools.ietf.org/html/rfc2989,` November 2000. accessed 2012-02-26.

[Zer08] E. Zermelo. Untersuchungen über die Grundlagen der Mengenlehre. I. *Mathematische Annalen*, 65(2):261–281, 1908.